FOR THOSE WHO

CAME IN LATE...

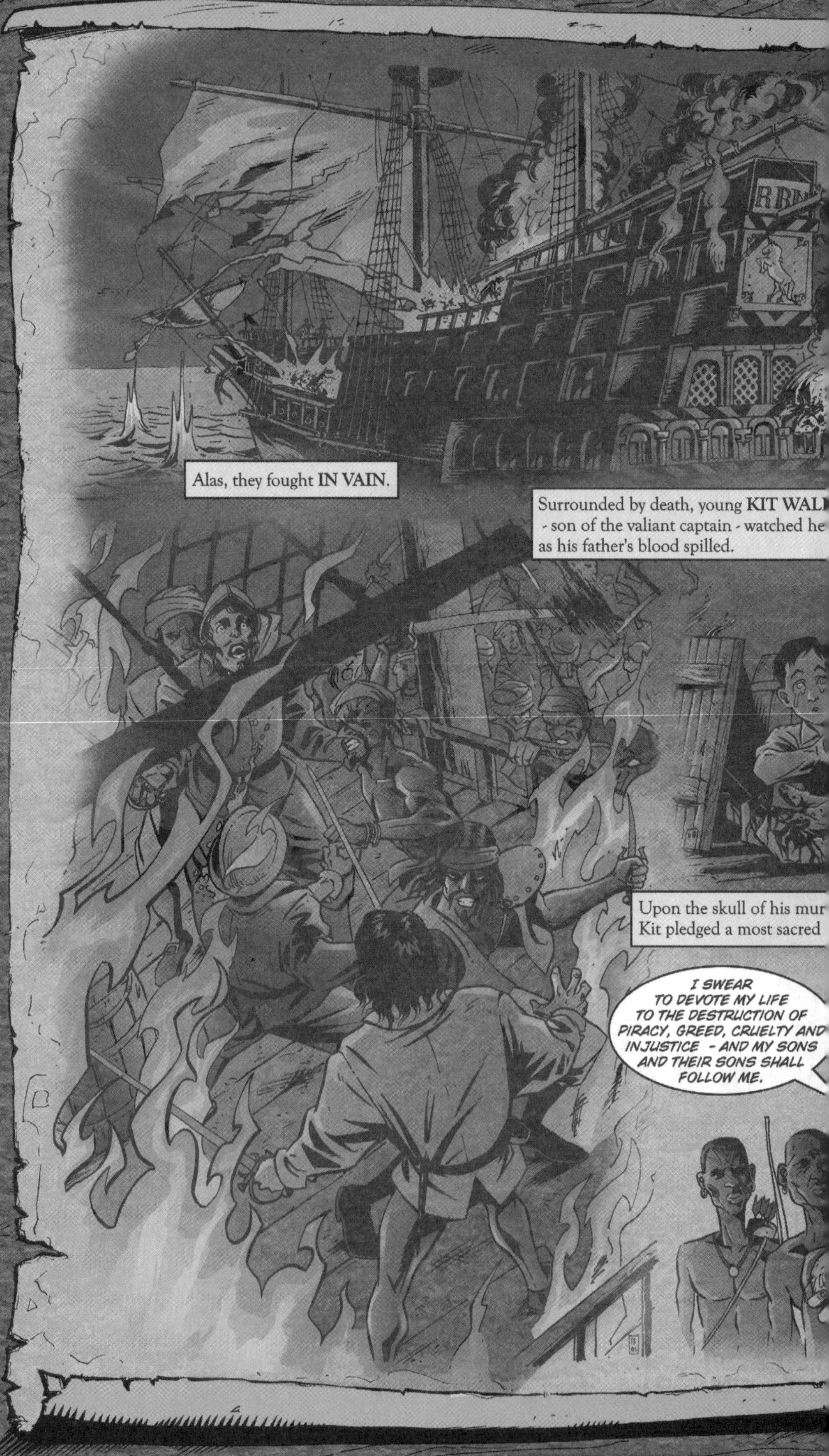
Alas, they fought IN VAIN.
Surrounded by death, young KIT WAL
- son of the valiant captain - watched he
as his father's blood spilled.
Upon the skull of his mur
Kit pledged a most sacred
I SWEAR TO DEVOTE MY LIFE TO THE DESTRUCTION OF PIRACY, GREED, CRUELTY AND INJUSTICE - AND MY SONS AND THEIR SONS SHALL FOLLOW ME.

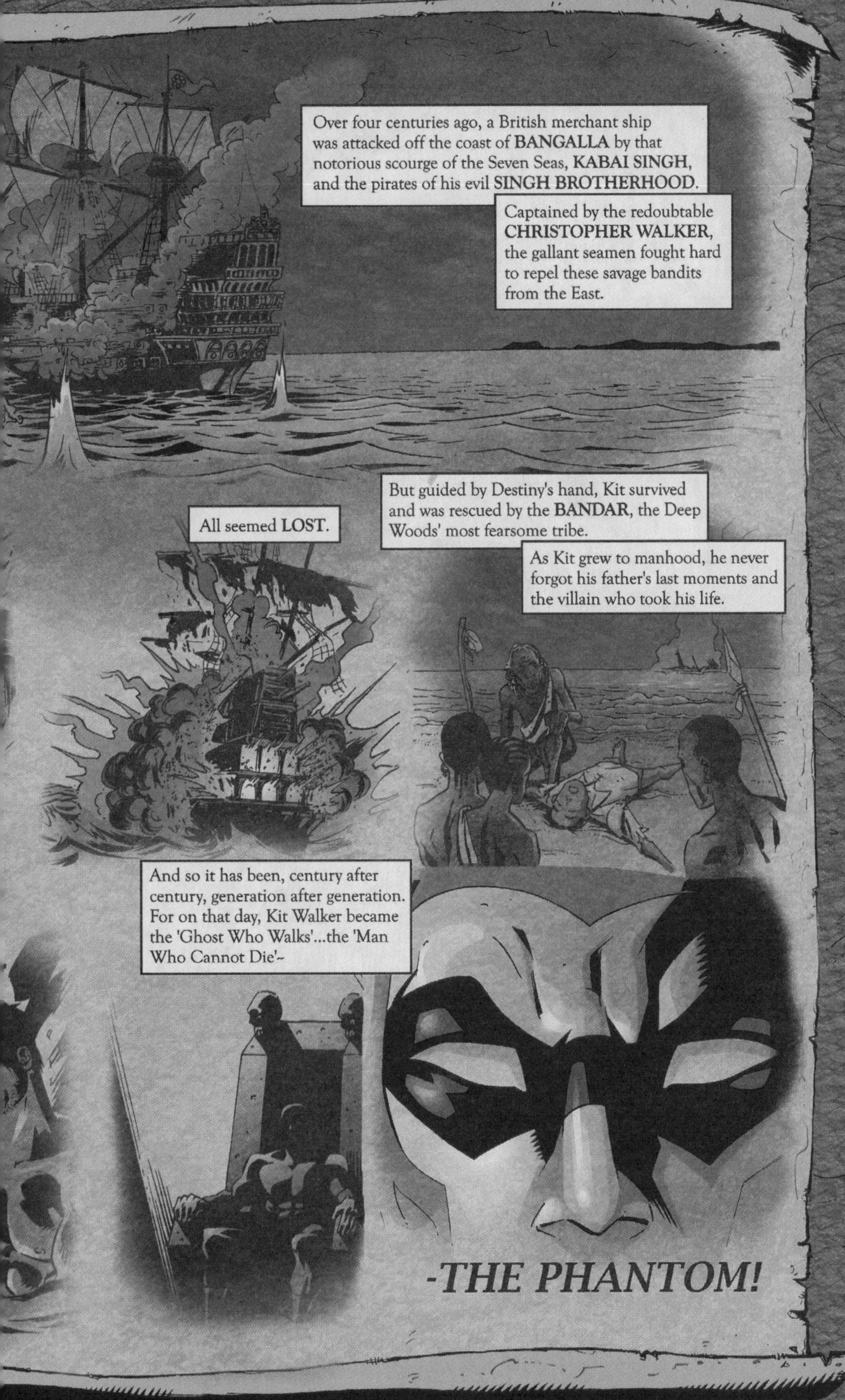
Over four centuries ago, a British merchant ship was attacked off the coast of BANGALLA by that notorious scourge of the Seven Seas, KABAI SINGH, and the pirates of his evil SINGH BROTHERHOOD.
Captained by the redoubtable CHRISTOPHER WALKER, the gallant seamen fought hard to repel these savage bandits from the East.
All seemed LOST.
But guided by Destiny's hand, Kit survived and was rescued by the BANDAR, the Deep Woods' most fearsome tribe.
As Kit grew to manhood, he never forgot his father's last moments and the villain who took his life.
And so it has been, century after century, generation after generation. For on that day, Kit Walker became the 'Ghost Who Walks'...the 'Man Who Cannot Die'~
-THE PHANTOM!

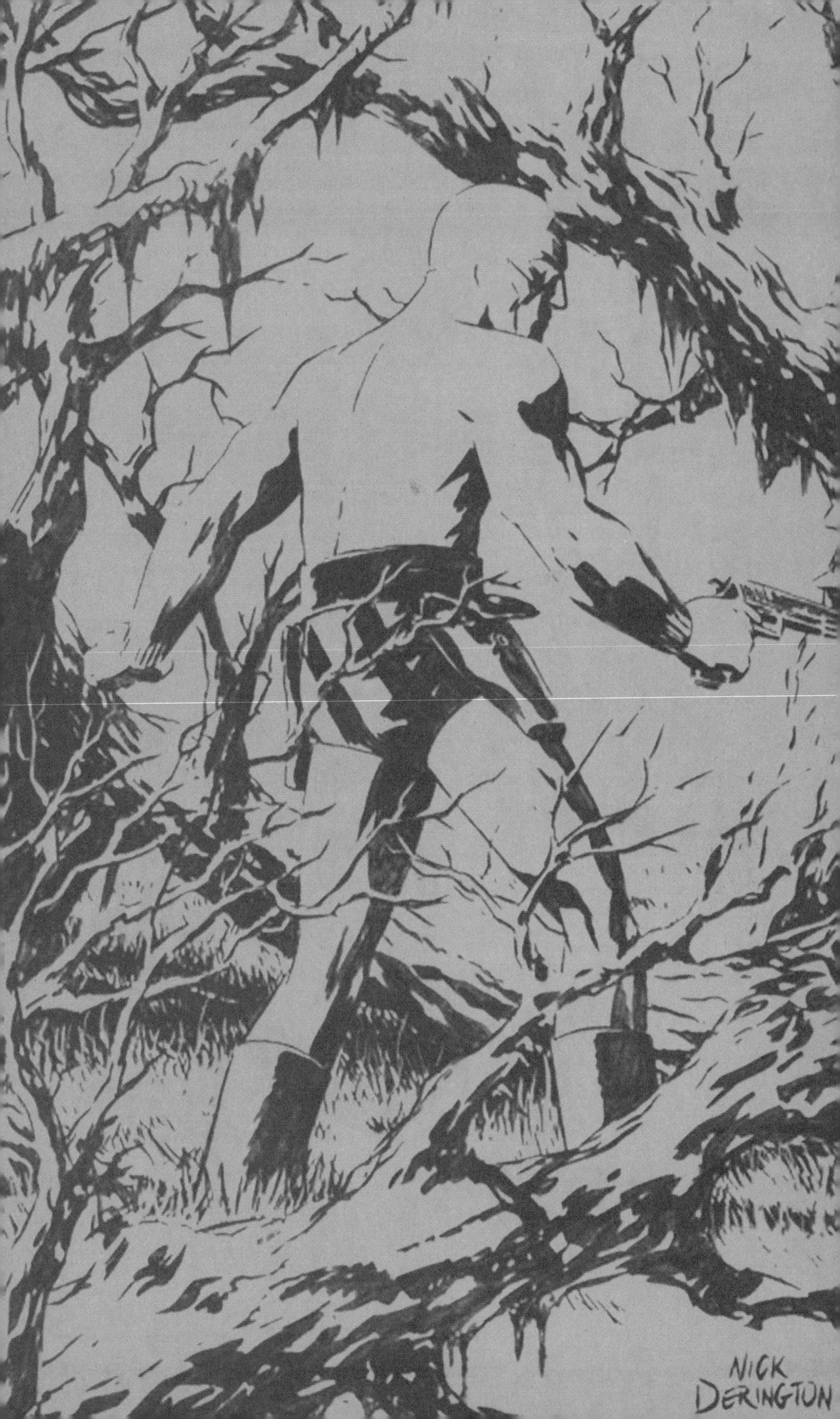
NICK
DERINGTON

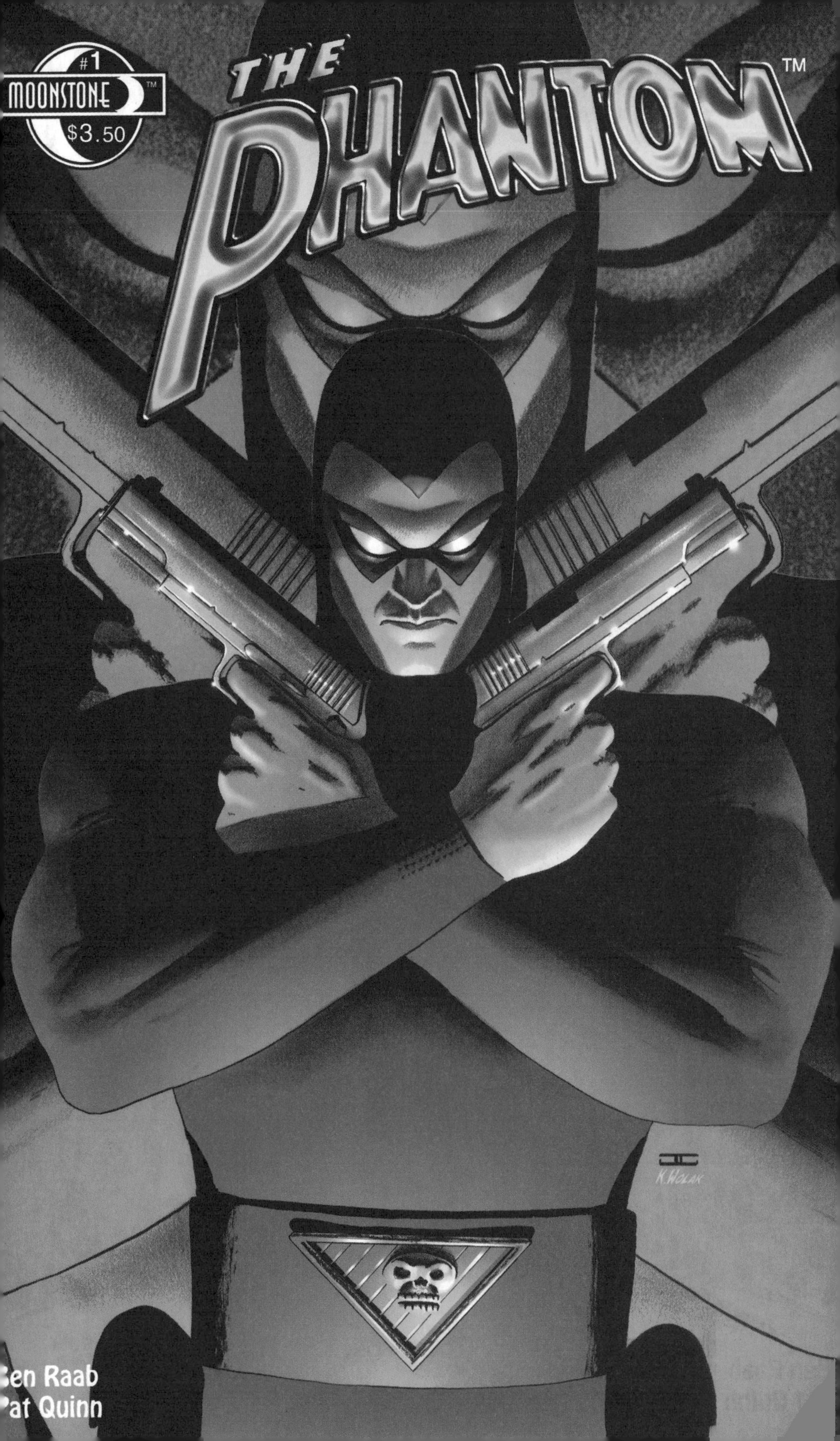
#1
MOONSTONE
$3.50
THE PHANTOM™
en Raab
at Quinn

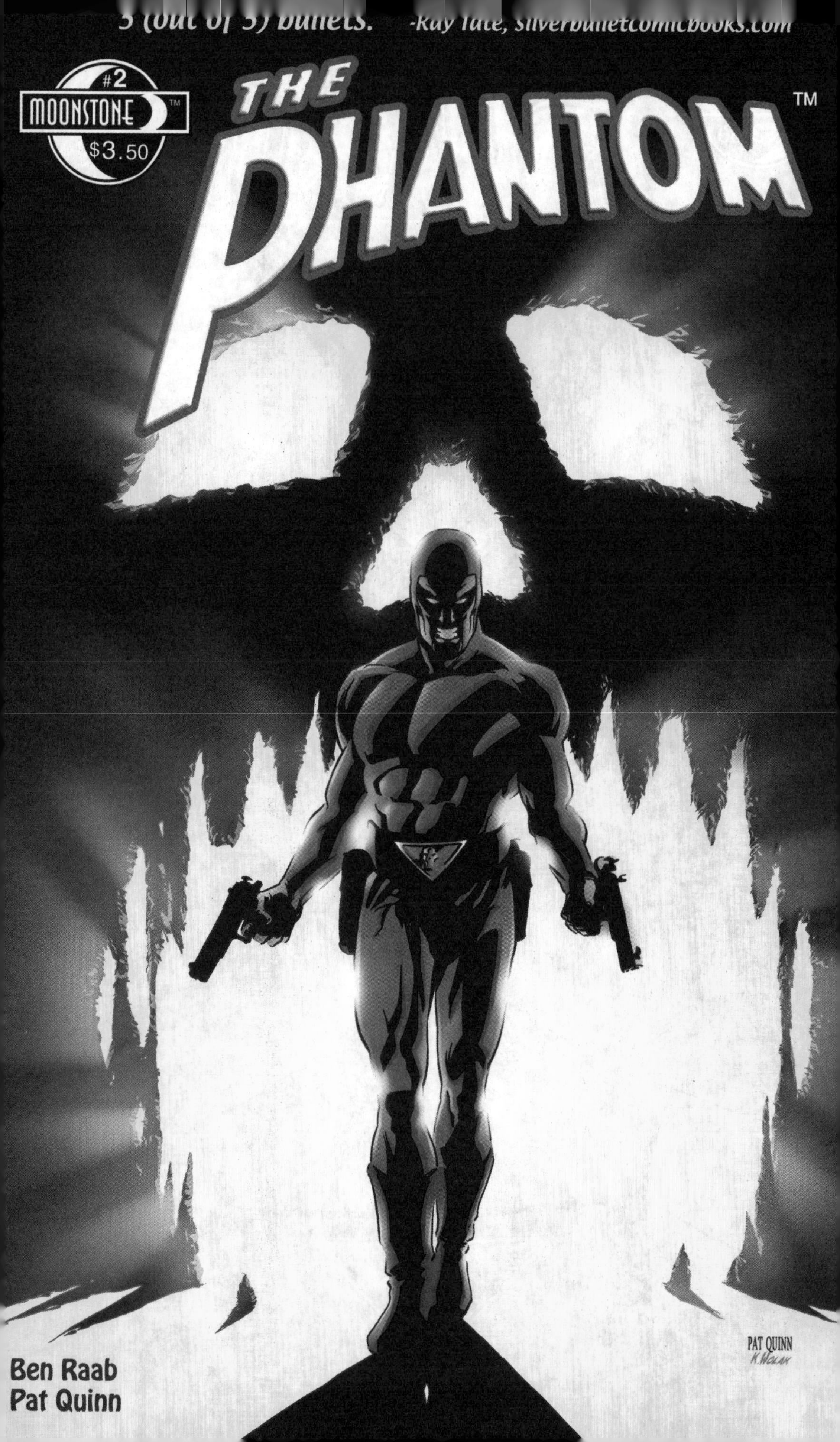
5 (out of 5) bullets. -Ray Tate, silverbulletcomicbooks.com
#2
MOONSTONE
$3.50
THE PHANTOM
TM
PAT QUINN
K. WOLAK
Ben Raab
Pat Quinn

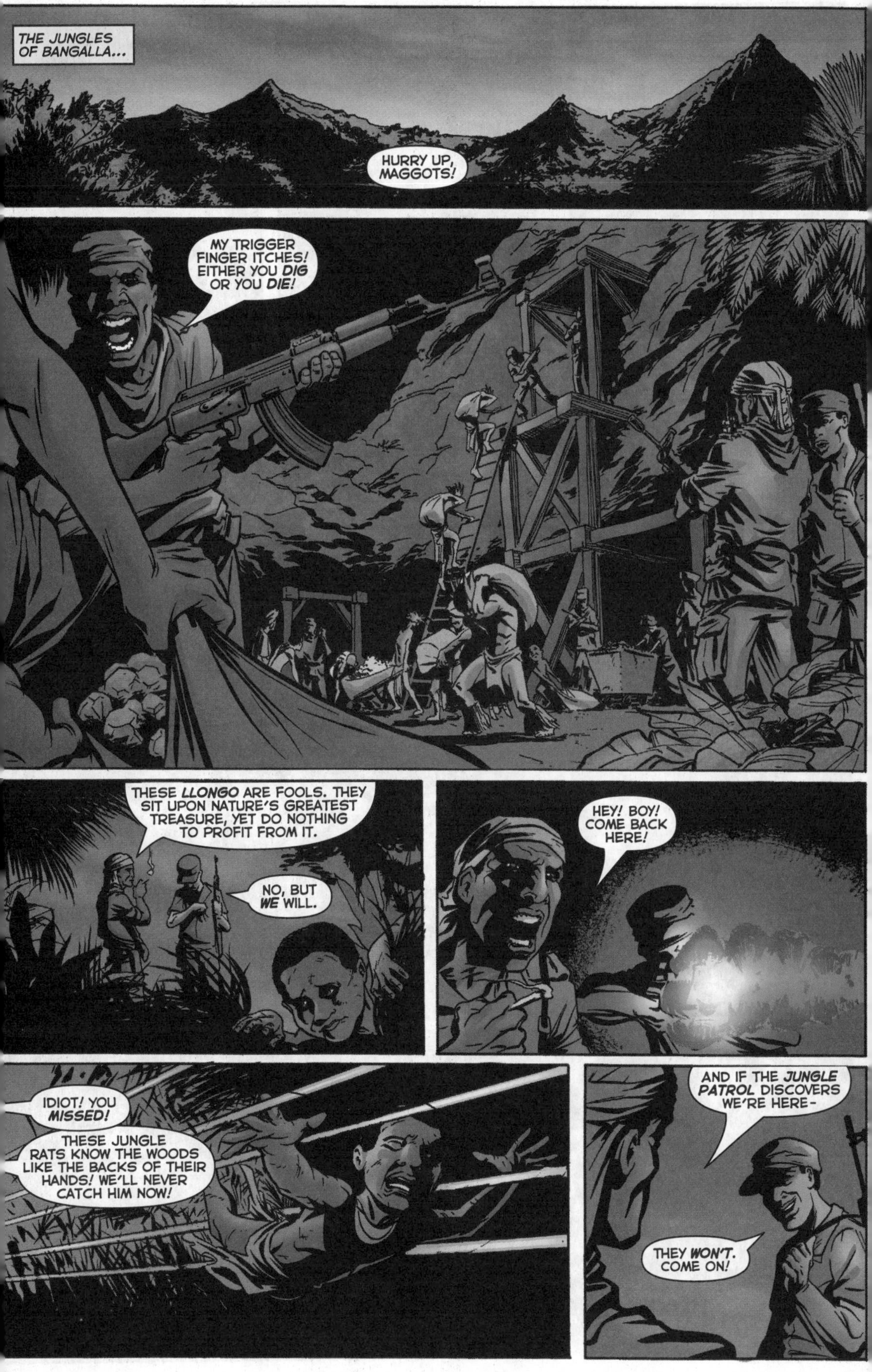
THE JUNGLES OF BANGALLA...
HURRY UP, MAGGOTS!
MY TRIGGER FINGER ITCHES! EITHER YOU DIG OR YOU DIE!
THESE LLONGO ARE FOOLS. THEY SIT UPON NATURE'S GREATEST TREASURE, YET DO NOTHING TO PROFIT FROM IT.
NO, BUT WE WILL.
HEY! BOY! COME BACK HERE!
IDIOT! YOU MISSED!
THESE JUNGLE RATS KNOW THE WOODS LIKE THE BACKS OF THEIR HANDS! WE'LL NEVER CATCH HIM NOW!
AND IF THE JUNGLE PATROL DISCOVERS WE'RE HERE-
THEY WON'T. COME ON!

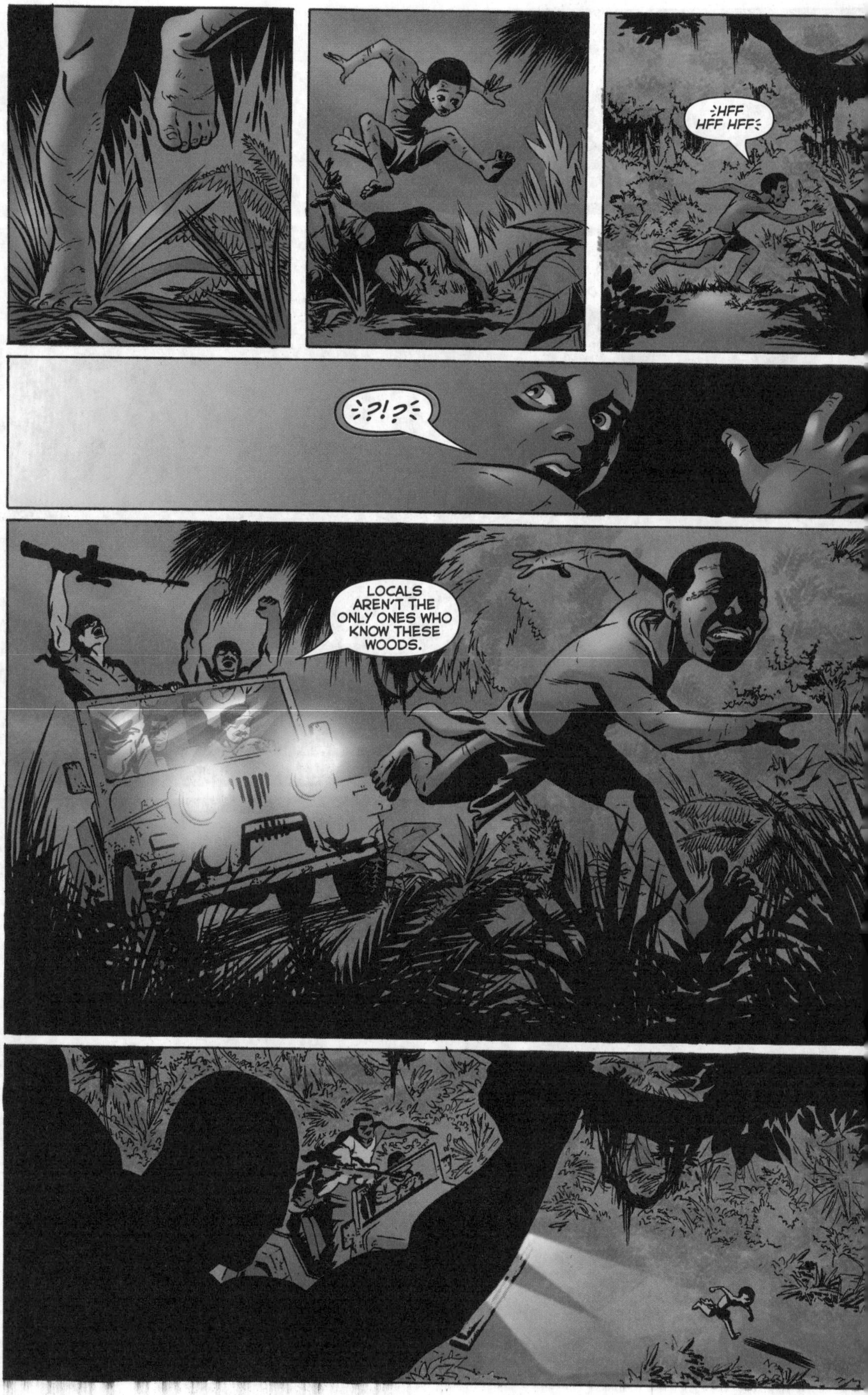
HFF HFF HFF
?!?
LOCALS AREN'T THE ONLY ONES WHO KNOW THESE WOODS.

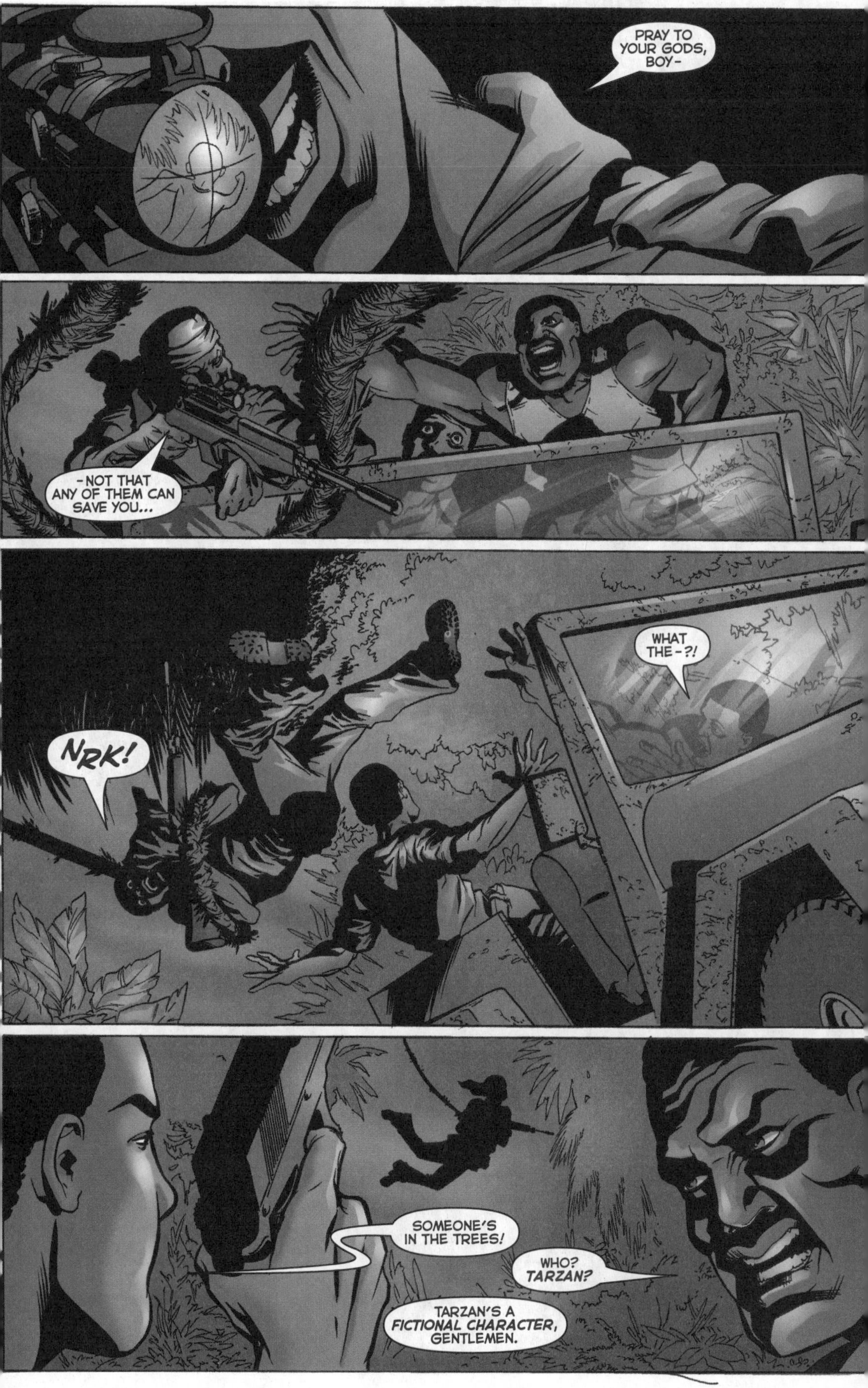

PRAY TO YOUR GODS, BOY-
-NOT THAT ANY OF THEM CAN SAVE YOU...
WHAT THE-?!
NRK!
SOMEONE'S IN THE TREES!
WHO? *TARZAN?*
TARZAN'S A *FICTIONAL CHARACTER,* GENTLEMEN.

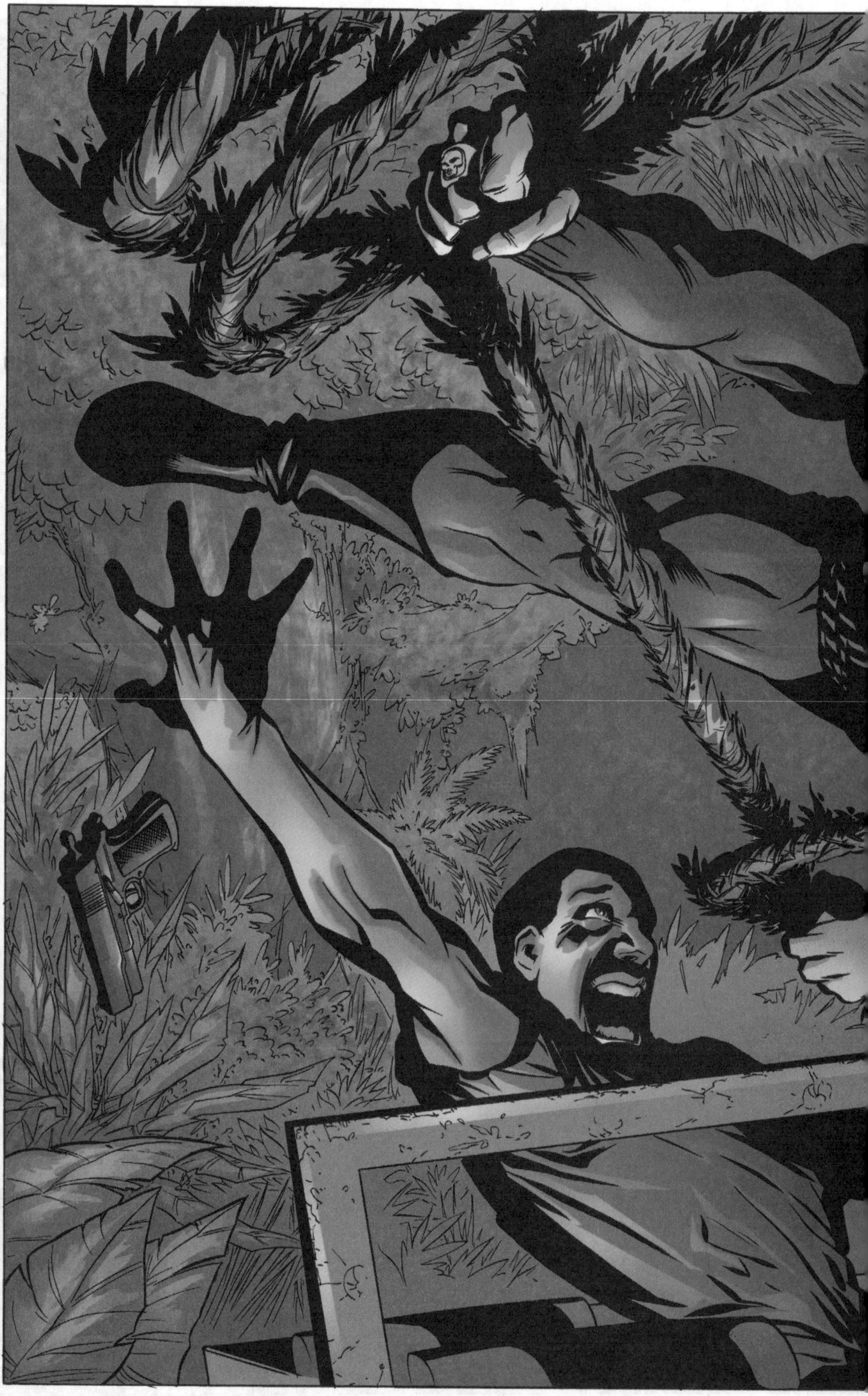

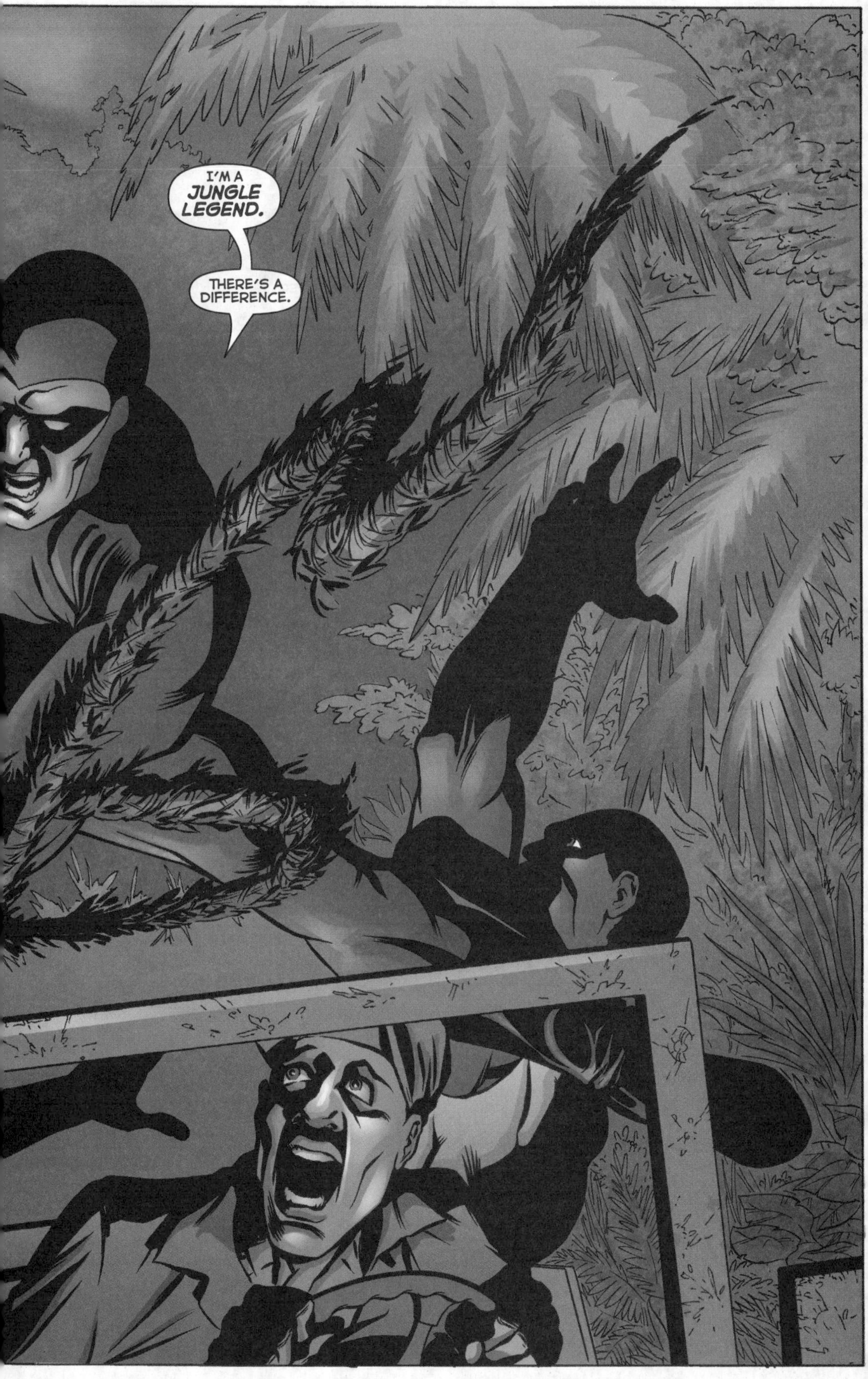
I'M A JUNGLE LEGEND.
THERE'S A DIFFERENCE.

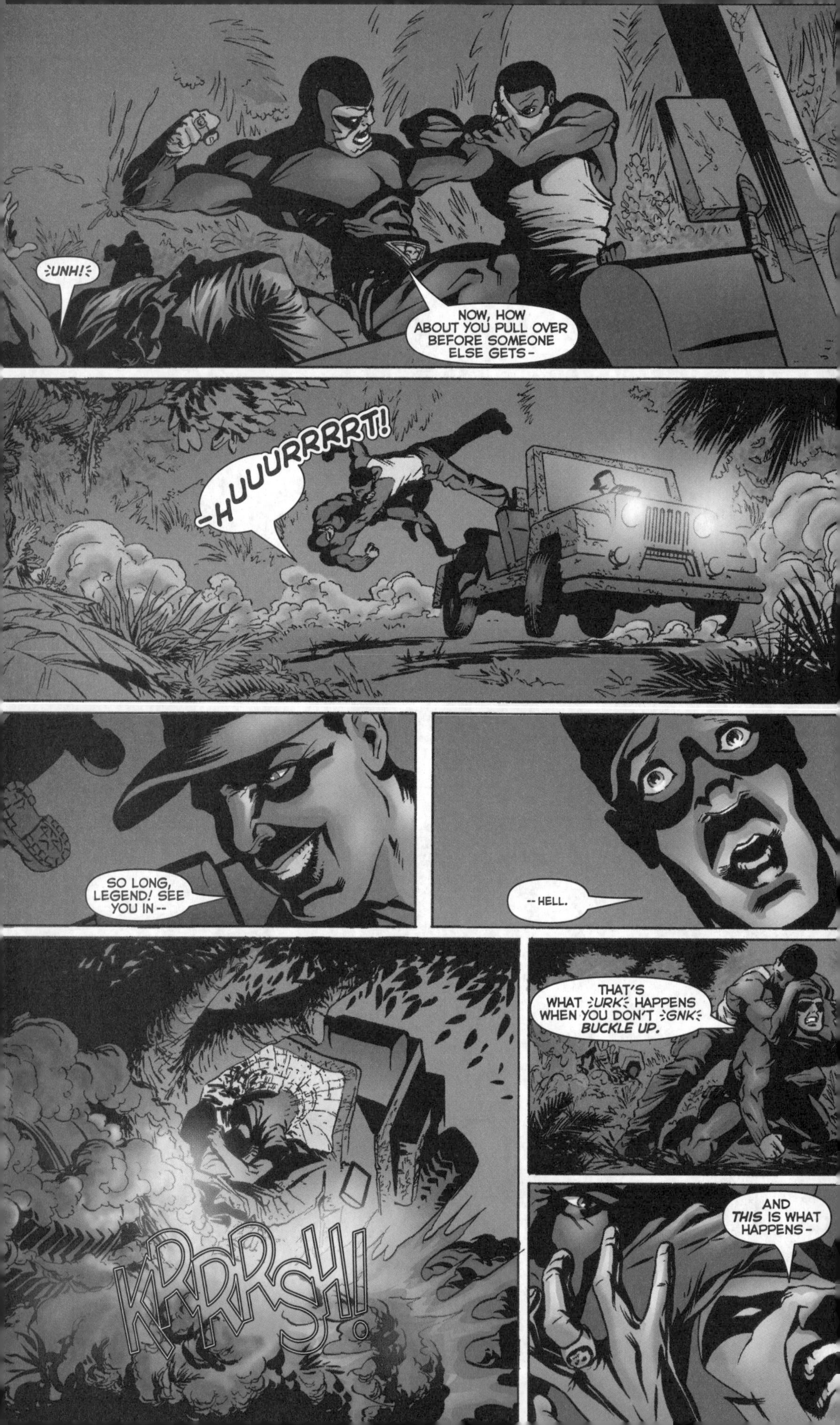

UNH!
NOW, HOW ABOUT YOU PULL OVER BEFORE SOMEONE ELSE GETS-
-HUUURRRRT!
SO LONG, LEGEND! SEE YOU IN--
--HELL.
KRRRSH!
THAT'S WHAT URK HAPPENS WHEN YOU DON'T GNK BUCKLE UP.
AND THIS IS WHAT HAPPENS-

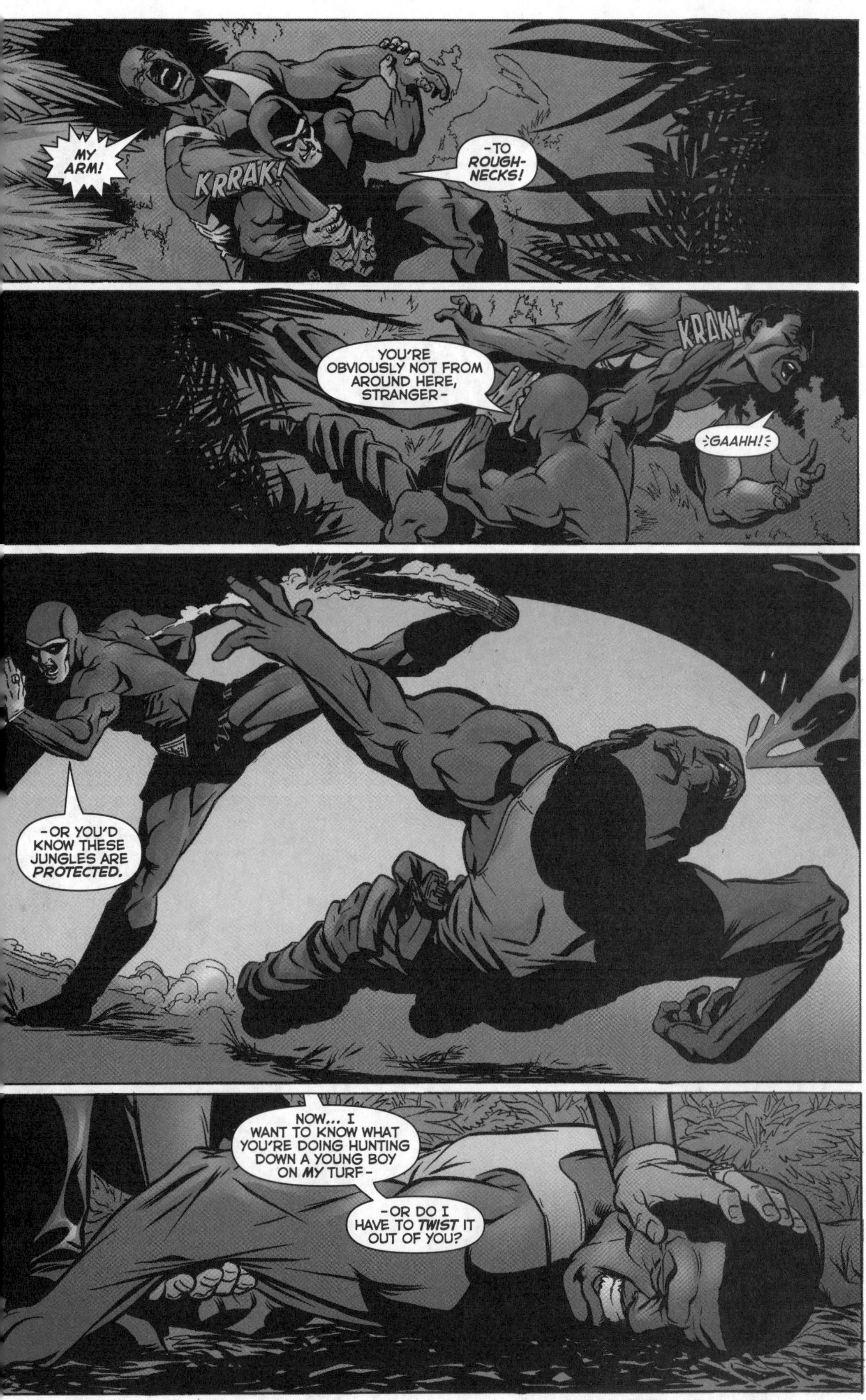
MY ARM!
KRRAK!
-TO ROUGH-NECKS!
YOU'RE OBVIOUSLY NOT FROM AROUND HERE, STRANGER-
KRAK!
GAAHH!
-OR YOU'D KNOW THESE JUNGLES ARE *PROTECTED.*
NOW... I WANT TO KNOW WHAT YOU'RE DOING HUNTING DOWN A YOUNG BOY ON *MY* TURF-
-OR DO I HAVE TO *TWIST* IT OUT OF YOU?

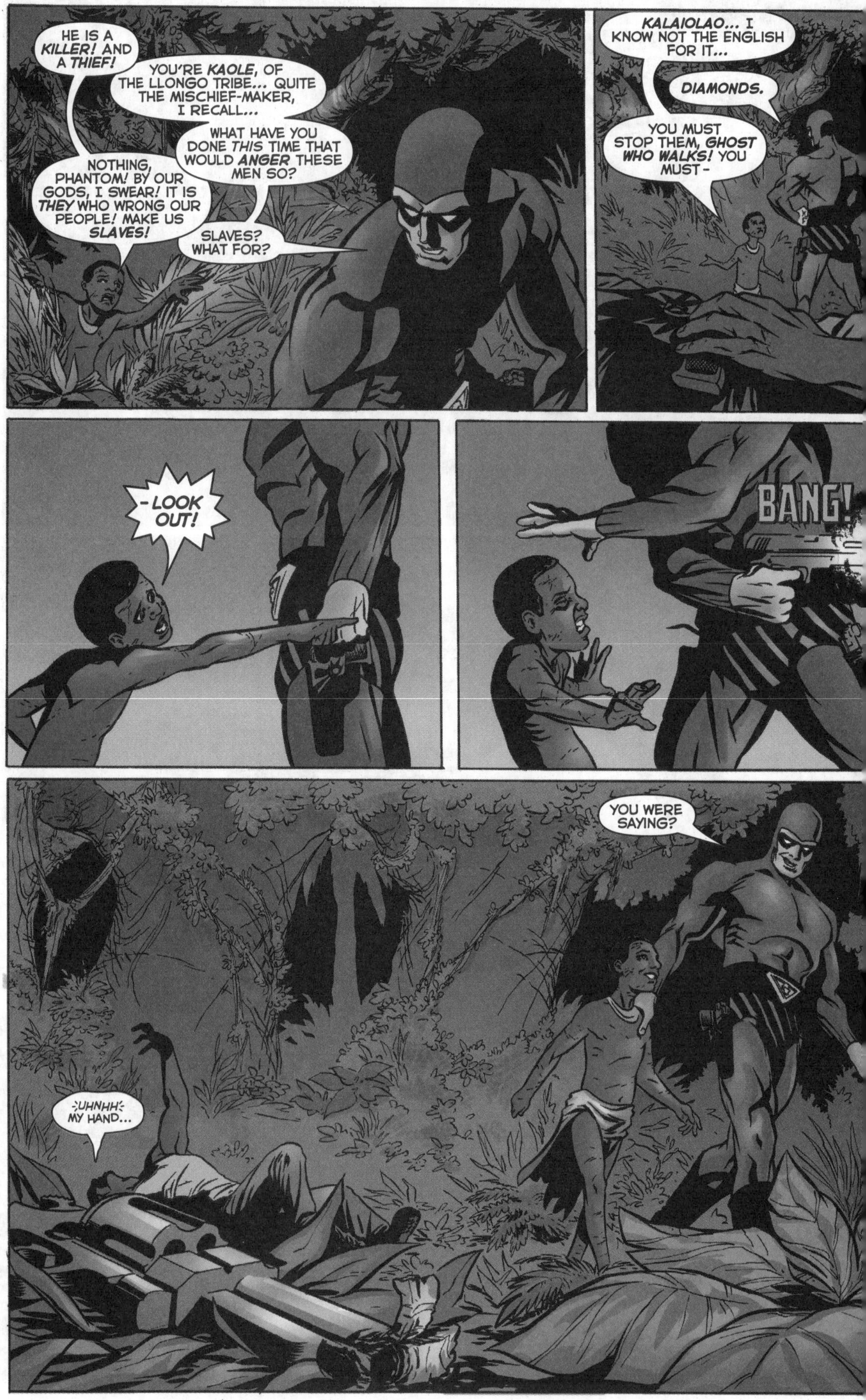
HE IS A KILLER! AND A THIEF!
YOU'RE KAOLE, OF THE LLONGO TRIBE... QUITE THE MISCHIEF-MAKER, I RECALL...
NOTHING, PHANTOM! BY OUR GODS, I SWEAR! IT IS THEY WHO WRONG OUR PEOPLE! MAKE US SLAVES!
WHAT HAVE YOU DONE THIS TIME THAT WOULD ANGER THESE MEN SO?
SLAVES? WHAT FOR?
KALAIOLAO... I KNOW NOT THE ENGLISH FOR IT...
DIAMONDS.
YOU MUST STOP THEM, GHOST WHO WALKS! YOU MUST-
-LOOK OUT!
BANG!
YOU WERE SAYING?
UHNHH MY HAND...

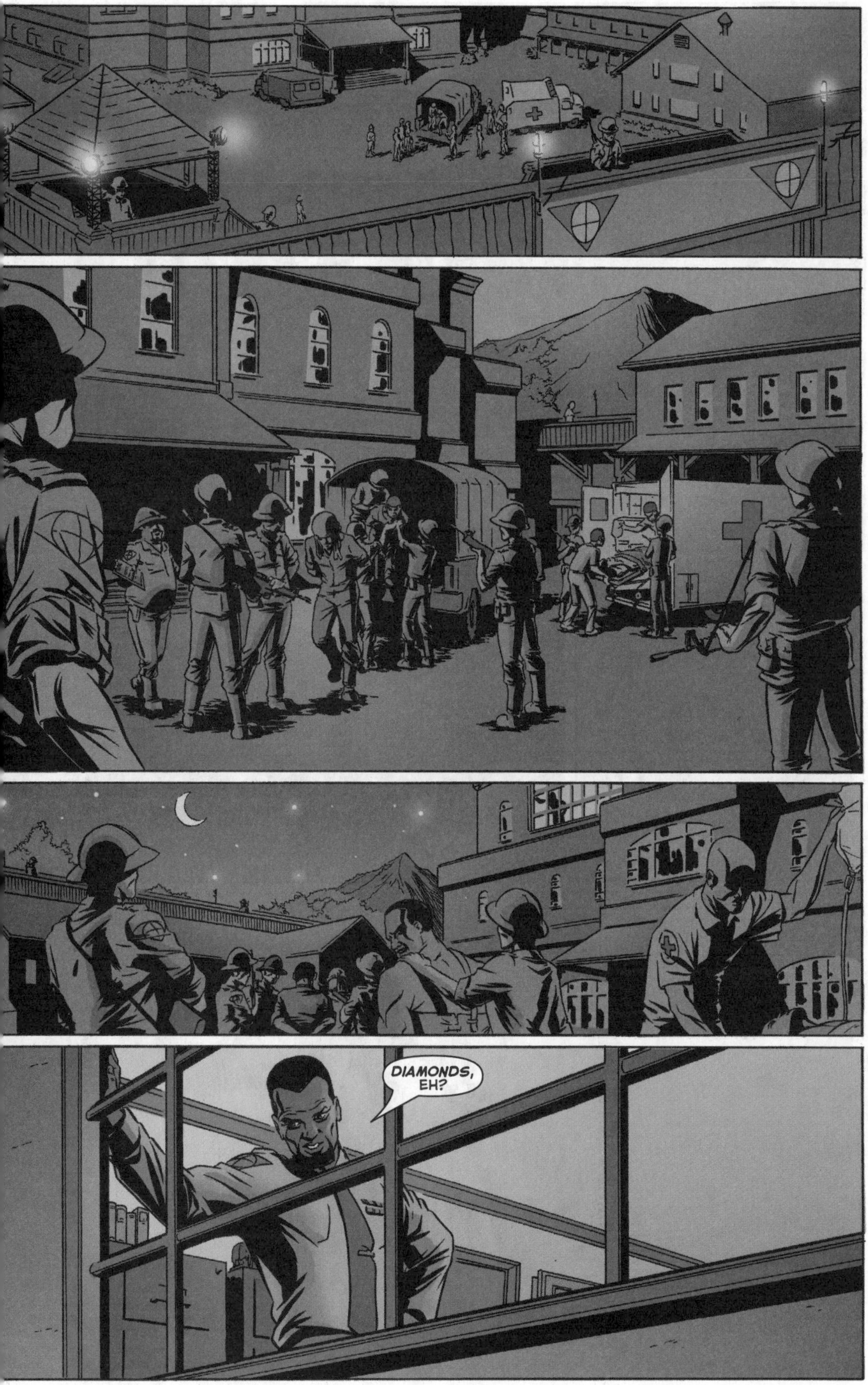
DIAMONDS, EH?

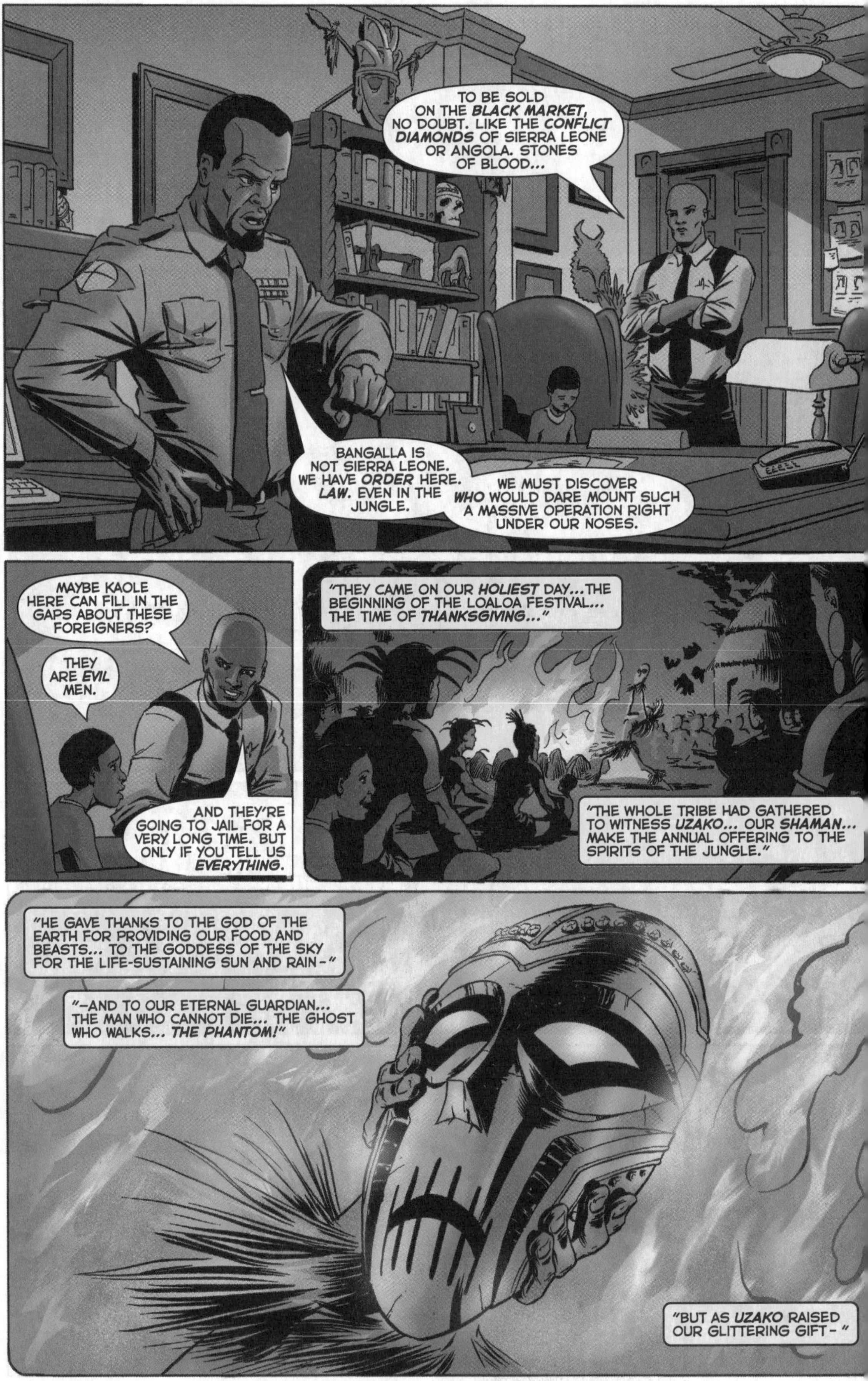
TO BE SOLD ON THE *BLACK MARKET*, NO DOUBT. LIKE THE *CONFLICT DIAMONDS* OF SIERRA LEONE OR ANGOLA. STONES OF BLOOD...
BANGALLA IS NOT SIERRA LEONE. WE HAVE *ORDER* HERE. *LAW*. EVEN IN THE JUNGLE.
WE MUST DISCOVER *WHO* WOULD DARE MOUNT SUCH A MASSIVE OPERATION RIGHT UNDER OUR NOSES.
MAYBE KAOLE HERE CAN FILL IN THE GAPS ABOUT THESE FOREIGNERS?
THEY ARE *EVIL* MEN.
AND THEY'RE GOING TO JAIL FOR A VERY LONG TIME. BUT ONLY IF YOU TELL US *EVERYTHING*.
"THEY CAME ON OUR *HOLIEST* DAY... THE BEGINNING OF THE LOALOA FESTIVAL... THE TIME OF *THANKSGIVING*..."
"THE WHOLE TRIBE HAD GATHERED TO WITNESS *UZAKO*... OUR *SHAMAN*... MAKE THE ANNUAL OFFERING TO THE SPIRITS OF THE JUNGLE."
"HE GAVE THANKS TO THE GOD OF THE EARTH FOR PROVIDING OUR FOOD AND BEASTS... TO THE GODDESS OF THE SKY FOR THE LIFE-SUSTAINING SUN AND RAIN-"
"-AND TO OUR ETERNAL GUARDIAN... THE MAN WHO CANNOT DIE... THE GHOST WHO WALKS... *THE PHANTOM!*"
"BUT AS *UZAKO* RAISED OUR GLITTERING GIFT-"

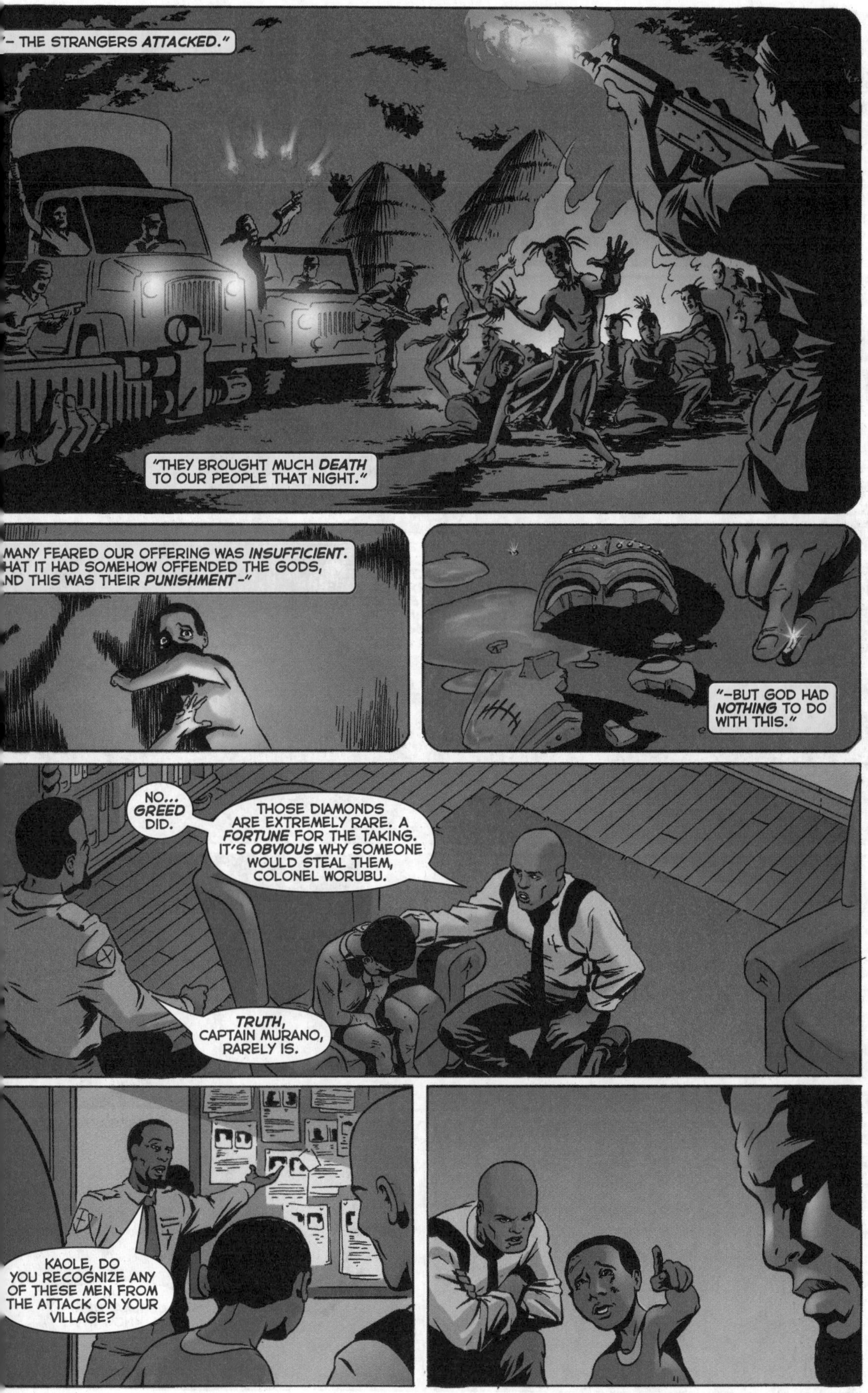
"– THE STRANGERS ATTACKED."
"THEY BROUGHT MUCH DEATH TO OUR PEOPLE THAT NIGHT."
MANY FEARED OUR OFFERING WAS INSUFFICIENT. HAT IT HAD SOMEHOW OFFENDED THE GODS, ND THIS WAS THEIR PUNISHMENT –"
"–BUT GOD HAD NOTHING TO DO WITH THIS."
NO... GREED DID.
THOSE DIAMONDS ARE EXTREMELY RARE. A FORTUNE FOR THE TAKING. IT'S OBVIOUS WHY SOMEONE WOULD STEAL THEM, COLONEL WORUBU.
TRUTH, CAPTAIN MURANO, RARELY IS.
KAOLE, DO YOU RECOGNIZE ANY OF THESE MEN FROM THE ATTACK ON YOUR VILLAGE?

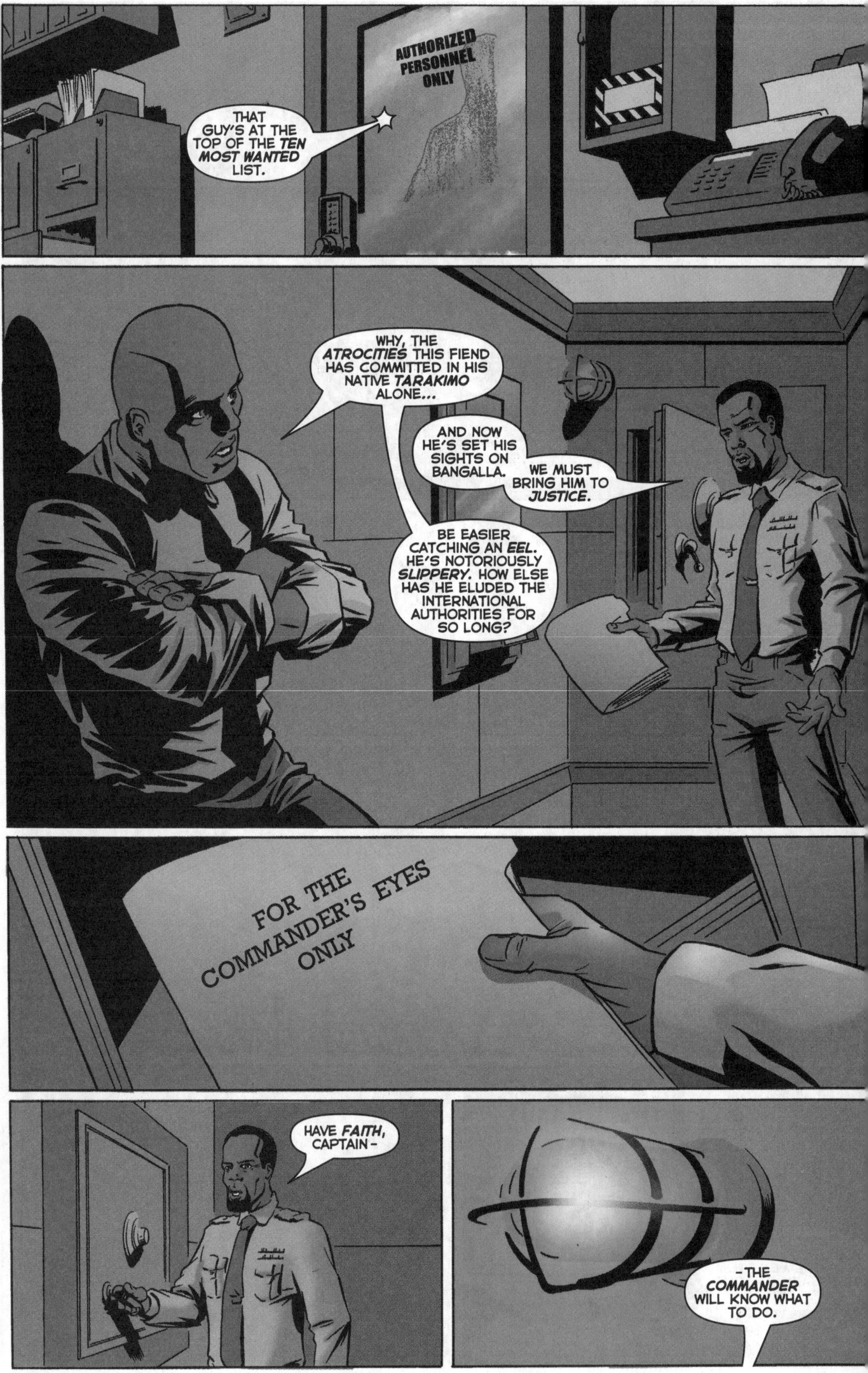
AUTHORIZED PERSONNEL ONLY
THAT GUY'S AT THE TOP OF THE TEN MOST WANTED LIST.
WHY, THE ATROCITIES THIS FIEND HAS COMMITTED IN HIS NATIVE TARAKIMO ALONE...
AND NOW HE'S SET HIS SIGHTS ON BANGALLA.
WE MUST BRING HIM TO JUSTICE.
BE EASIER CATCHING AN EEL. HE'S NOTORIOUSLY SLIPPERY. HOW ELSE HAS HE ELUDED THE INTERNATIONAL AUTHORITIES FOR SO LONG?
FOR THE COMMANDER'S EYES ONLY
HAVE FAITH, CAPTAIN -
- THE COMMANDER WILL KNOW WHAT TO DO.

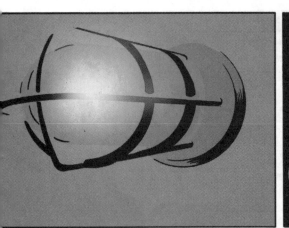

WANTED – DEAD OR ALIVE
ALI GUTAALE

DESCRIPTION

Date of Birth:
December 14, 1965
Place of Birth:
Tarakimo
Height: 6' 2"/188 cm
Weight:190 lbs/86 kg

Hair: Bald
Eyes: Brown
Complexion: Dark
Sex: Male
Build: Muscular
Race: Black/Arab

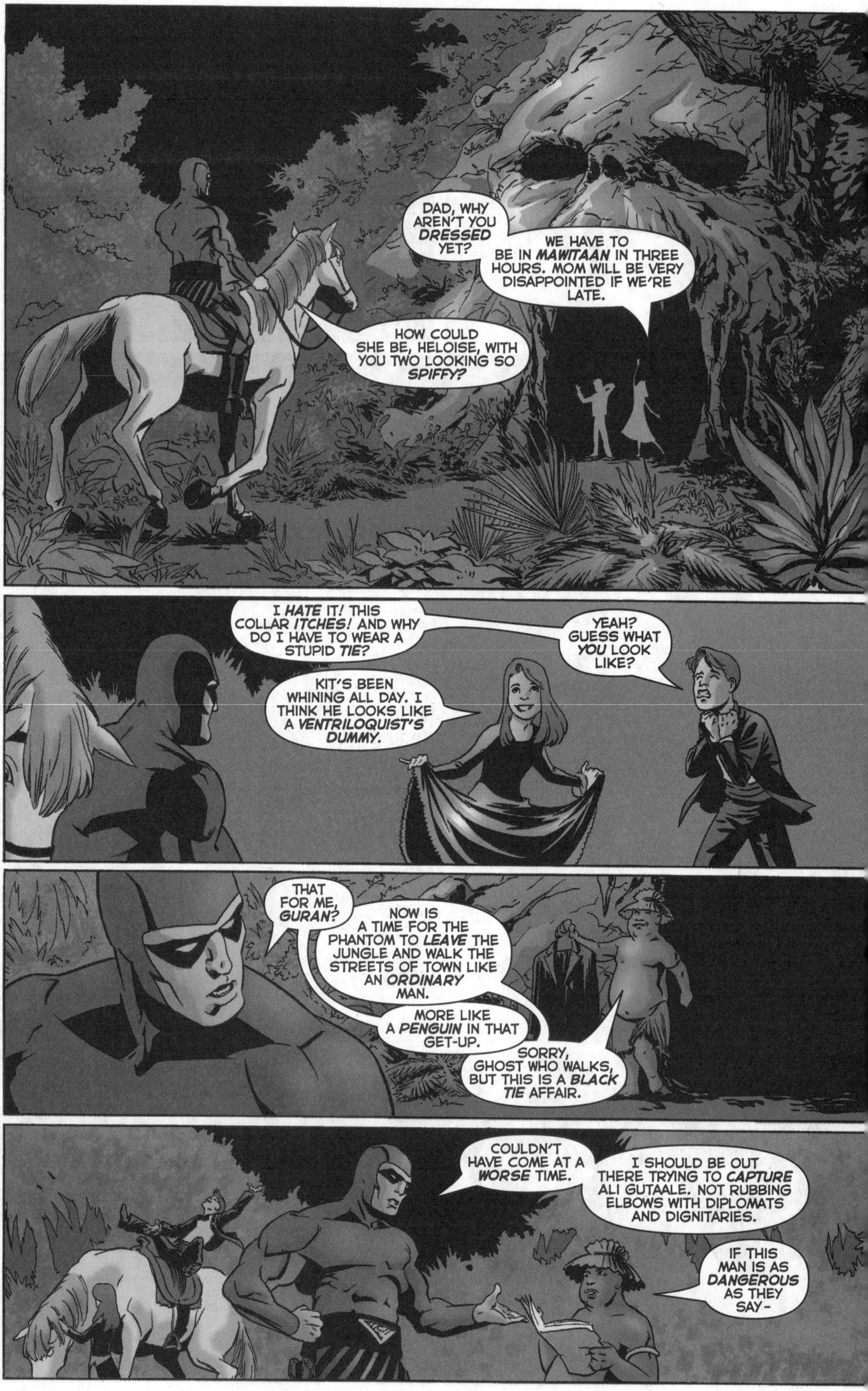
DAD, WHY AREN'T YOU *DRESSED* YET?
WE HAVE TO BE IN *MAWITAAN* IN THREE HOURS. MOM WILL BE VERY DISAPPOINTED IF WE'RE LATE.
HOW COULD SHE BE, HELOISE, WITH YOU TWO LOOKING SO *SPIFFY?*
I *HATE* IT! THIS COLLAR *ITCHES!* AND WHY DO I HAVE TO WEAR A STUPID *TIE?*
YEAH? GUESS WHAT *YOU* LOOK LIKE?
KIT'S BEEN WHINING ALL DAY. I THINK HE LOOKS LIKE A *VENTRILOQUIST'S DUMMY.*
THAT FOR ME, *GURAN?*
NOW IS A TIME FOR THE PHANTOM TO *LEAVE* THE JUNGLE AND WALK THE STREETS OF TOWN LIKE AN *ORDINARY* MAN.
MORE LIKE A *PENGUIN* IN THAT GET-UP.
SORRY, GHOST WHO WALKS, BUT THIS IS A *BLACK TIE* AFFAIR.
COULDN'T HAVE COME AT A *WORSE* TIME.
I SHOULD BE OUT THERE TRYING TO *CAPTURE* ALI GUTAALE. NOT RUBBING ELBOWS WITH DIPLOMATS AND DIGNITARIES.
IF THIS MAN IS AS *DANGEROUS* AS THEY SAY-

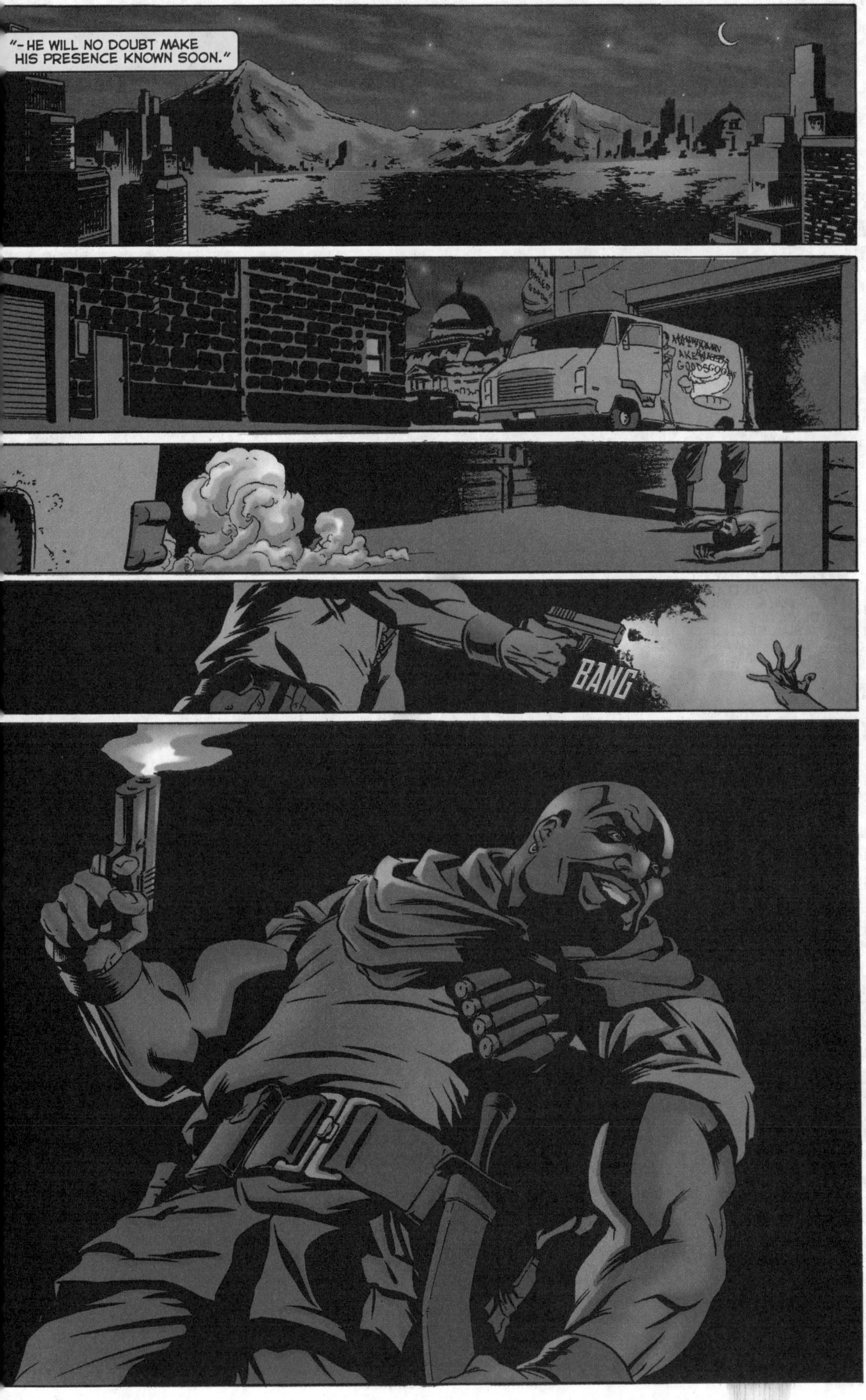
"– HE WILL NO DOUBT MAKE HIS PRESENCE KNOWN SOON."
BANG

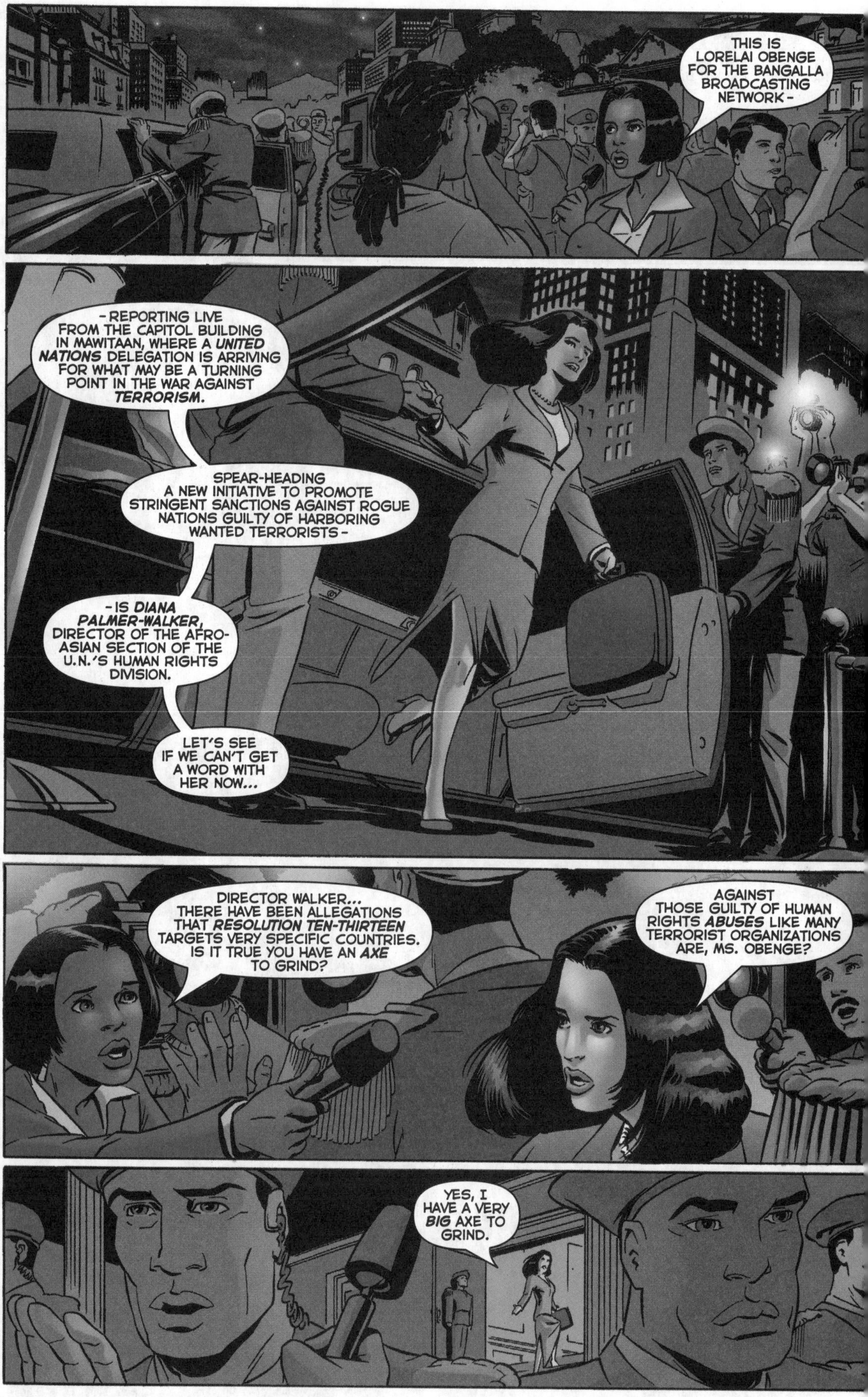
THIS IS LORELAI OBENGE FOR THE BANGALLA BROADCASTING NETWORK-
-REPORTING LIVE FROM THE CAPITOL BUILDING IN MAWITAAN, WHERE A UNITED NATIONS DELEGATION IS ARRIVING FOR WHAT MAY BE A TURNING POINT IN THE WAR AGAINST TERRORISM.
SPEAR-HEADING A NEW INITIATIVE TO PROMOTE STRINGENT SANCTIONS AGAINST ROGUE NATIONS GUILTY OF HARBORING WANTED TERRORISTS-
-IS DIANA PALMER-WALKER, DIRECTOR OF THE AFRO-ASIAN SECTION OF THE U.N.'S HUMAN RIGHTS DIVISION.
LET'S SEE IF WE CAN'T GET A WORD WITH HER NOW...
DIRECTOR WALKER... THERE HAVE BEEN ALLEGATIONS THAT RESOLUTION TEN-THIRTEEN TARGETS VERY SPECIFIC COUNTRIES. IS IT TRUE YOU HAVE AN AXE TO GRIND?
AGAINST THOSE GUILTY OF HUMAN RIGHTS ABUSES LIKE MANY TERRORIST ORGANIZATIONS ARE, MS. OBENGE?
YES, I HAVE A VERY BIG AXE TO GRIND.

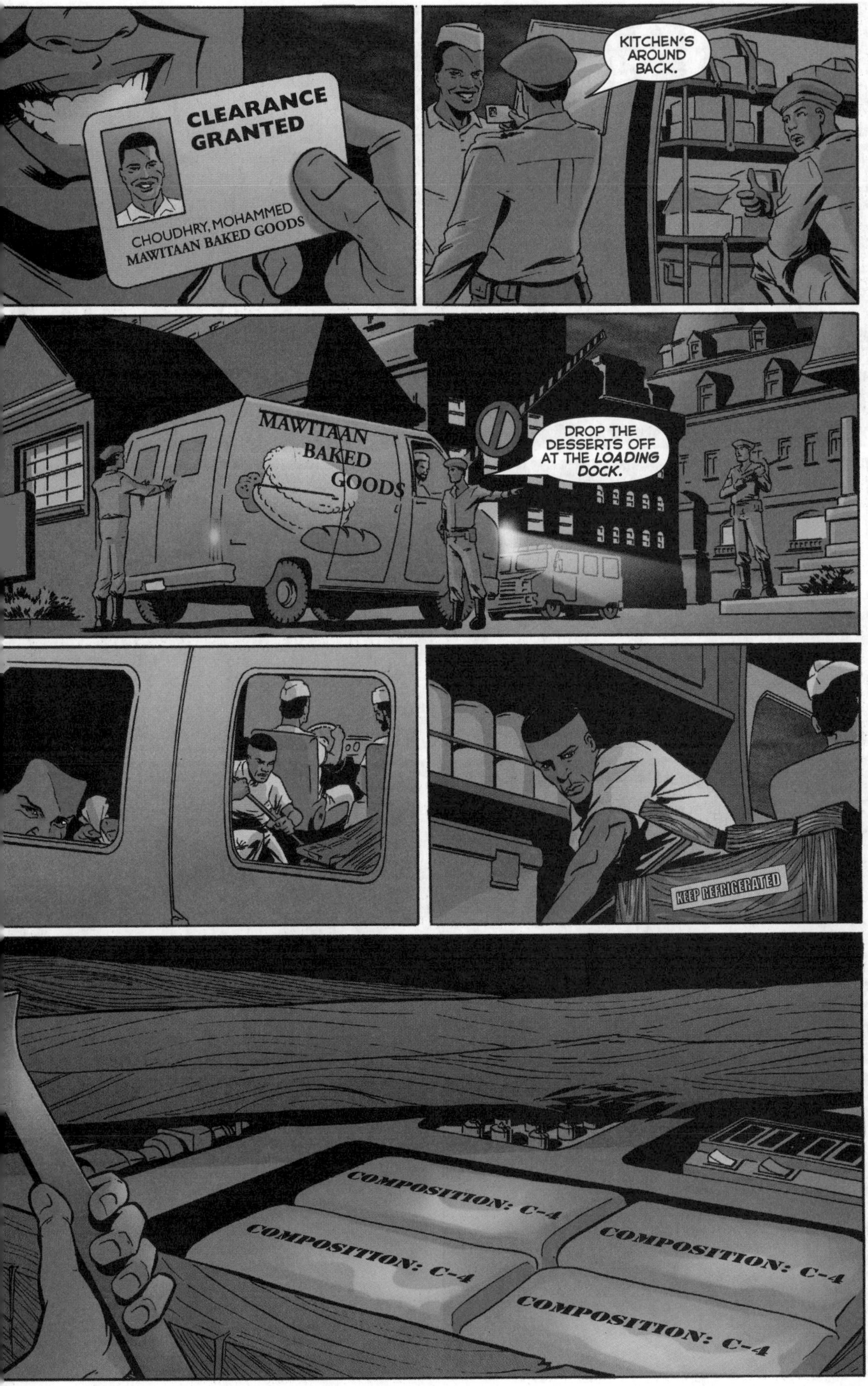
CLEARANCE GRANTED
CHOUDHRY, MOHAMMED
MAWITAAN BAKED GOODS
KITCHEN'S AROUND BACK.
MAWITAAN BAKED GOODS
DROP THE DESSERTS OFF AT THE *LOADING DOCK.*
KEEP REFRIGERATED
COMPOSITION: C-4
COMPOSITION: C-4
COMPOSITION: C-4
COMPOSITION: C-4

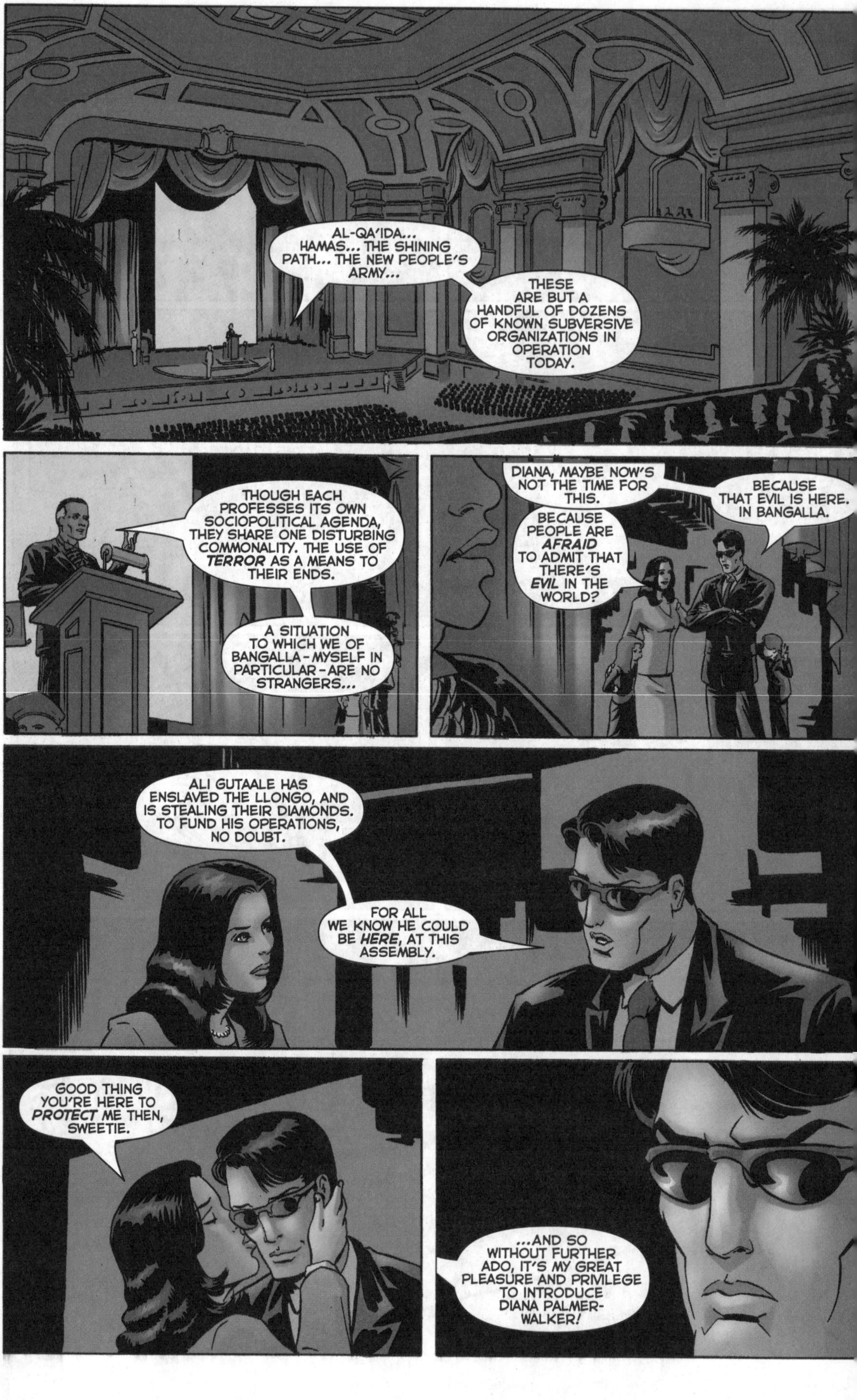
AL-QA'IDA... HAMAS... THE SHINING PATH... THE NEW PEOPLE'S ARMY...
THESE ARE BUT A HANDFUL OF DOZENS OF KNOWN SUBVERSIVE ORGANIZATIONS IN OPERATION TODAY.
THOUGH EACH PROFESSES ITS OWN SOCIOPOLITICAL AGENDA, THEY SHARE ONE DISTURBING COMMONALITY. THE USE OF *TERROR* AS A MEANS TO THEIR ENDS.
A SITUATION TO WHICH WE OF BANGALLA - MYSELF IN PARTICULAR - ARE NO STRANGERS...
DIANA, MAYBE NOW'S NOT THE TIME FOR THIS.
BECAUSE PEOPLE ARE *AFRAID* TO ADMIT THAT THERE'S *EVIL* IN THE WORLD?
BECAUSE THAT EVIL IS HERE. IN BANGALLA.
ALI GUTAALE HAS ENSLAVED THE LLONGO, AND IS STEALING THEIR DIAMONDS. TO FUND HIS OPERATIONS, NO DOUBT.
FOR ALL WE KNOW HE COULD BE *HERE*, AT THIS ASSEMBLY.
GOOD THING YOU'RE HERE TO *PROTECT* ME THEN, SWEETIE.
...AND SO WITHOUT FURTHER ADO, IT'S MY GREAT PLEASURE AND PRIVILEGE TO INTRODUCE DIANA PALMER-WALKER!

THANK YOU, PRESIDENT LUAGA—

—AND THANK ALL OF YOU FOR COMING IN THE NAME OF INTERNATIONAL PEACE.

WE STARE DOWN A LONG ROAD AT AN UNCERTAIN FUTURE. BUT AS EVERY JOURNEY BEGINS WITH A SINGLE STEP, SO DOES EVERY FUTURE BEGIN WITH A SINGLE ACT OF *DETERMINATION.*

RESOLUTION TEN-THIRTEEN *IS* SUCH AN ACT.

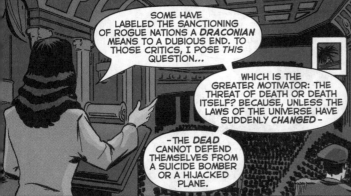

SOME HAVE LABELED THE SANCTIONING OF ROGUE NATIONS A *DRACONIAN* MEANS TO A DUBIOUS END. TO THOSE CRITICS, I POSE *THIS* QUESTION...

WHICH IS THE GREATER MOTIVATOR: THE THREAT OF DEATH OR DEATH ITSELF? BECAUSE, UNLESS THE LAWS OF THE UNIVERSE HAVE SUDDENLY *CHANGED*—

—THE *DEAD* CANNOT DEFEND THEMSELVES FROM A SUICIDE BOMBER OR A HIJACKED PLANE.

BUT *WE* CAN.

UHNH!

DIANA!

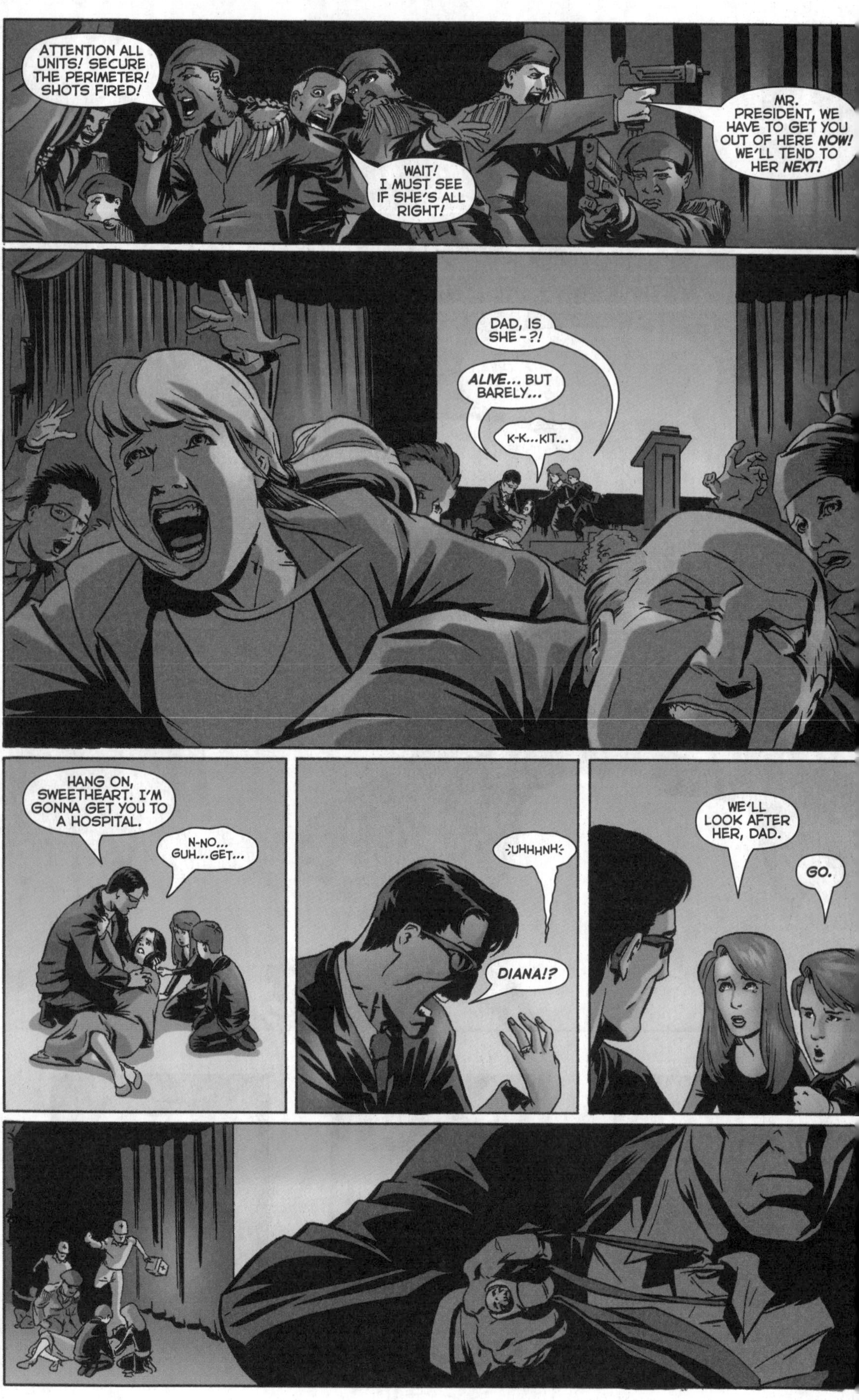
ATTENTION ALL UNITS! SECURE THE PERIMETER! SHOTS FIRED!
WAIT! I MUST SEE IF SHE'S ALL RIGHT!
MR. PRESIDENT, WE HAVE TO GET YOU OUT OF HERE NOW! WE'LL TEND TO HER NEXT!
DAD, IS SHE-?!
ALIVE... BUT BARELY...
K-K...KIT...
HANG ON, SWEETHEART. I'M GONNA GET YOU TO A HOSPITAL.
N-NO... GUH...GET...
UHHHNH
DIANA!?
WE'LL LOOK AFTER HER, DAD.
GO.

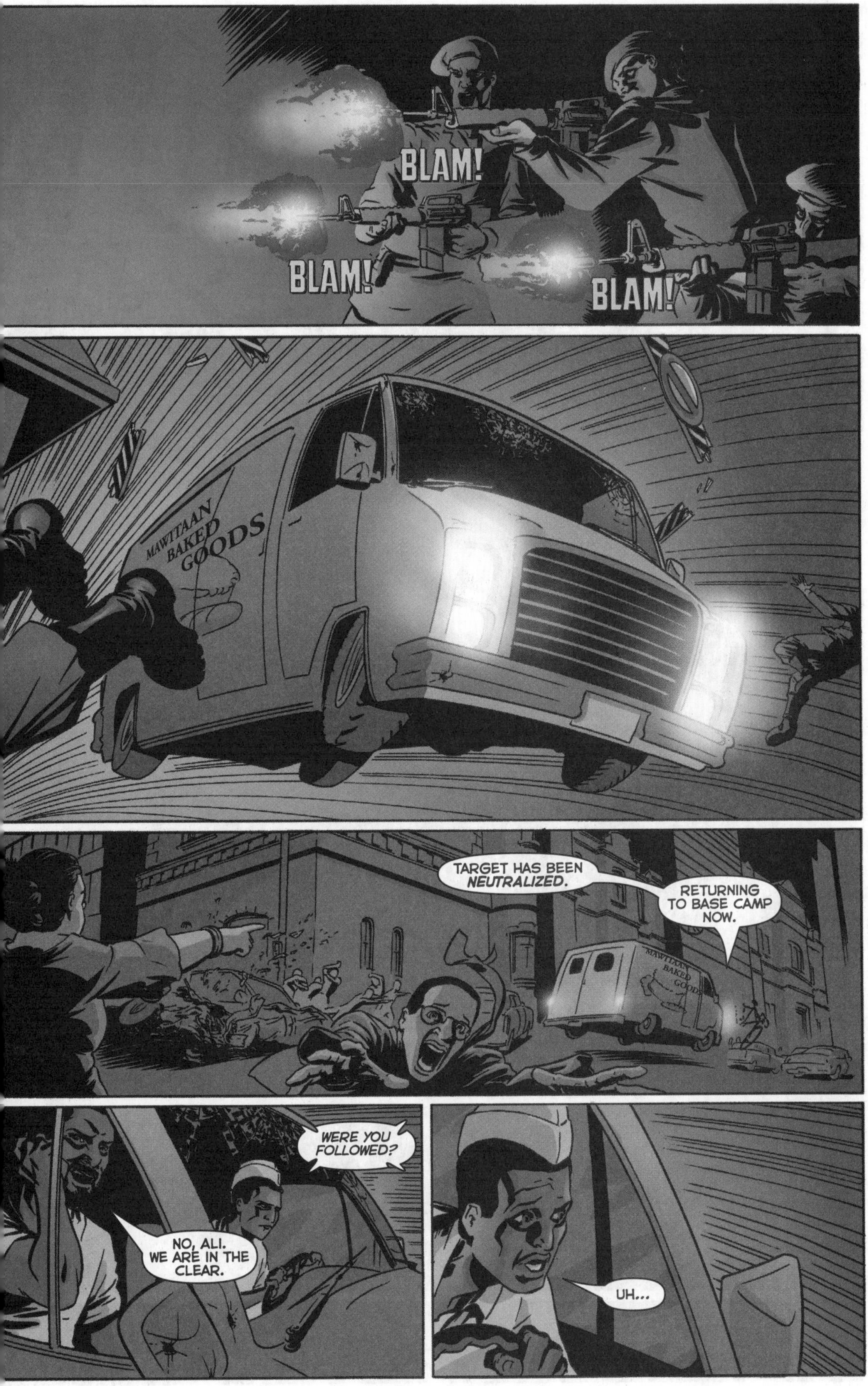
BLAM!
BLAM!
BLAM!
MAWITAAN BAKED GOODS
TARGET HAS BEEN *NEUTRALIZED*.
RETURNING TO BASE CAMP NOW.
WERE YOU FOLLOWED?
NO, ALI. WE ARE IN THE CLEAR.
UH...

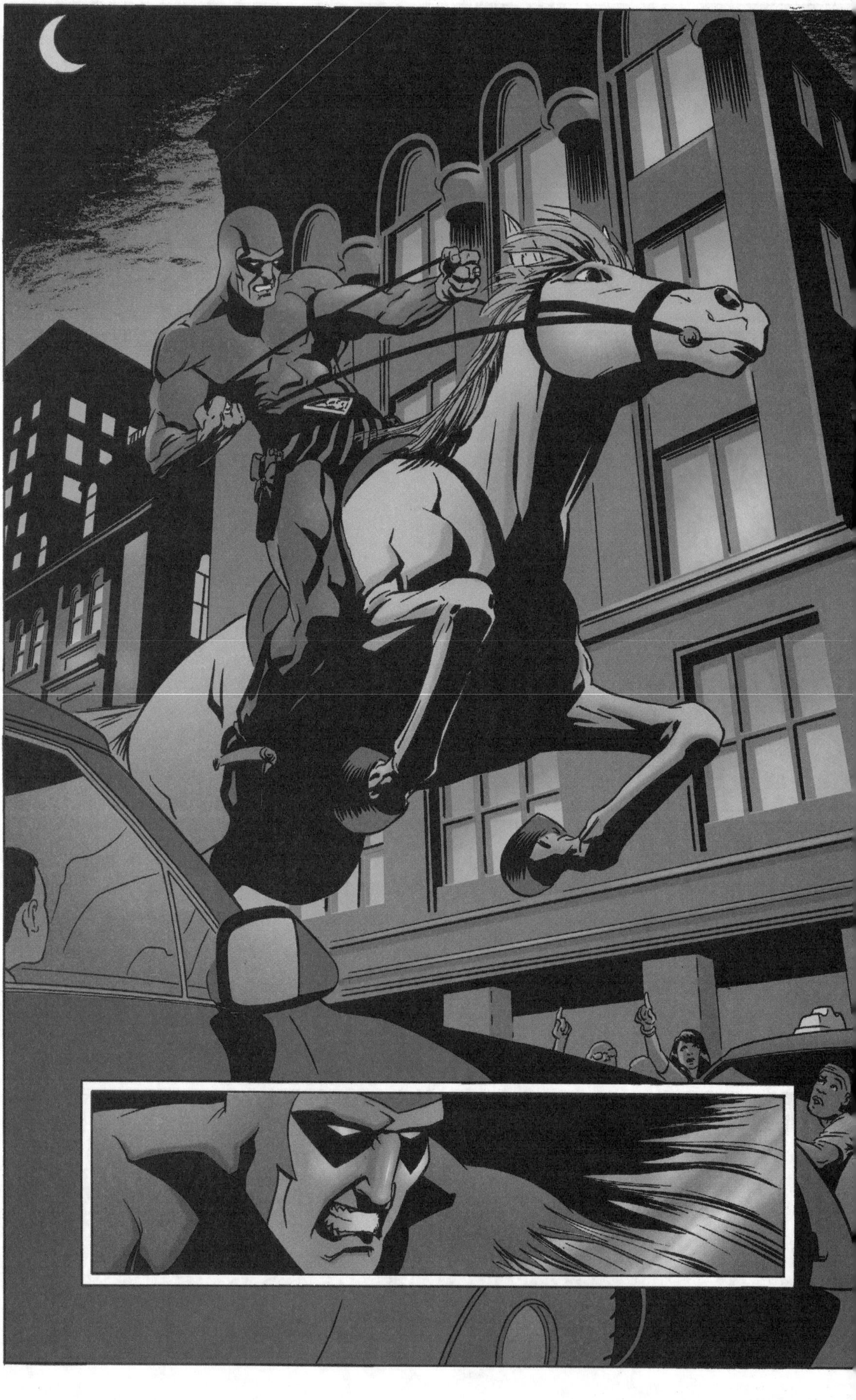

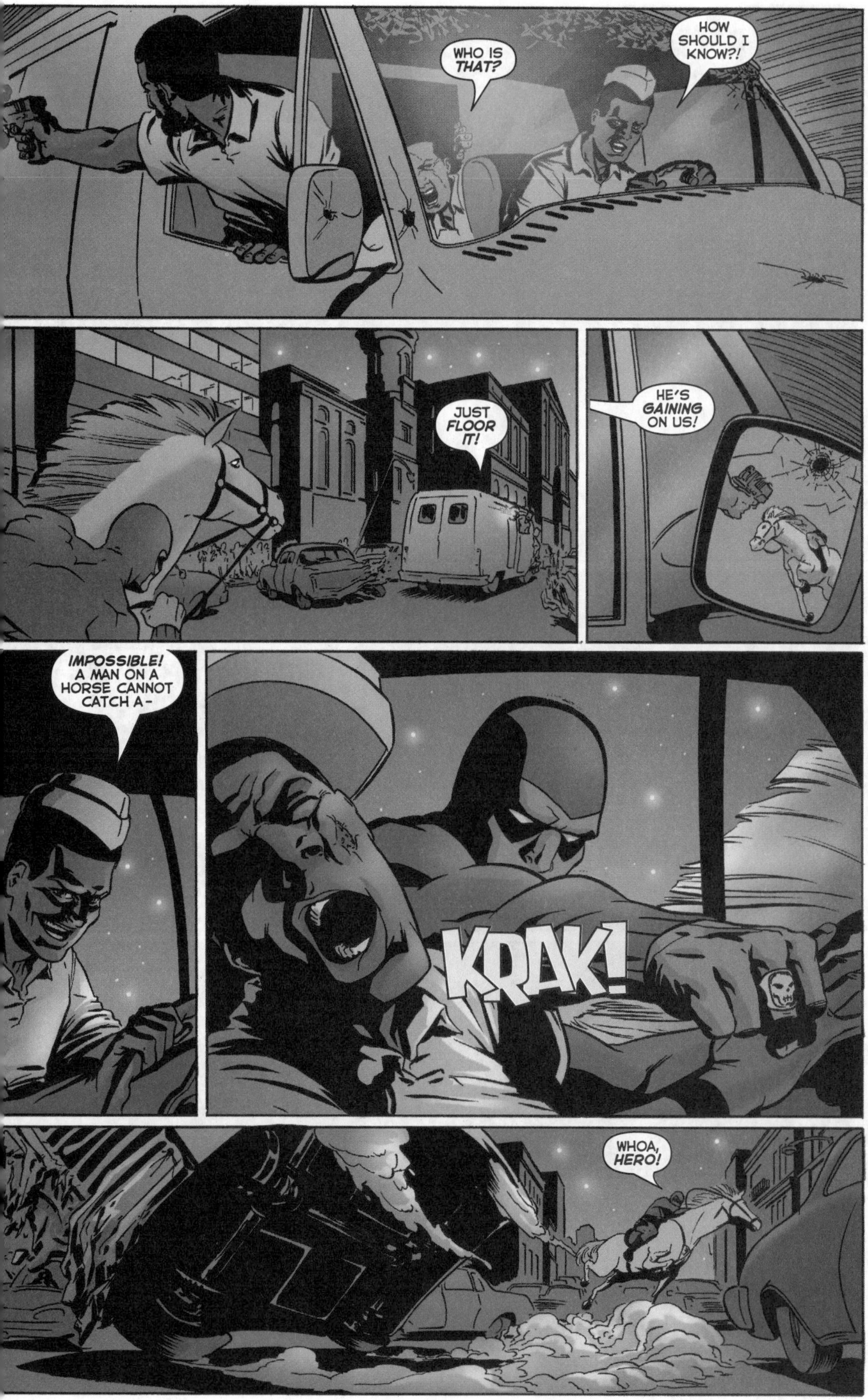
WHO IS THAT?
HOW SHOULD I KNOW?!
JUST FLOOR IT!
HE'S GAINING ON US!
IMPOSSIBLE! A MAN ON A HORSE CANNOT CATCH A-
KRAK!
WHOA, HERO!

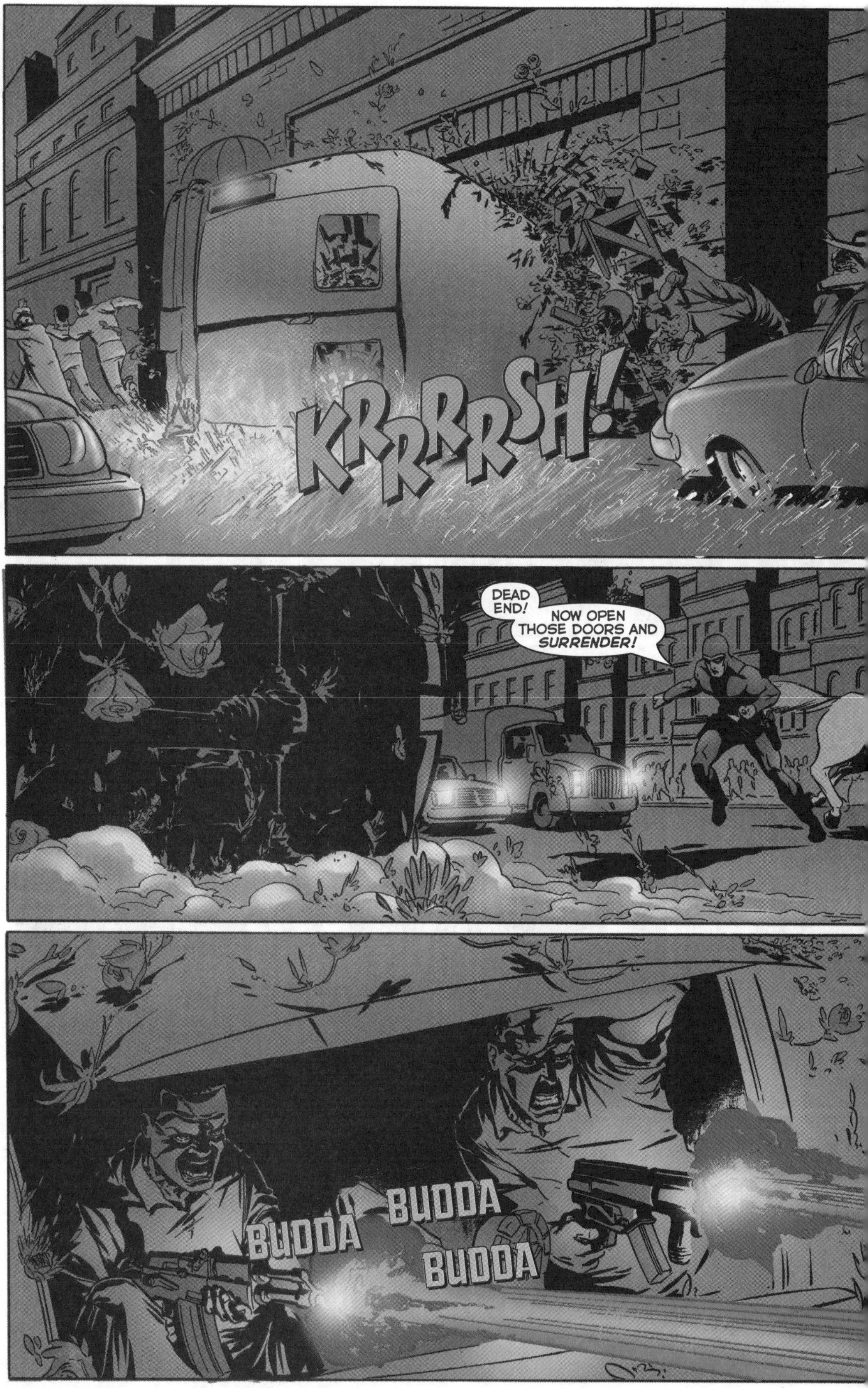
KRRRRRSH!
DEAD END!
NOW OPEN THOSE DOORS AND SURRENDER!
BUDDA
BUDDA
BUDDA

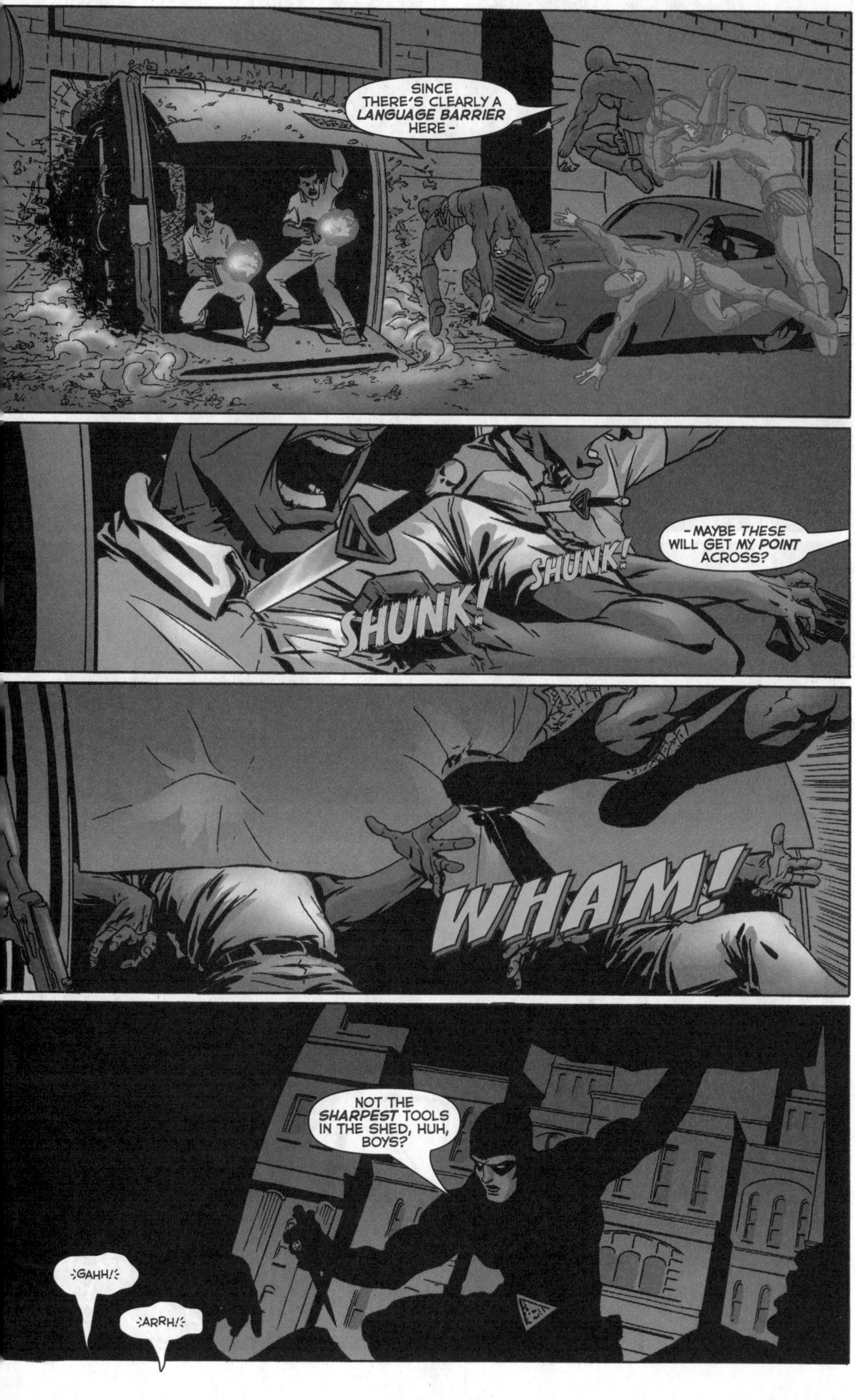
SINCE THERE'S CLEARLY A LANGUAGE BARRIER HERE -
- MAYBE THESE WILL GET MY POINT ACROSS?
SHUNK!
SHUNK!
WHAM!
NOT THE SHARPEST TOOLS IN THE SHED, HUH, BOYS?
GAHH!
ARRH!

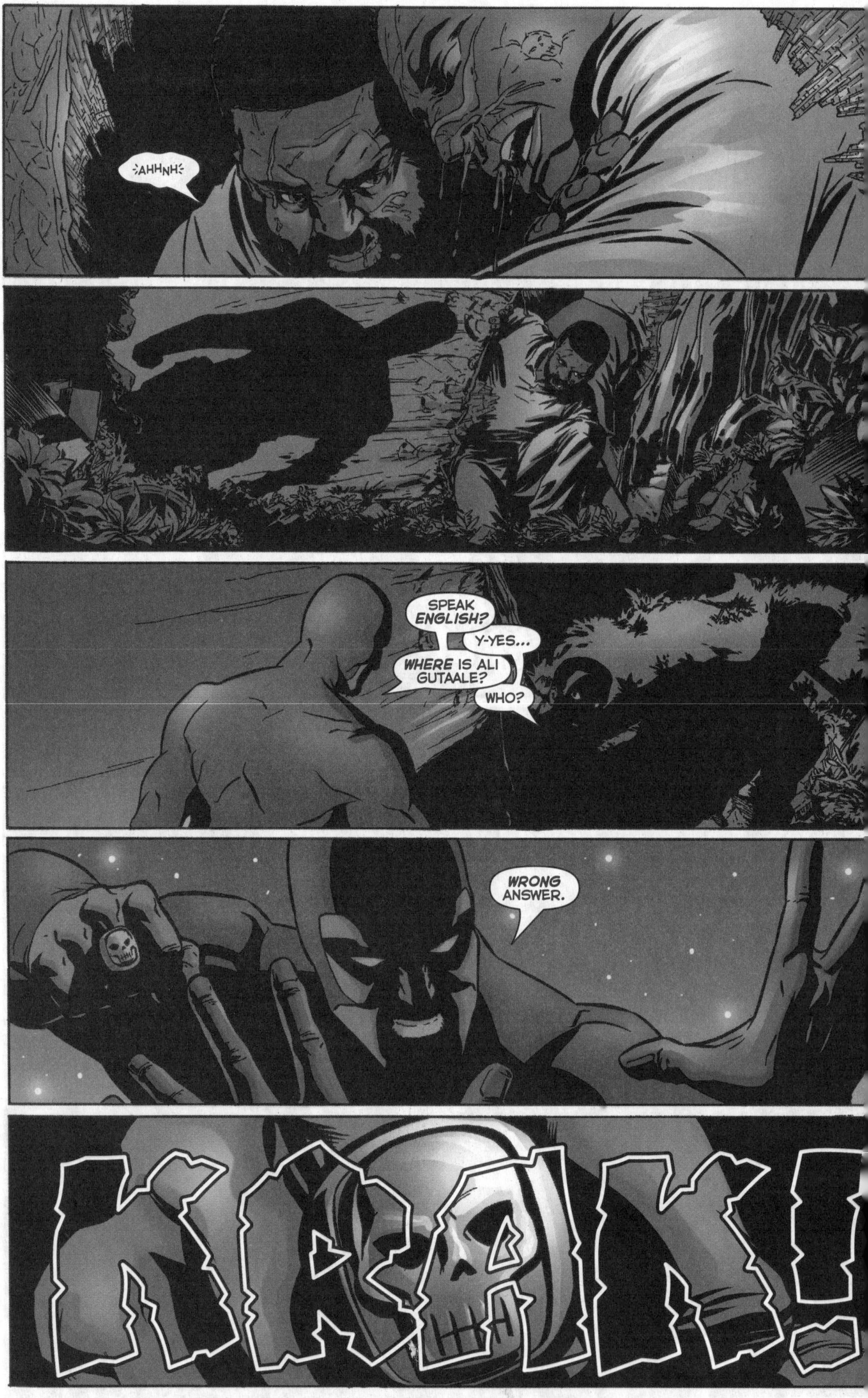
AHHNH
SPEAK ENGLISH?
Y-YES...
WHERE IS ALI GUTAALE?
WHO?
WRONG ANSWER.
KRAK!

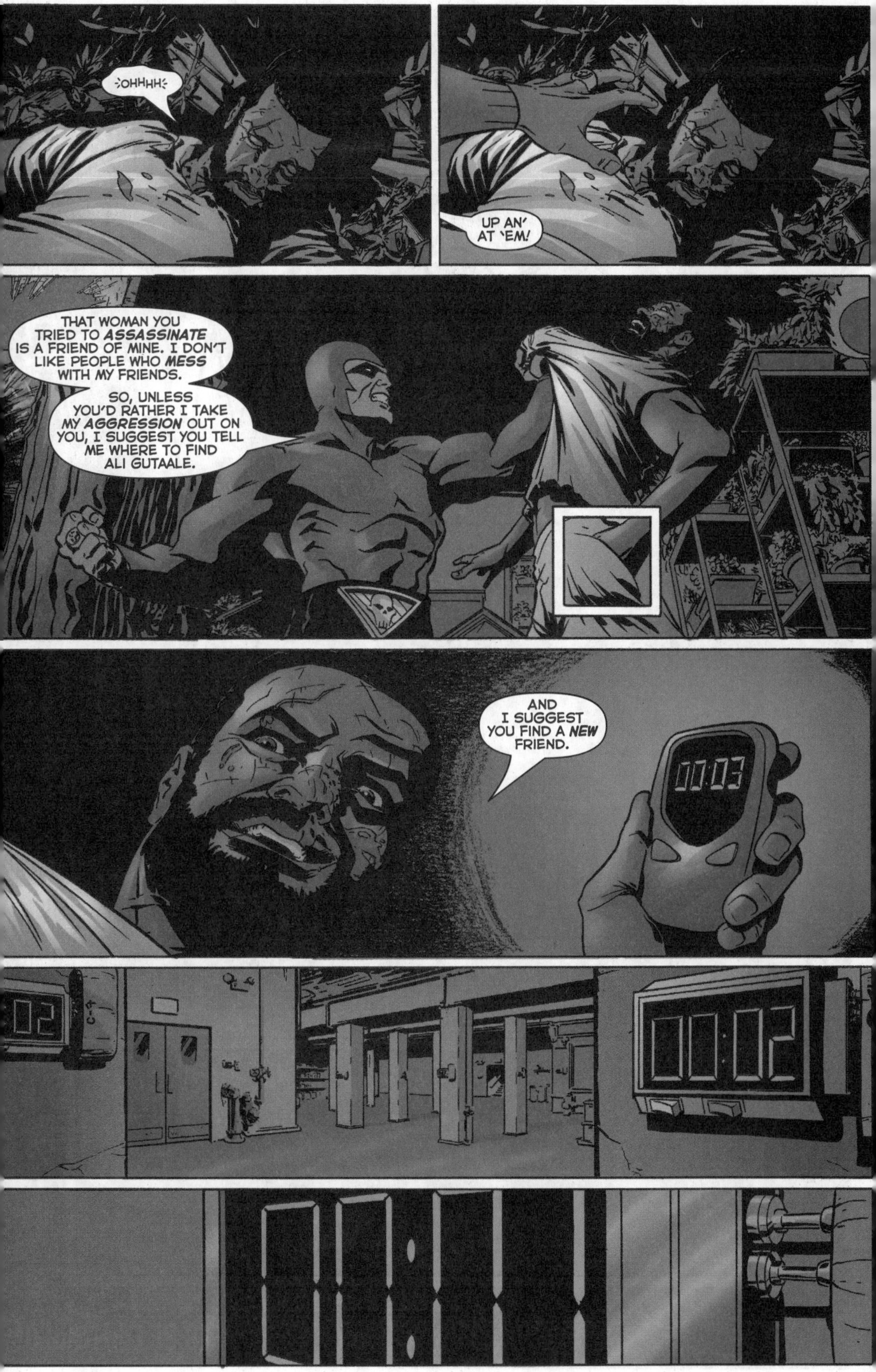

OHHHH
UP AN' AT 'EM!
THAT WOMAN YOU TRIED TO ASSASSINATE IS A FRIEND OF MINE. I DON'T LIKE PEOPLE WHO MESS WITH MY FRIENDS.
SO, UNLESS YOU'D RATHER I TAKE MY AGGRESSION OUT ON YOU, I SUGGEST YOU TELL ME WHERE TO FIND ALI GUTAALE.
AND I SUGGEST YOU FIND A NEW FRIEND.
00:03
00:02

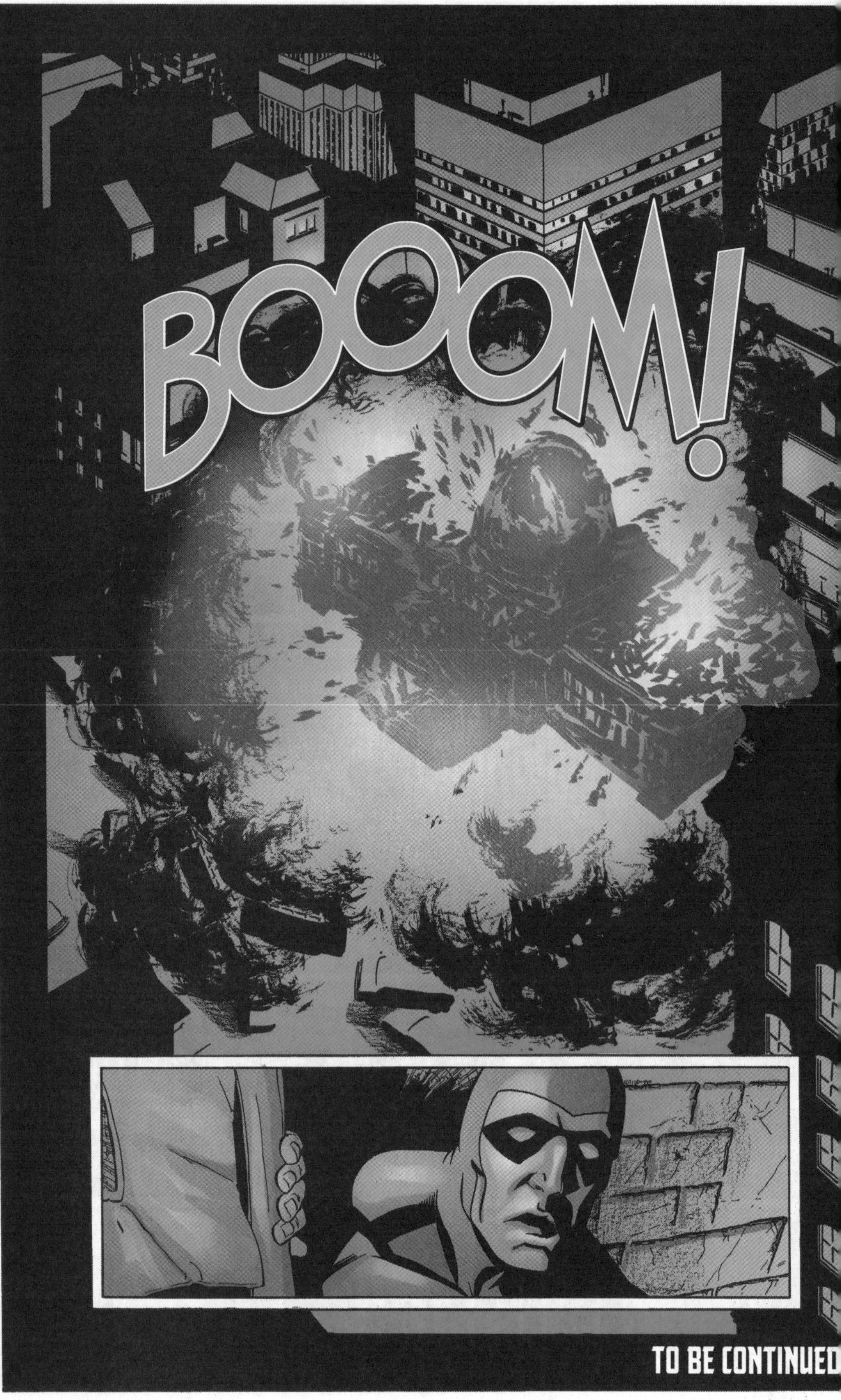
BOOOM!
TO BE CONTINUED

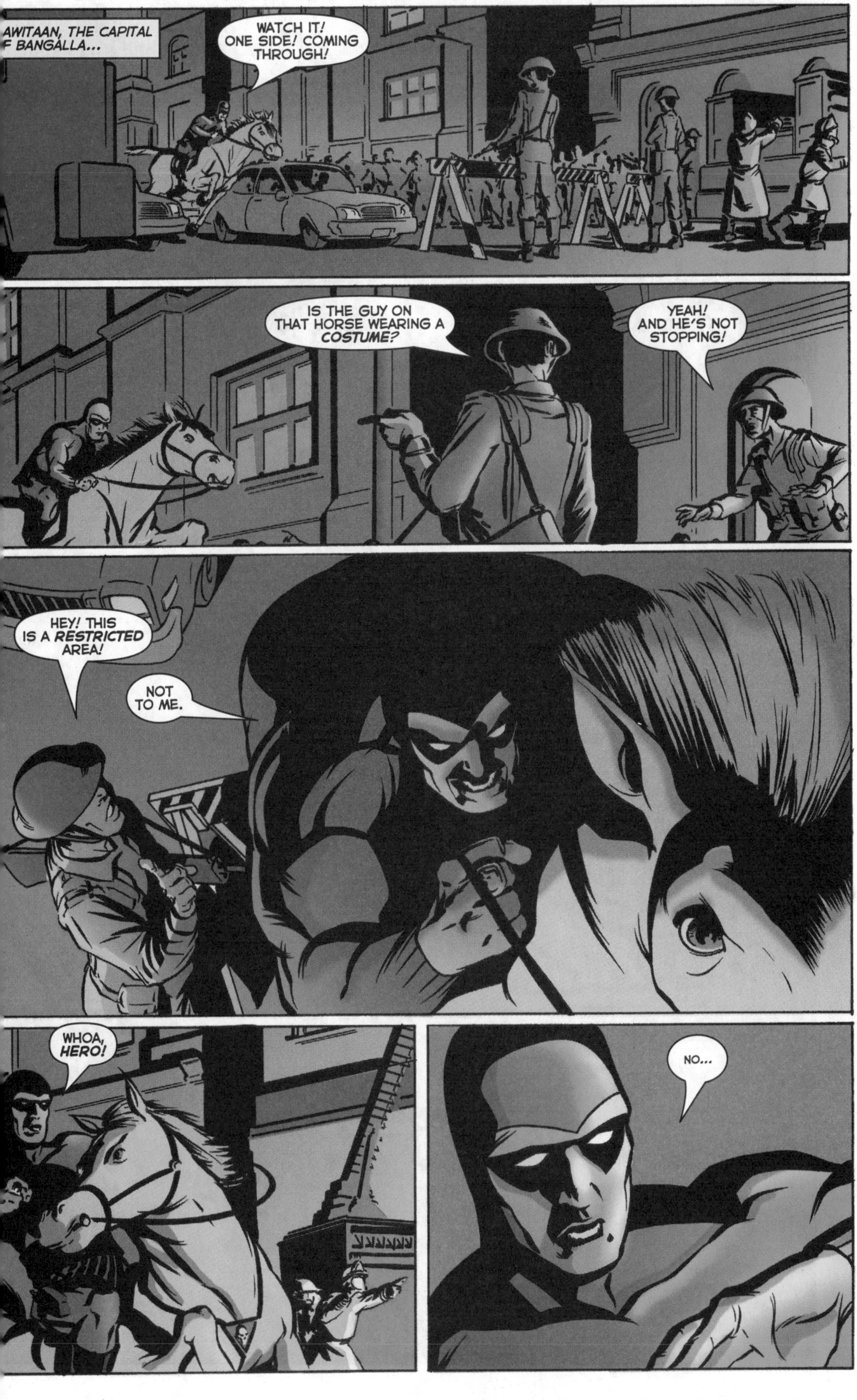
AWITAAN, THE CAPITAL
F BANGALLA...
WATCH IT! ONE SIDE! COMING THROUGH!
IS THE GUY ON THAT HORSE WEARING A *COSTUME?*
YEAH! AND HE'S NOT STOPPING!
HEY! THIS IS A *RESTRICTED* AREA!
NOT TO ME.
WHOA, *HERO!*
NO...

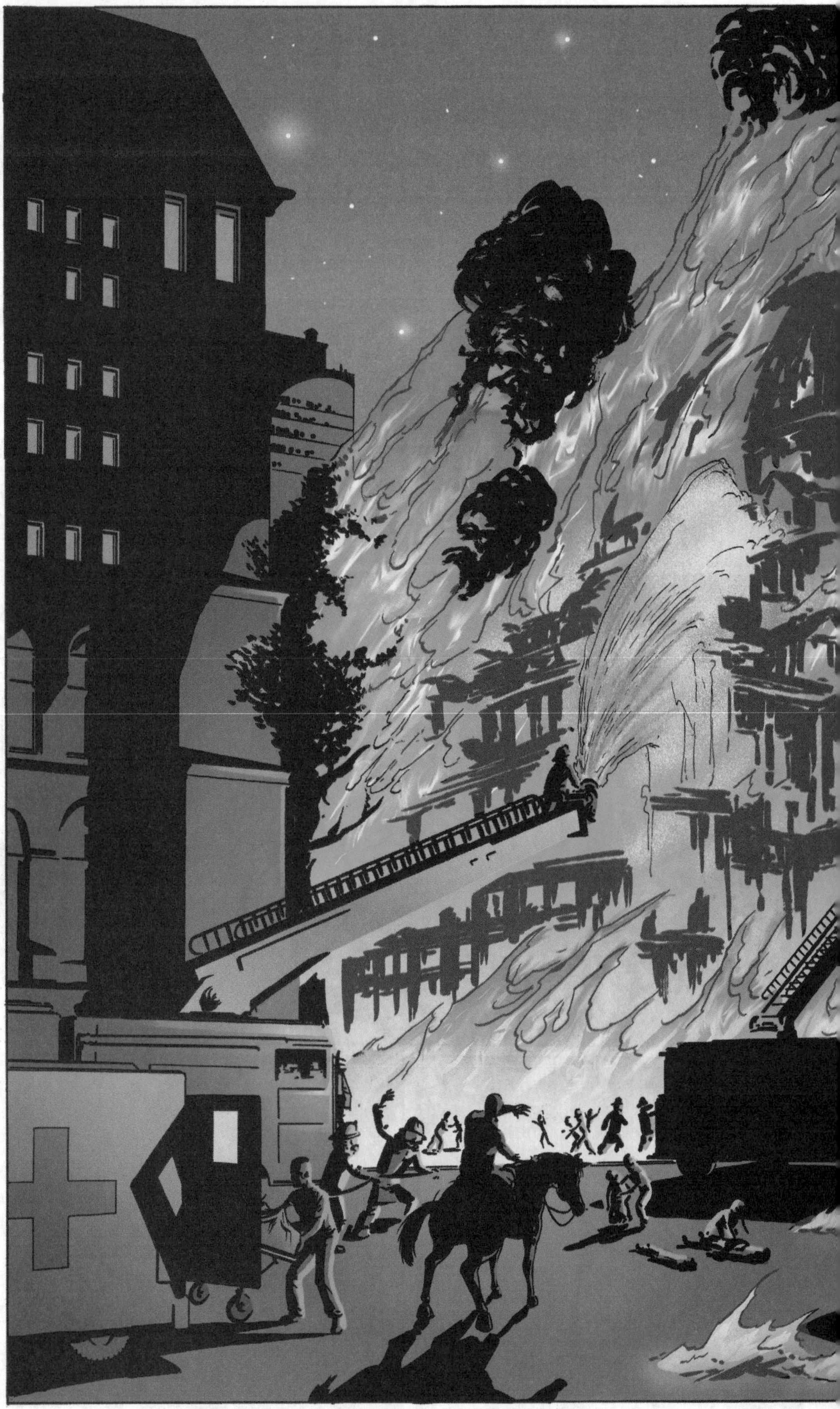

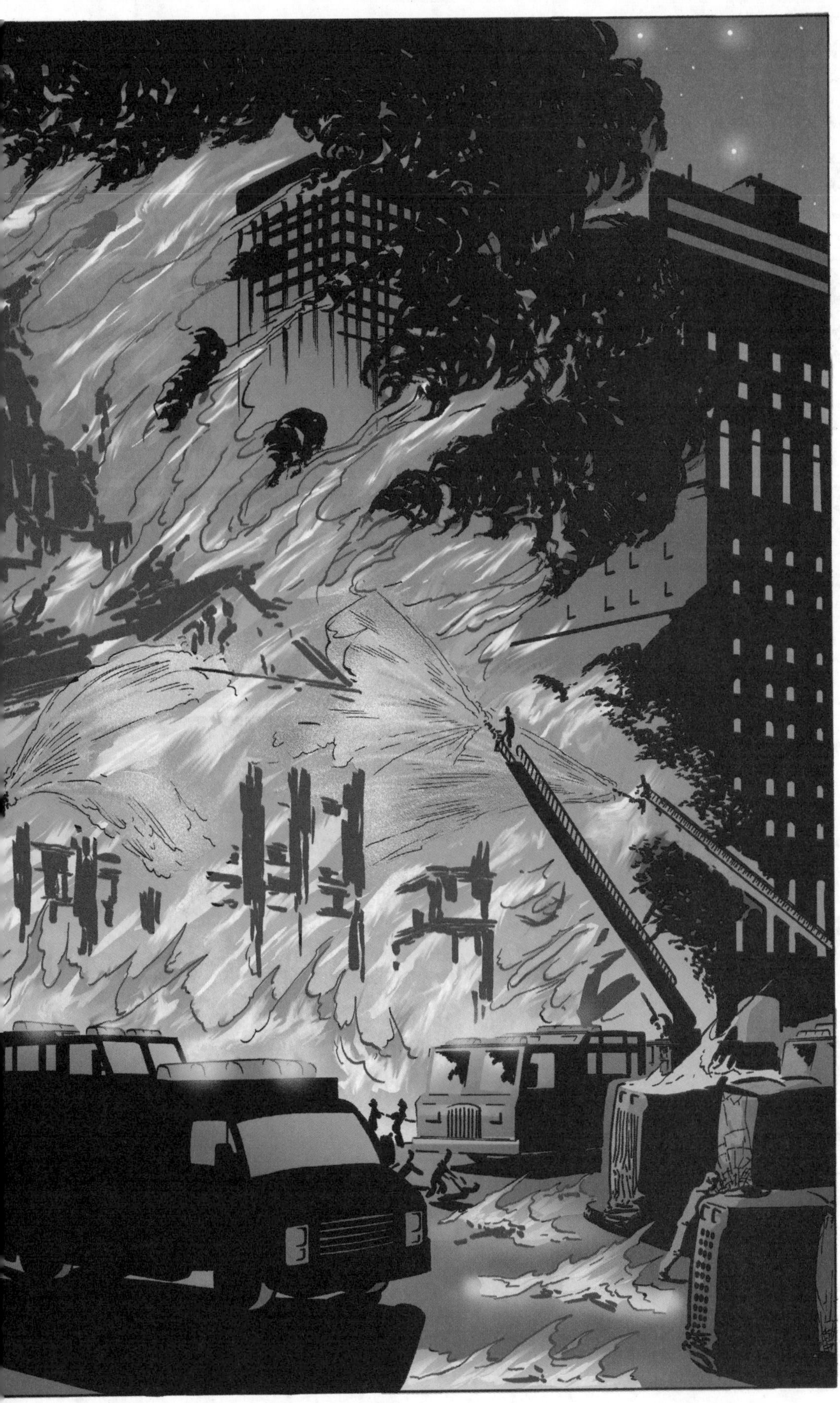

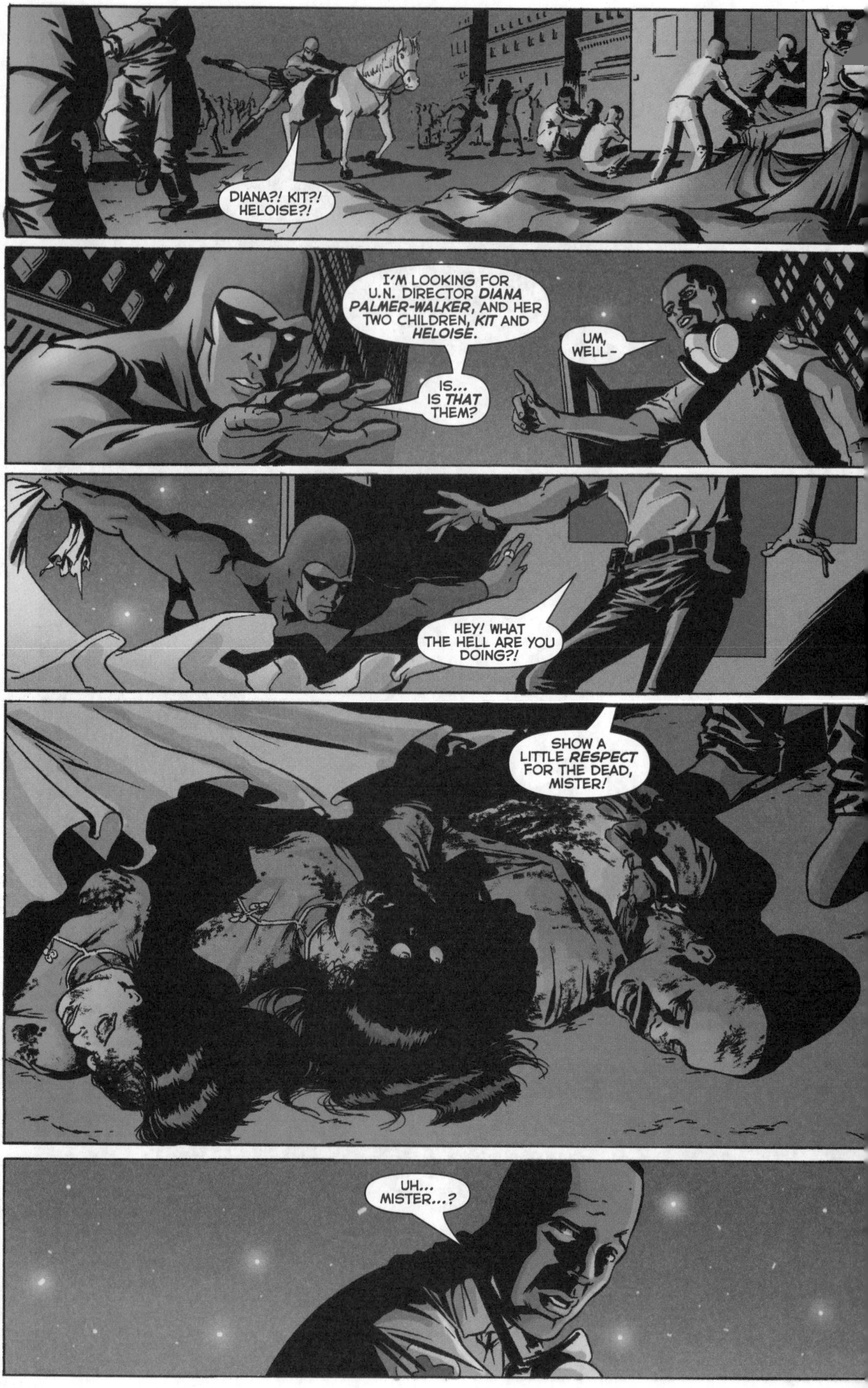
DIANA?! KIT?! HELOISE?!
I'M LOOKING FOR U.N. DIRECTOR DIANA PALMER-WALKER, AND HER TWO CHILDREN, KIT AND HELOISE.
IS... IS THAT THEM?
UM, WELL-
HEY! WHAT THE HELL ARE YOU DOING?!
SHOW A LITTLE RESPECT FOR THE DEAD, MISTER!
UH... MISTER...?

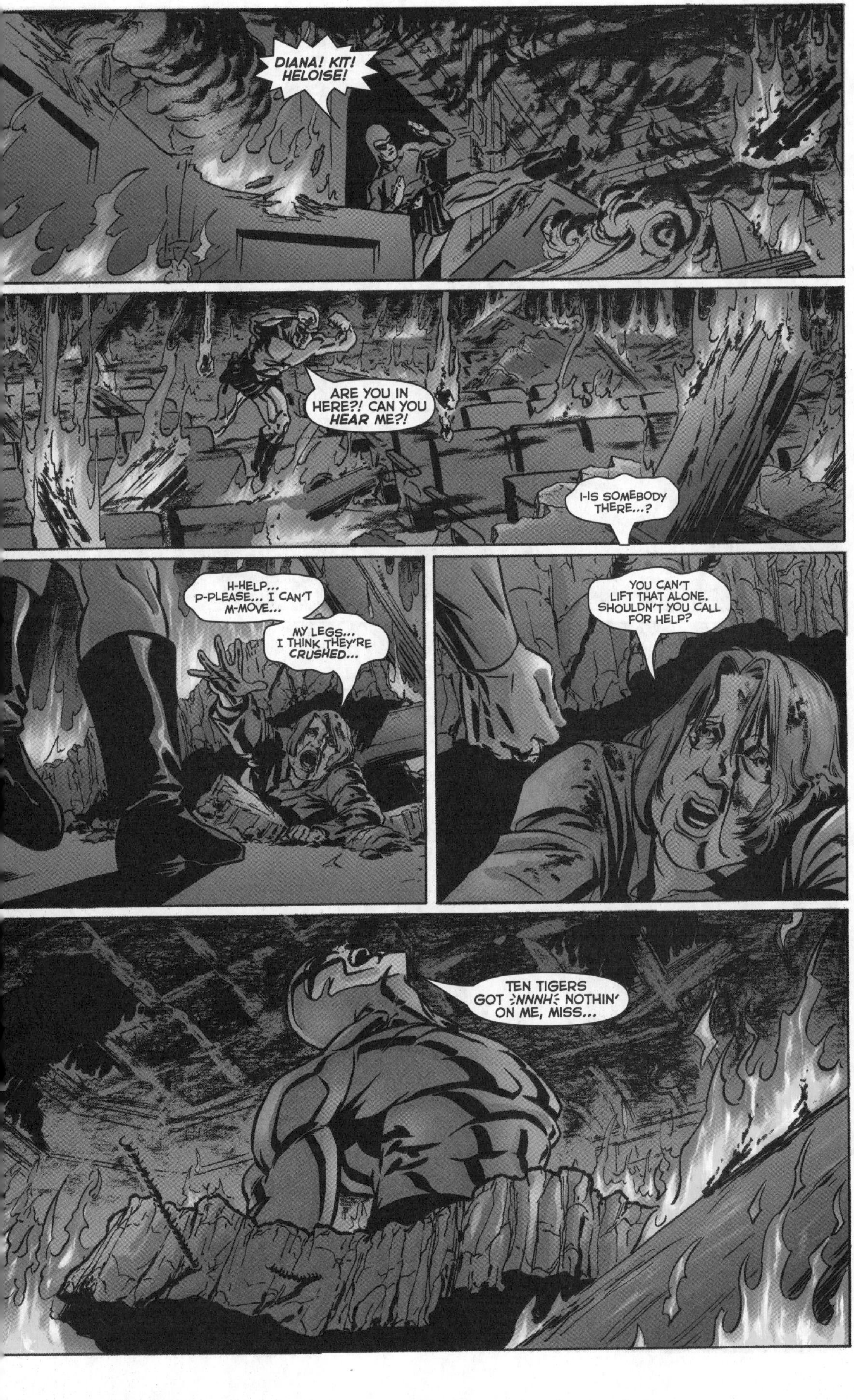
DIANA! KIT! HELOISE!
ARE YOU IN HERE?! CAN YOU HEAR ME?!
I-IS SOMEBODY THERE...?
H-HELP... P-PLEASE... I CAN'T M-MOVE...
MY LEGS... I THINK THEY'RE CRUSHED...
YOU CAN'T LIFT THAT ALONE. SHOULDN'T YOU CALL FOR HELP?
TEN TIGERS GOT NNNH NOTHIN' ON ME, MISS...

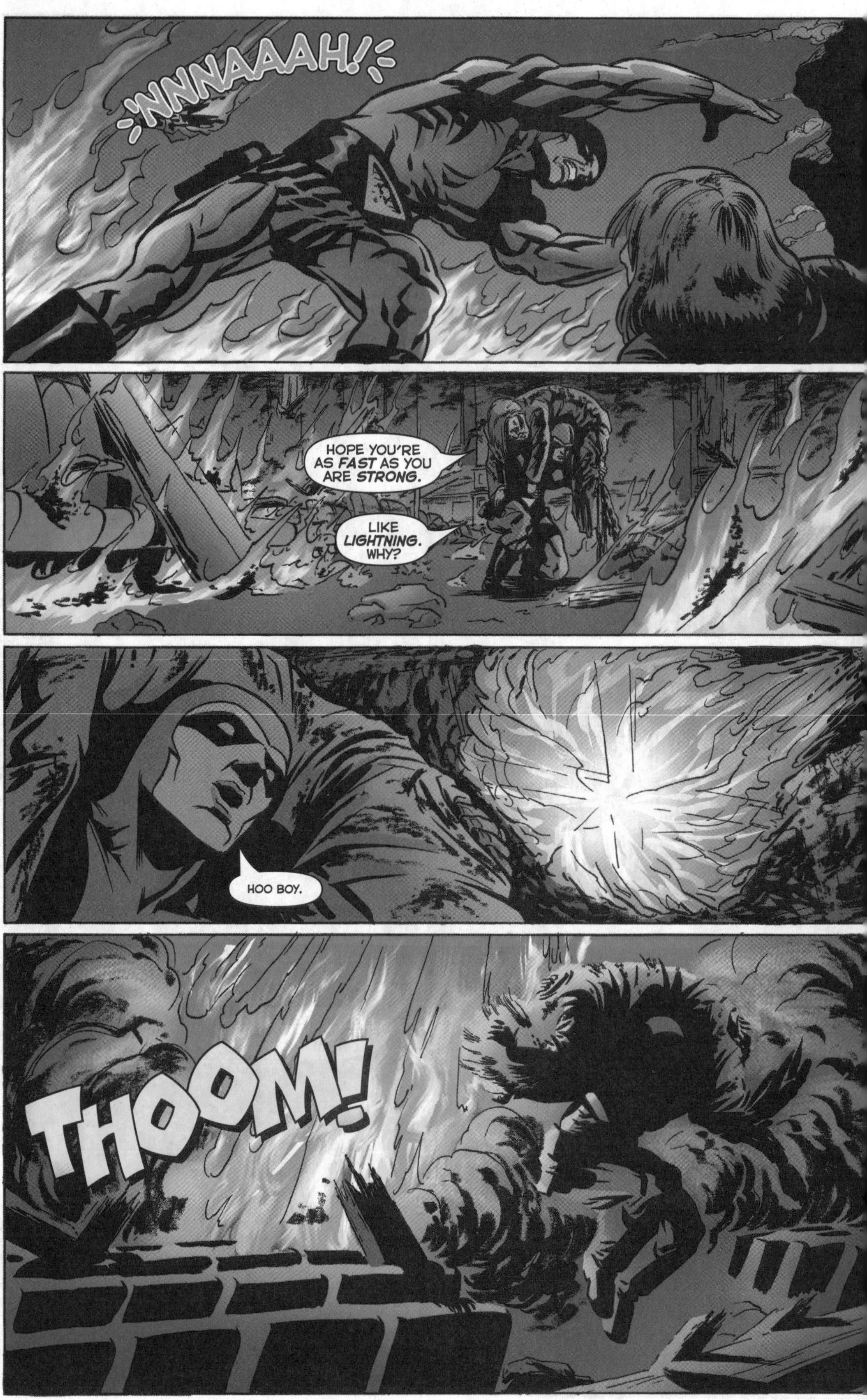
NNNAAAH!
HOPE YOU'RE AS *FAST* AS YOU ARE *STRONG*.
LIKE *LIGHTNING*. WHY?
HOO BOY.
THOOM!

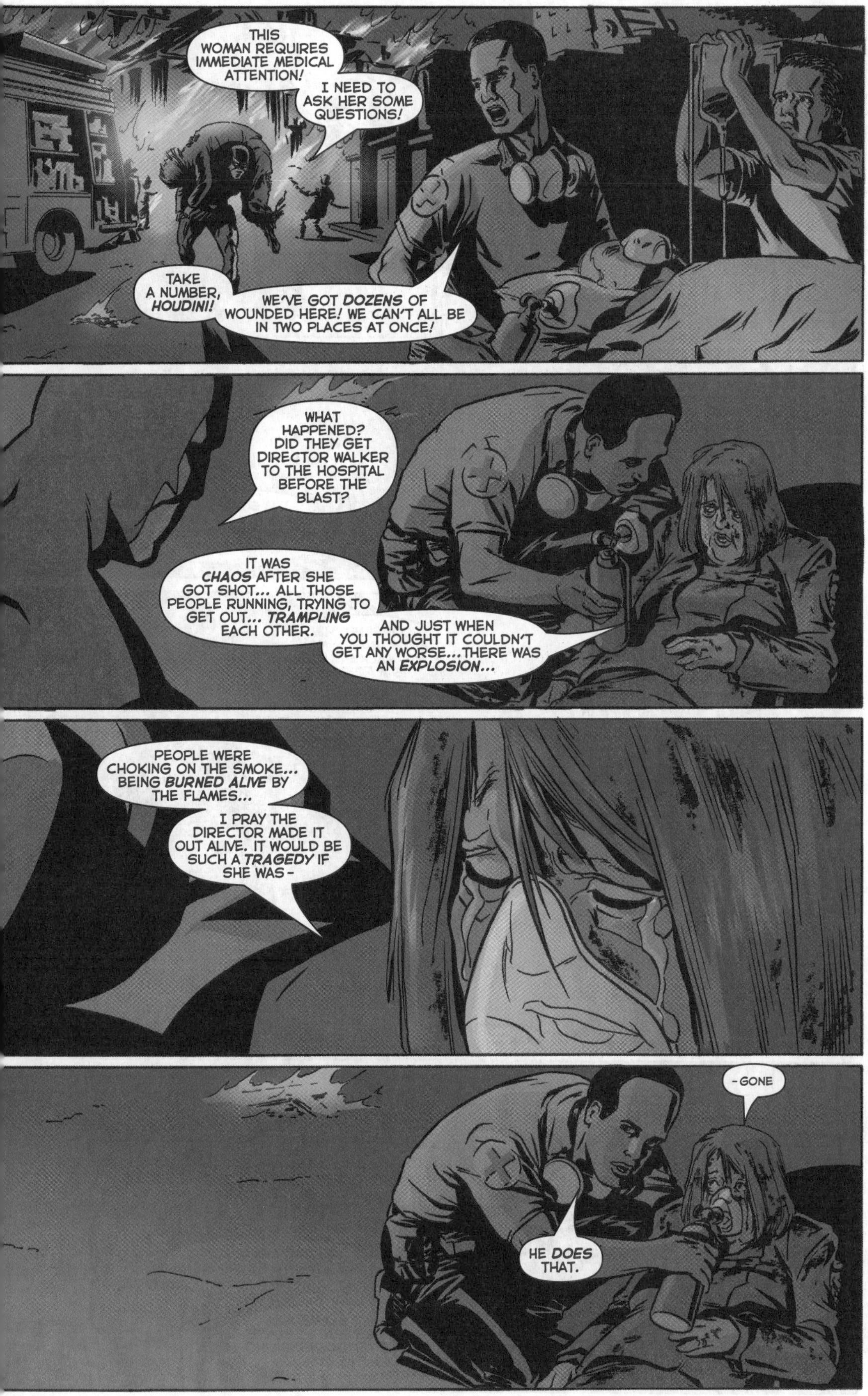
THIS WOMAN REQUIRES IMMEDIATE MEDICAL ATTENTION!
I NEED TO ASK HER SOME QUESTIONS!
TAKE A NUMBER, HOUDINI!
WE'VE GOT DOZENS OF WOUNDED HERE! WE CAN'T ALL BE IN TWO PLACES AT ONCE!
WHAT HAPPENED? DID THEY GET DIRECTOR WALKER TO THE HOSPITAL BEFORE THE BLAST?
IT WAS CHAOS AFTER SHE GOT SHOT... ALL THOSE PEOPLE RUNNING, TRYING TO GET OUT... TRAMPLING EACH OTHER.
AND JUST WHEN YOU THOUGHT IT COULDN'T GET ANY WORSE...THERE WAS AN EXPLOSION...
PEOPLE WERE CHOKING ON THE SMOKE... BEING BURNED ALIVE BY THE FLAMES...
I PRAY THE DIRECTOR MADE IT OUT ALIVE. IT WOULD BE SUCH A TRAGEDY IF SHE WAS -
-GONE
HE DOES THAT.

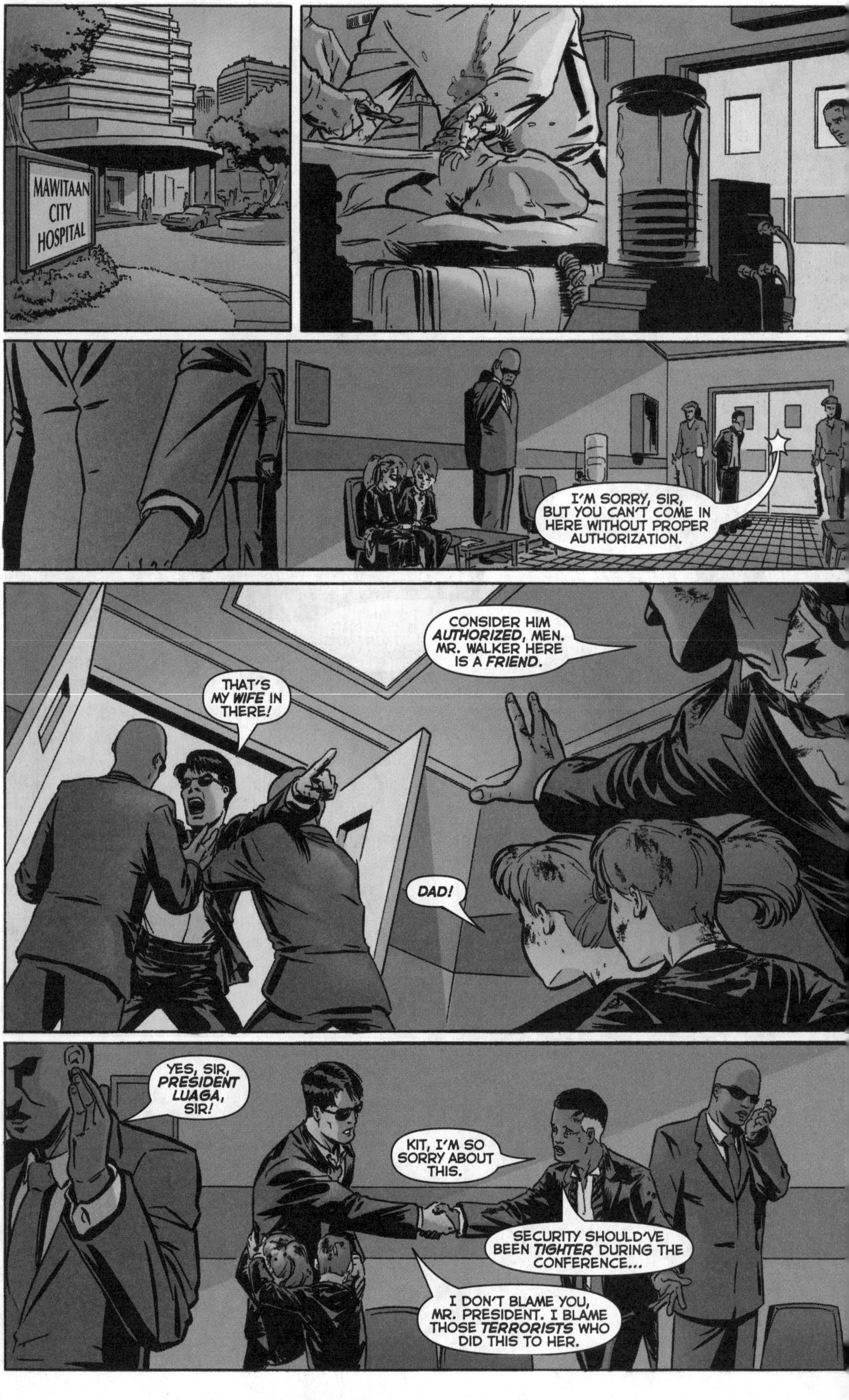
MAWITAAN CITY HOSPITAL
I'M SORRY, SIR, BUT YOU CAN'T COME IN HERE WITHOUT PROPER AUTHORIZATION.
CONSIDER HIM AUTHORIZED, MEN. MR. WALKER HERE IS A FRIEND.
THAT'S MY WIFE IN THERE!
DAD!
YES, SIR, PRESIDENT LUAGA, SIR!
KIT, I'M SO SORRY ABOUT THIS.
SECURITY SHOULD'VE BEEN TIGHTER DURING THE CONFERENCE...
I DON'T BLAME YOU, MR. PRESIDENT. I BLAME THOSE TERRORISTS WHO DID THIS TO HER.

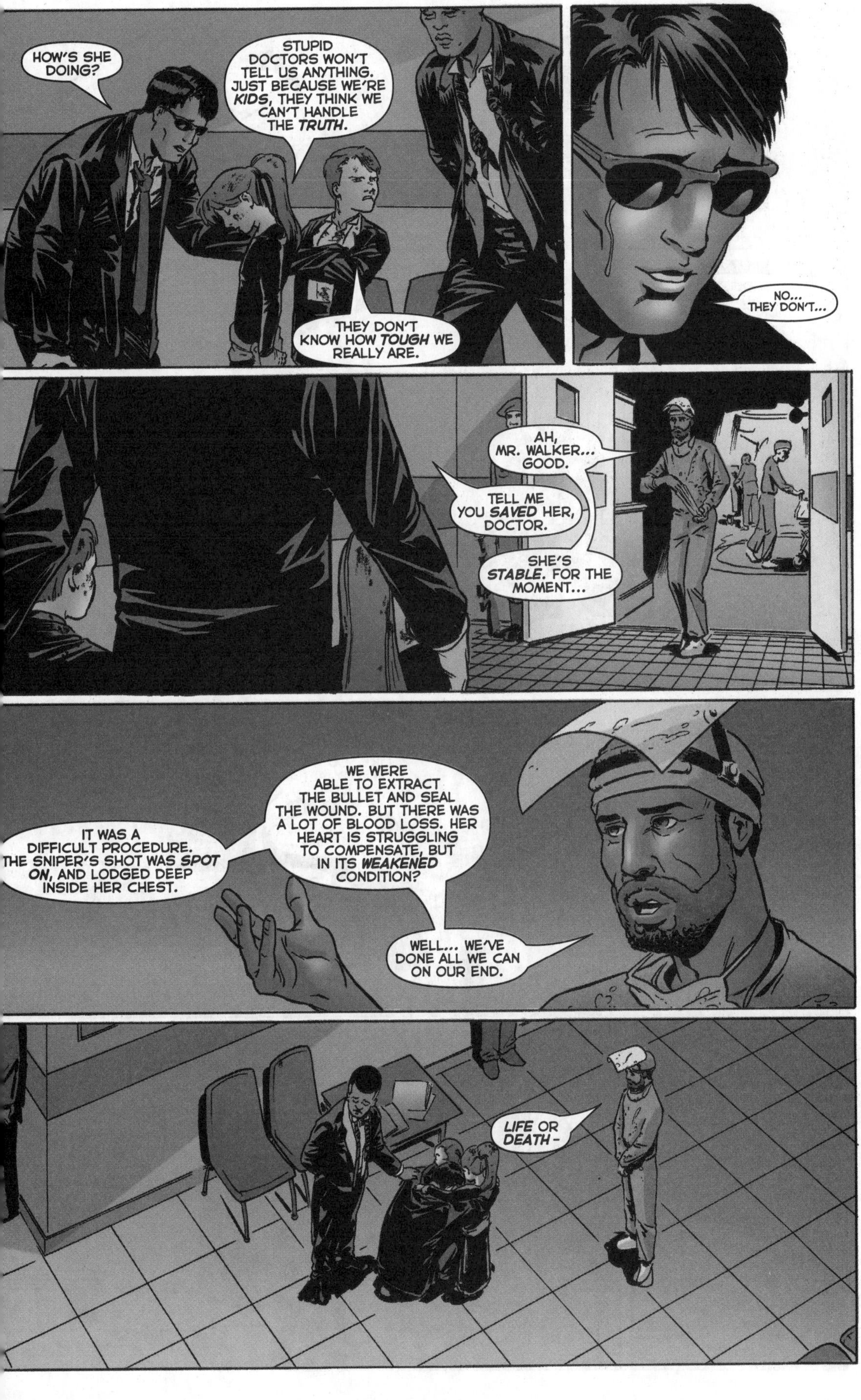
HOW'S SHE DOING?
STUPID DOCTORS WON'T TELL US ANYTHING. JUST BECAUSE WE'RE KIDS, THEY THINK WE CAN'T HANDLE THE TRUTH.
THEY DON'T KNOW HOW TOUGH WE REALLY ARE.
NO... THEY DON'T...
AH, MR. WALKER... GOOD.
TELL ME YOU SAVED HER, DOCTOR.
SHE'S STABLE. FOR THE MOMENT...
IT WAS A DIFFICULT PROCEDURE. THE SNIPER'S SHOT WAS SPOT ON, AND LODGED DEEP INSIDE HER CHEST.
WE WERE ABLE TO EXTRACT THE BULLET AND SEAL THE WOUND. BUT THERE WAS A LOT OF BLOOD LOSS. HER HEART IS STRUGGLING TO COMPENSATE, BUT IN ITS WEAKENED CONDITION?
WELL... WE'VE DONE ALL WE CAN ON OUR END.
LIFE OR DEATH-

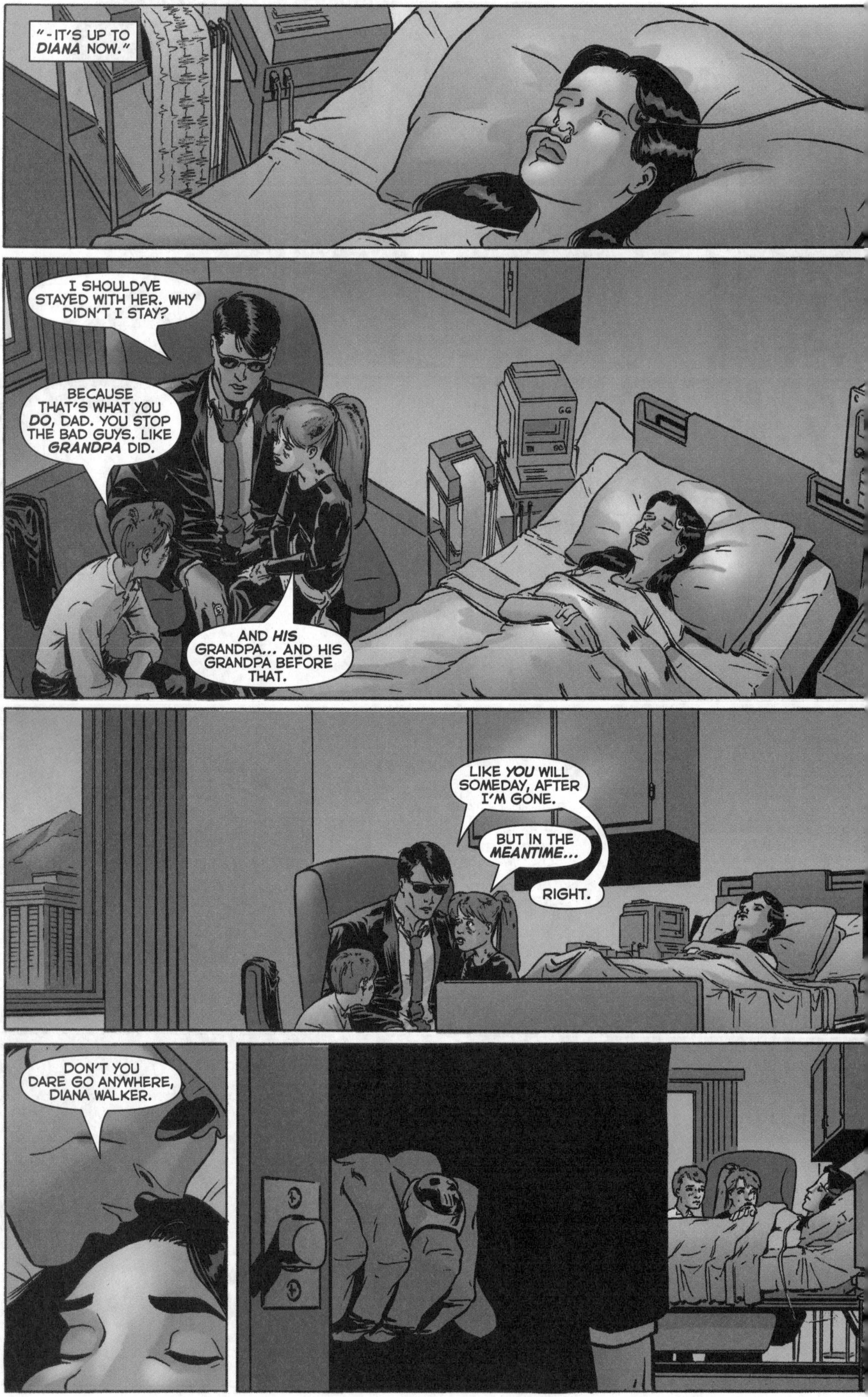
"-IT'S UP TO DIANA NOW."
I SHOULD'VE STAYED WITH HER. WHY DIDN'T I STAY?
BECAUSE THAT'S WHAT YOU DO, DAD. YOU STOP THE BAD GUYS. LIKE GRANDPA DID.
AND HIS GRANDPA... AND HIS GRANDPA BEFORE THAT.
LIKE YOU WILL SOMEDAY, AFTER I'M GONE.
BUT IN THE MEANTIME...
RIGHT.
DON'T YOU DARE GO ANYWHERE, DIANA WALKER.

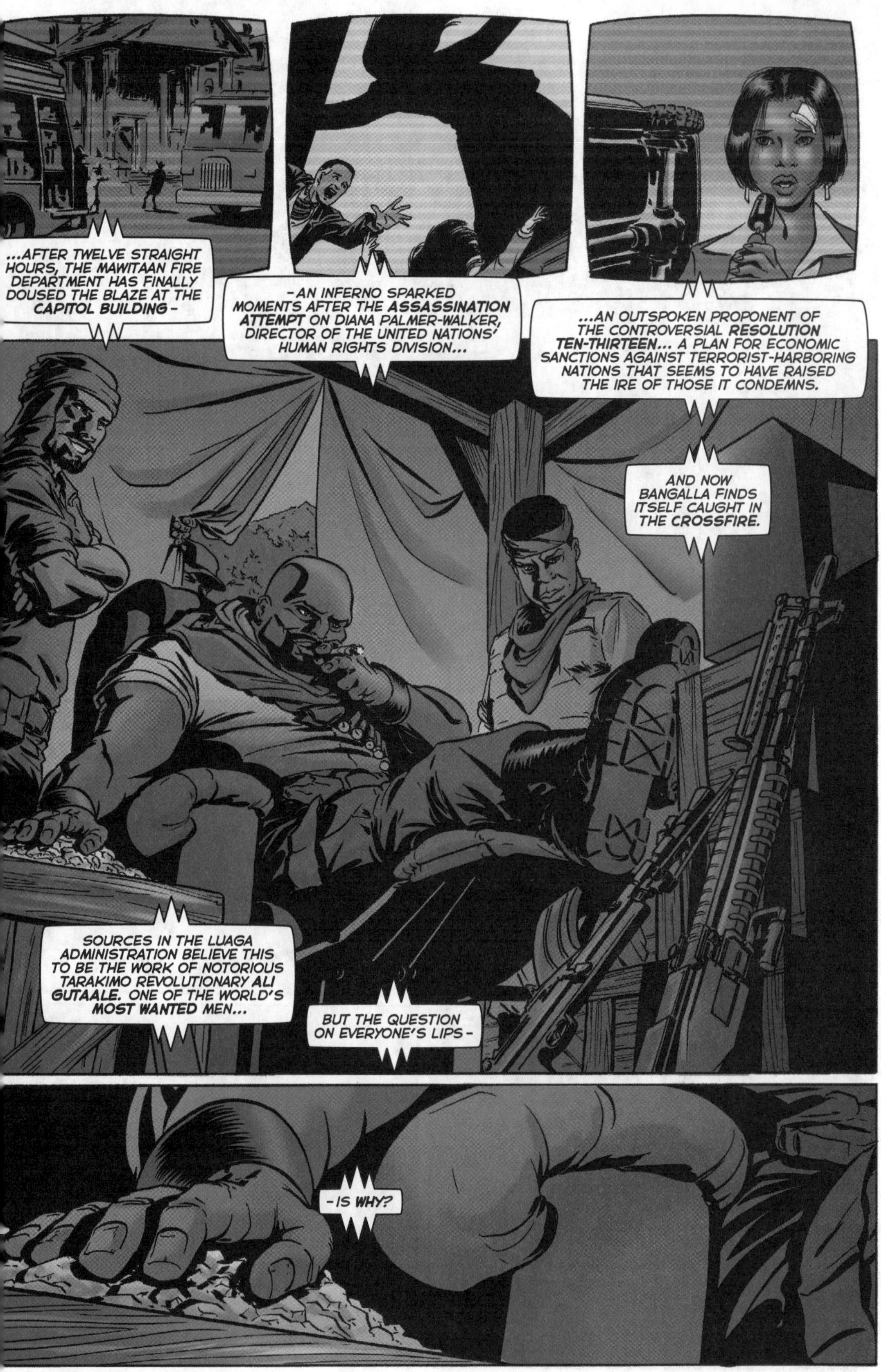
...AFTER TWELVE STRAIGHT HOURS, THE MAWITAAN FIRE DEPARTMENT HAS FINALLY DOUSED THE BLAZE AT THE CAPITOL BUILDING-
-AN INFERNO SPARKED MOMENTS AFTER THE ASSASSINATION ATTEMPT ON DIANA PALMER-WALKER, DIRECTOR OF THE UNITED NATIONS' HUMAN RIGHTS DIVISION...
...AN OUTSPOKEN PROPONENT OF THE CONTROVERSIAL RESOLUTION TEN-THIRTEEN... A PLAN FOR ECONOMIC SANCTIONS AGAINST TERRORIST-HARBORING NATIONS THAT SEEMS TO HAVE RAISED THE IRE OF THOSE IT CONDEMNS.
AND NOW BANGALLA FINDS ITSELF CAUGHT IN THE CROSSFIRE.
SOURCES IN THE LUAGA ADMINISTRATION BELIEVE THIS TO BE THE WORK OF NOTORIOUS TARAKIMO REVOLUTIONARY ALI GUTAALE. ONE OF THE WORLD'S MOST WANTED MEN...
BUT THE QUESTION ON EVERYONE'S LIPS-
-IS WHY?

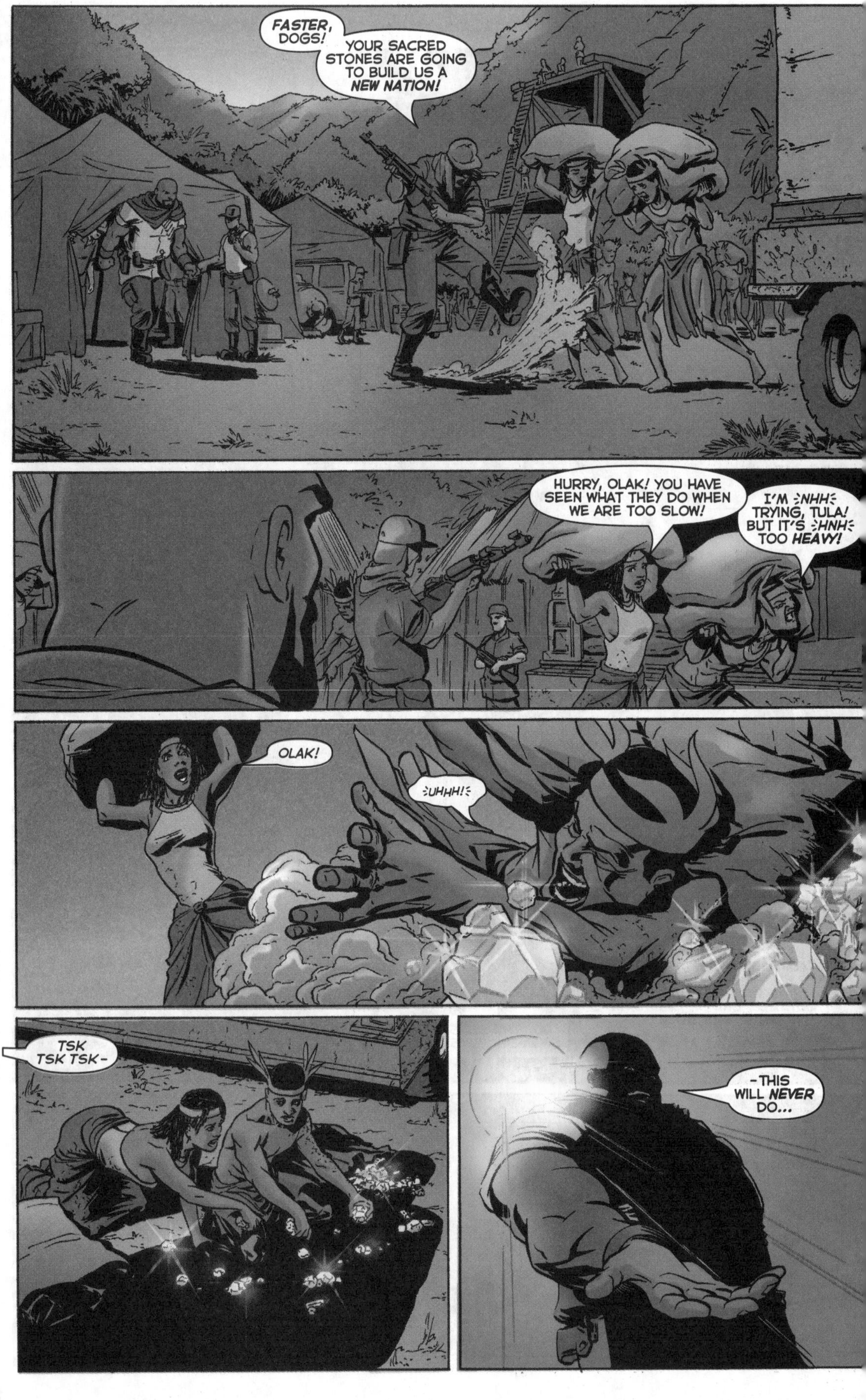
FASTER, DOGS!
YOUR SACRED STONES ARE GOING TO BUILD US A NEW NATION!
HURRY, OLAK! YOU HAVE SEEN WHAT THEY DO WHEN WE ARE TOO SLOW!
I'M -NHH- TRYING, TULA! BUT IT'S -HNH- TOO HEAVY!
OLAK!
-UHHH!-
TSK TSK TSK-
-THIS WILL NEVER DO...

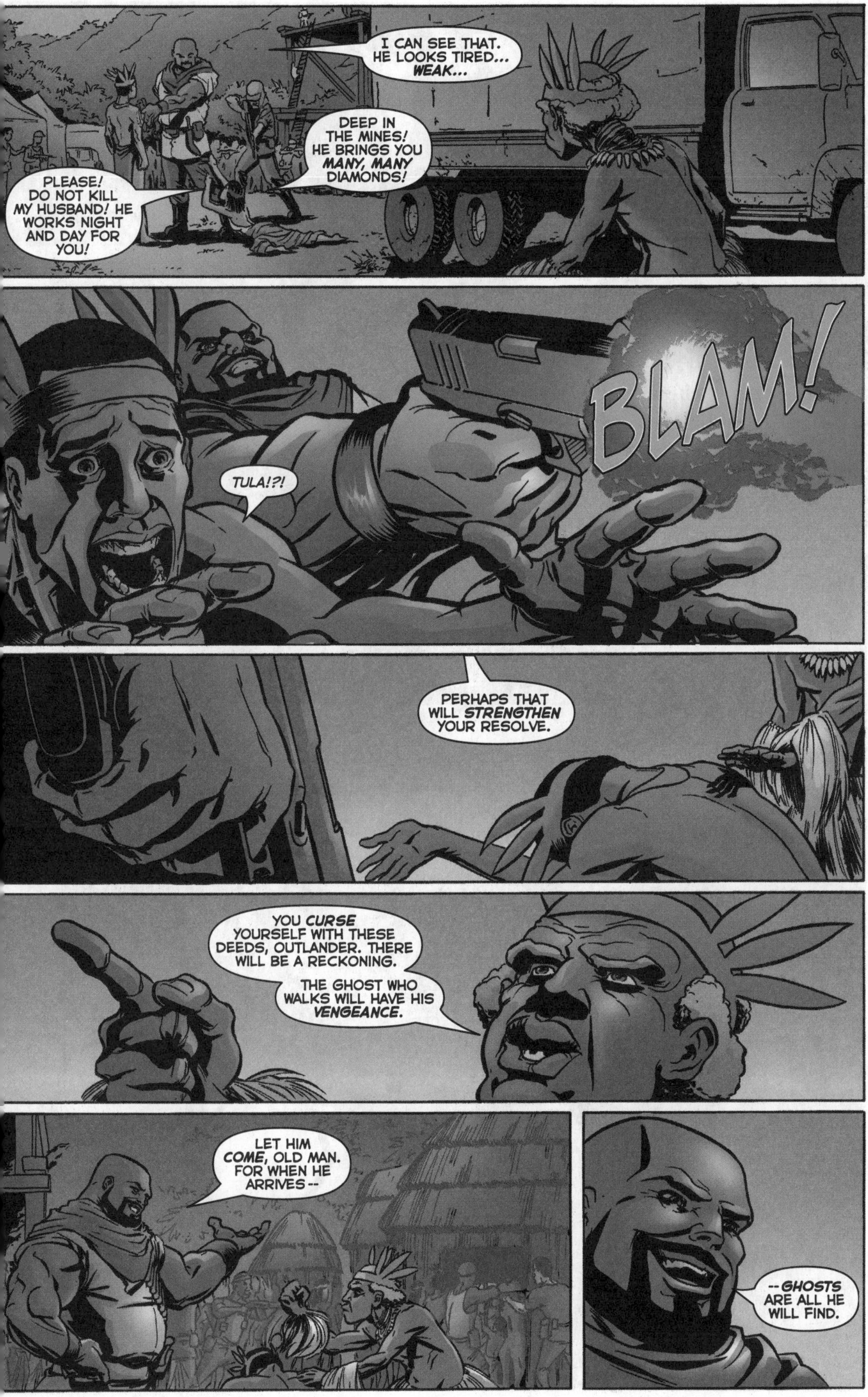
PLEASE! DO NOT KILL MY HUSBAND! HE WORKS NIGHT AND DAY FOR YOU!
I CAN SEE THAT. HE LOOKS TIRED... WEAK...
DEEP IN THE MINES! HE BRINGS YOU MANY, MANY DIAMONDS!
BLAM!
TULA!?!
PERHAPS THAT WILL STRENGTHEN YOUR RESOLVE.
YOU CURSE YOURSELF WITH THESE DEEDS, OUTLANDER. THERE WILL BE A RECKONING.
THE GHOST WHO WALKS WILL HAVE HIS VENGEANCE.
LET HIM COME, OLD MAN. FOR WHEN HE ARRIVES --
-- GHOSTS ARE ALL HE WILL FIND.

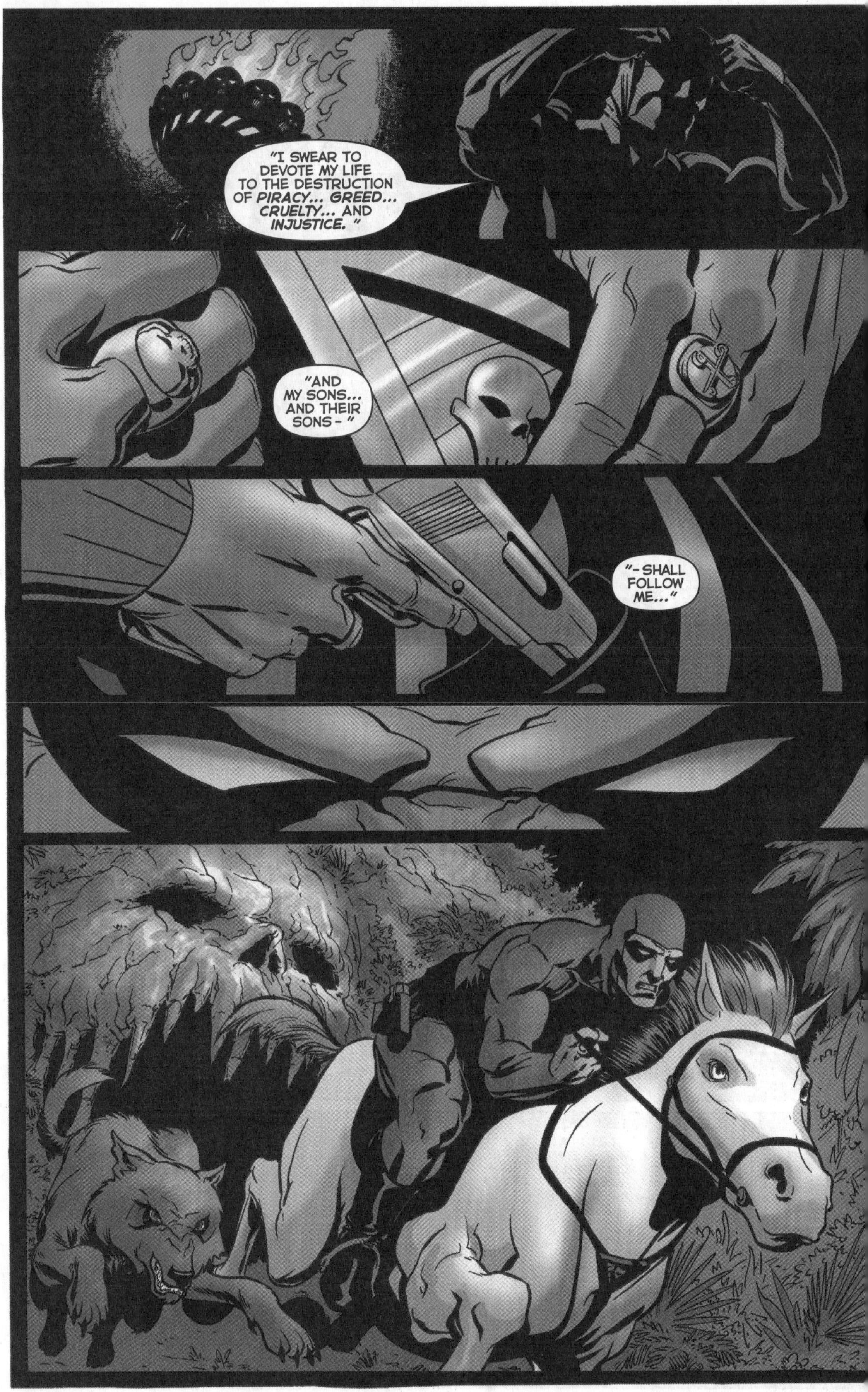
"I SWEAR TO DEVOTE MY LIFE TO THE DESTRUCTION OF *PIRACY*... *GREED*... *CRUELTY*... AND *INJUSTICE*."
"AND MY SONS... AND THEIR SONS-"
"-SHALL FOLLOW ME..."

IF THESE STONES ARE *ILLEGAL* OUTSIDE BANGALLA–

–WHAT COUNTRY WOULD VIOLATE INTERNATIONAL LAW TO PURCHASE THEM?

ANY OF THE SO-CALLED *'ROGUE NATIONS'* THAT HAVE GRANTED US ASYLUM WILL PAY TOP DOLLAR. ENOUGH TO ENSURE THE SUCCESS OF OUR *COUP.*

BUT, ALI... HAVE WE NOT DEALT WITH SUCH *DEVILS* ENOUGH? THEIR REPUTATION *TAINTS* OUR CAUSE IN THE WORLD'S EYES.

A SMALL PRICE TO PAY TO FINALLY WREST CONTROL OF TARAKIMO FROM THE *WARLORDS* WHO OPPRESS OUR PEOPLE.

NATIONS ARE BUILT UPON *TWO* FOUNDATIONS, MY FRIEND. *SACRIFICE...* AND *BLOOD...*

ALI! COME QUICK! THE VILLAGERS!

HAVE THEY FINALLY GROWN THE SPINE TO *REVOLT?*

WORSE!

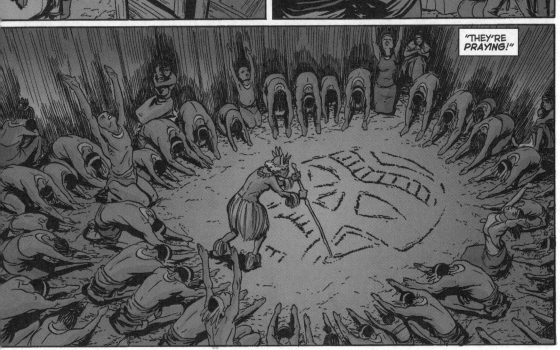

"THEY'RE *PRAYING!*"

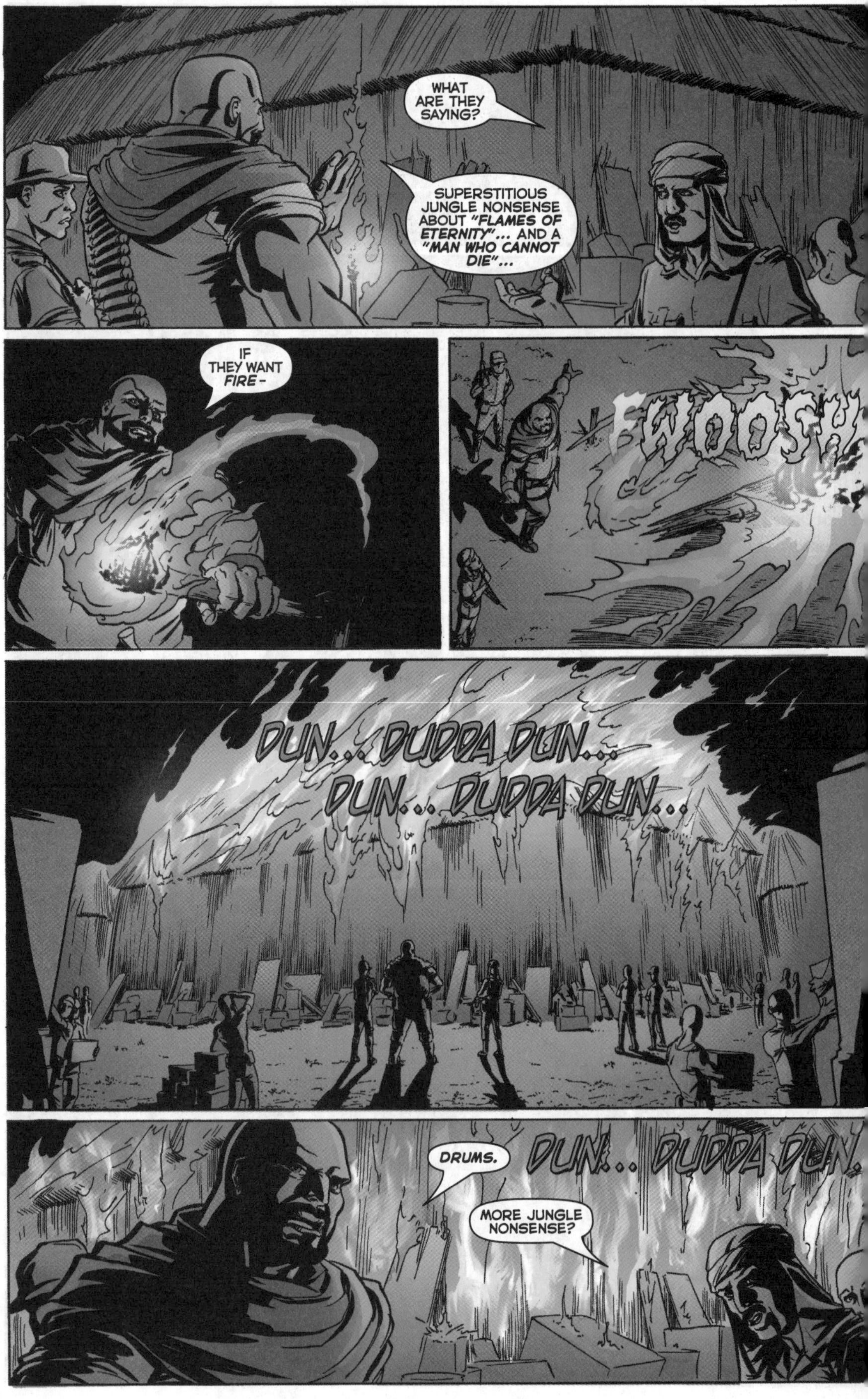

WHAT ARE THEY SAYING?
SUPERSTITIOUS JUNGLE NONSENSE ABOUT *"FLAMES OF ETERNITY"*... AND A *"MAN WHO CANNOT DIE"*...
IF THEY WANT *FIRE*-
FWOOSH
DUN... DUDDA DUN...
DUN... DUDDA DUN...
DRUMS.
DUN... DUDDA DUN.
MORE JUNGLE NONSENSE?

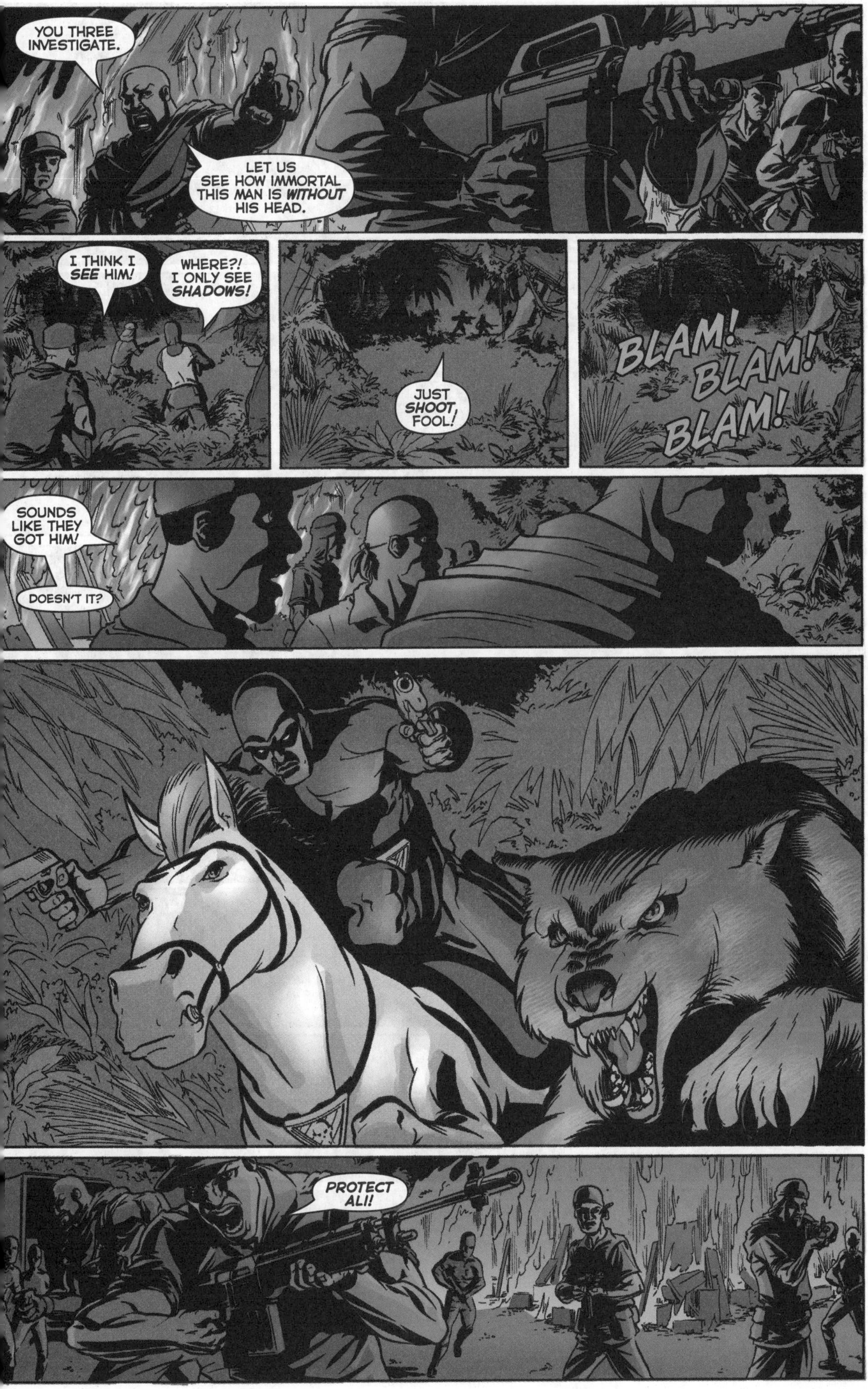
YOU THREE INVESTIGATE.
LET US SEE HOW IMMORTAL THIS MAN IS WITHOUT HIS HEAD.
I THINK I SEE HIM!
WHERE?! I ONLY SEE SHADOWS!
JUST SHOOT, FOOL!
BLAM! BLAM! BLAM!
SOUNDS LIKE THEY GOT HIM!
DOESN'T IT?
PROTECT ALI!

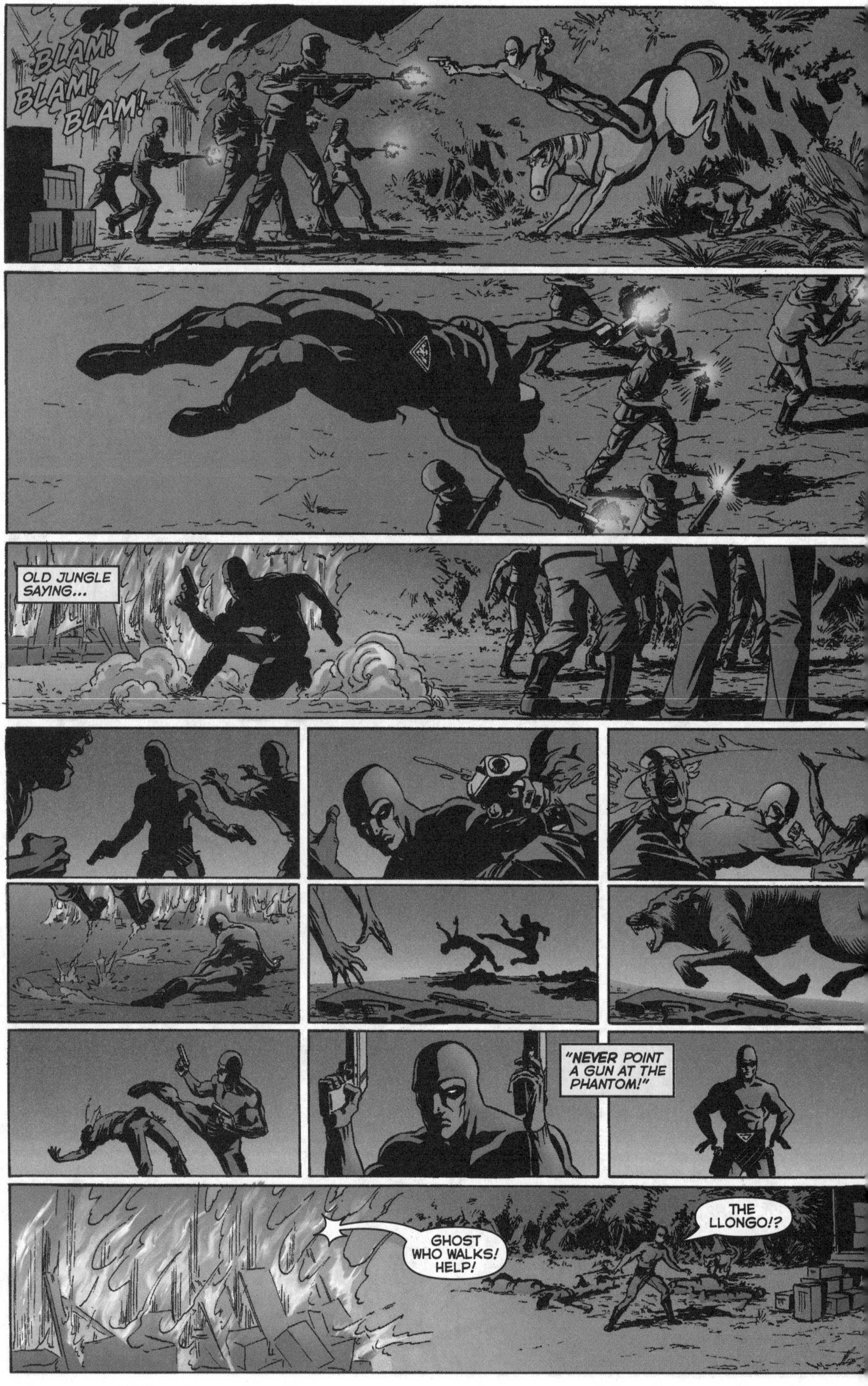
BLAM!
BLAM!
BLAM!
OLD JUNGLE SAYING...
"NEVER POINT A GUN AT THE PHANTOM!"
GHOST WHO WALKS! HELP!
THE LLONGO!?

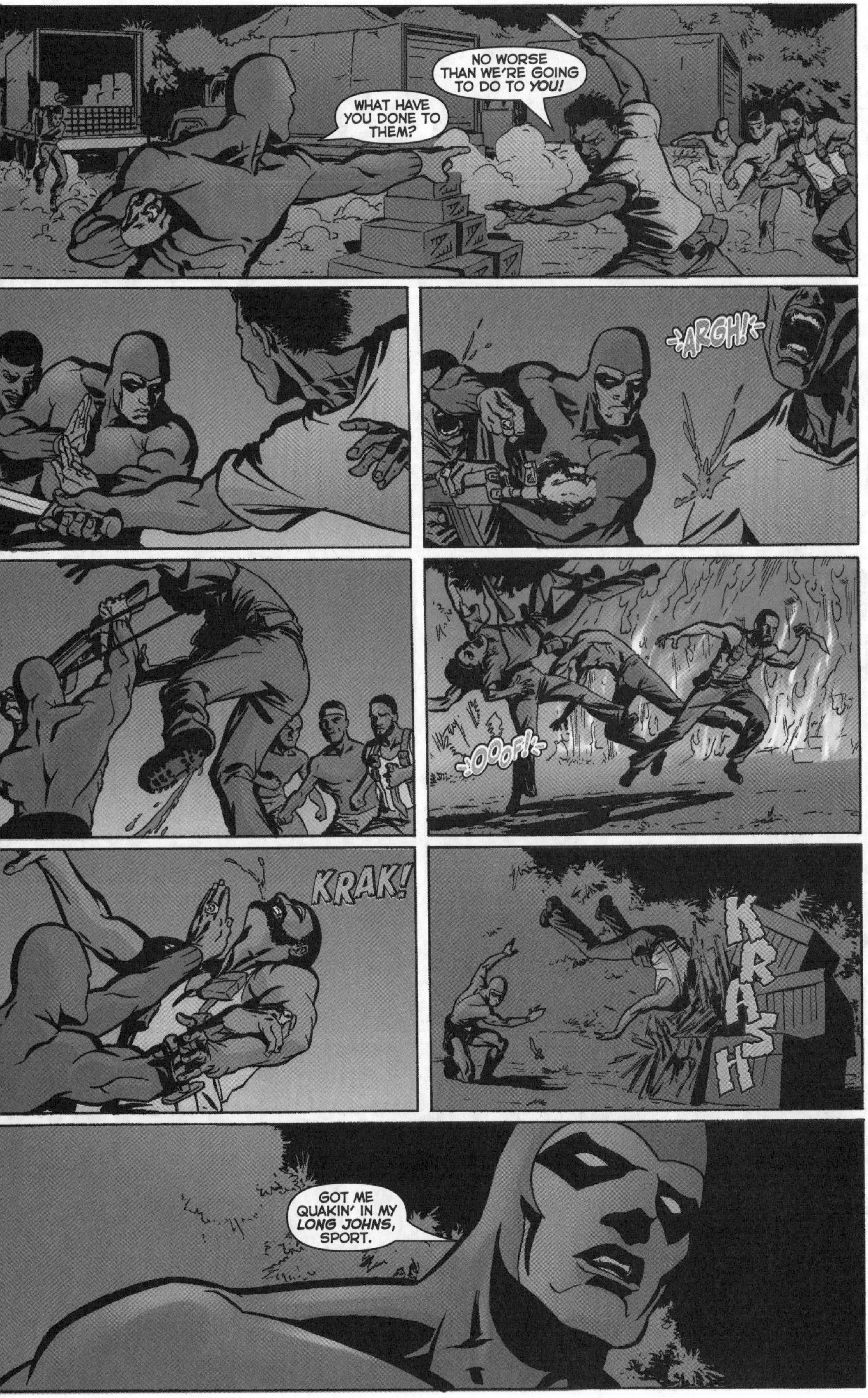
WHAT HAVE YOU DONE TO THEM?
NO WORSE THAN WE'RE GOING TO DO TO YOU!
ARGH!
OOOF!
KRAK!
KRASH
GOT ME QUAKIN' IN MY LONG JOHNS, SPORT.

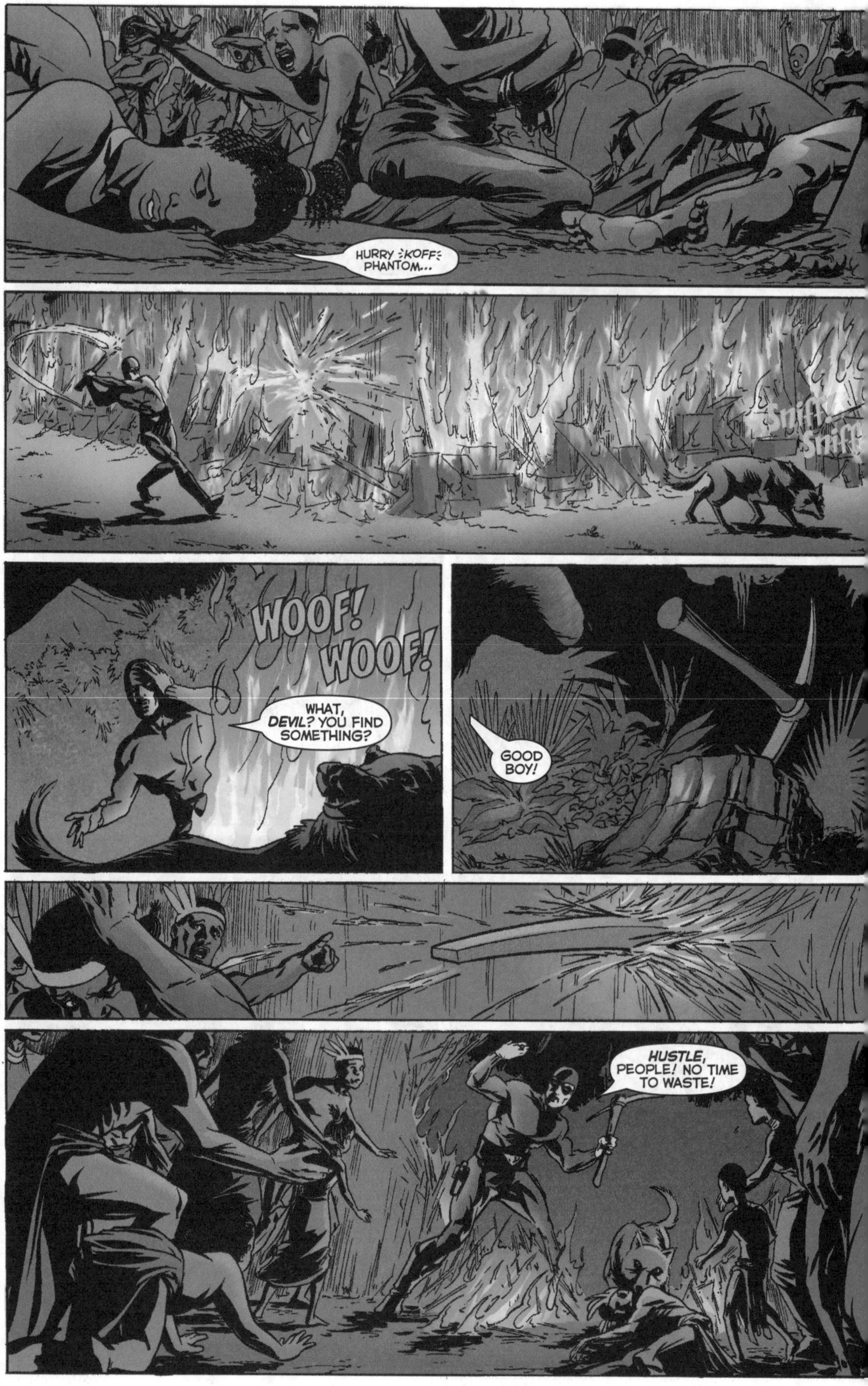
HURRY KOFF PHANTOM...
WOOF! WOOF!
WHAT, DEVIL? YOU FIND SOMETHING?
GOOD BOY!
HUSTLE, PEOPLE! NO TIME TO WASTE!

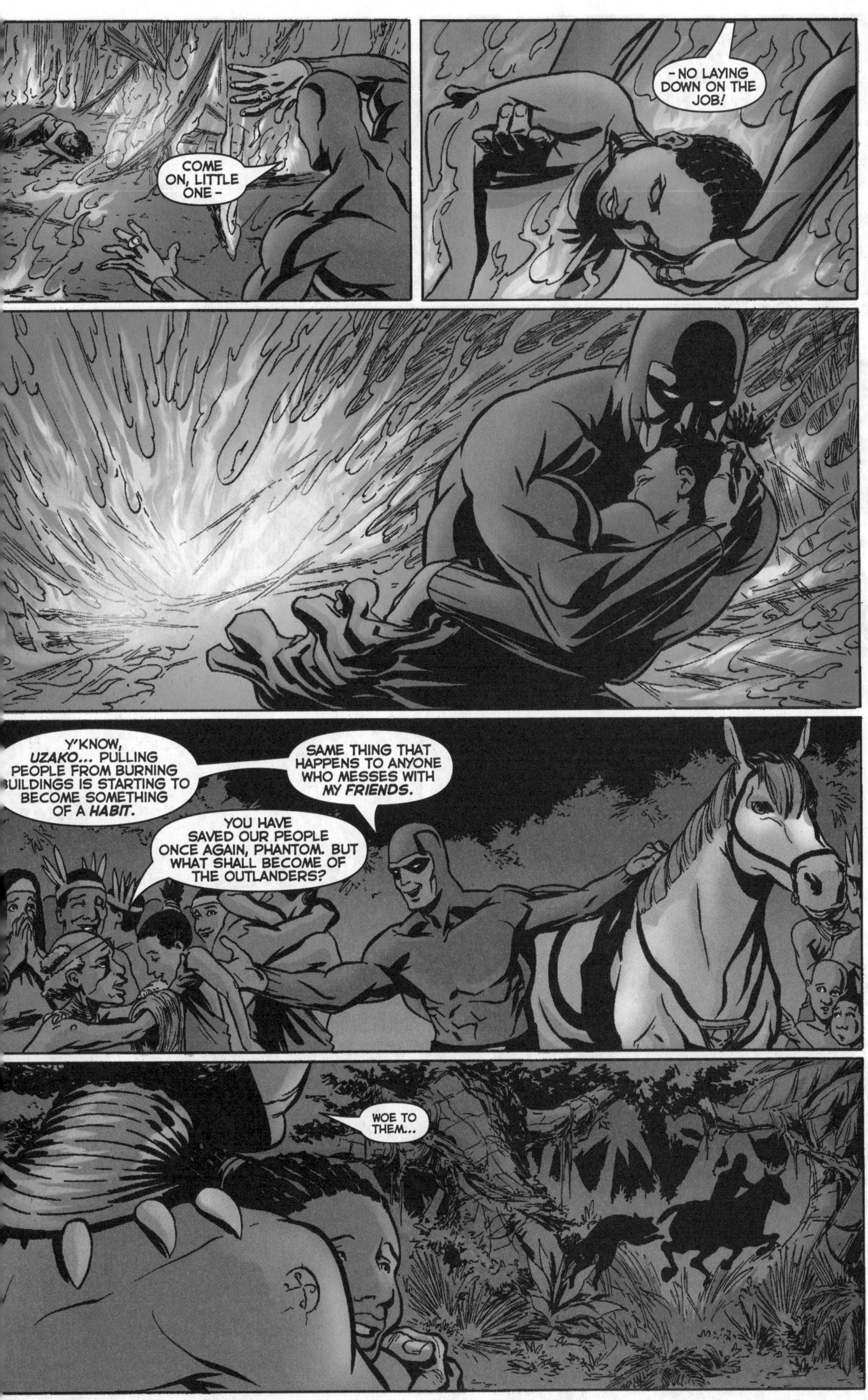
COME ON, LITTLE ONE -
- NO LAYING DOWN ON THE JOB!
Y'KNOW, UZAKO... PULLING PEOPLE FROM BURNING BUILDINGS IS STARTING TO BECOME SOMETHING OF A HABIT.
YOU HAVE SAVED OUR PEOPLE ONCE AGAIN, PHANTOM. BUT WHAT SHALL BECOME OF THE OUTLANDERS?
SAME THING THAT HAPPENS TO ANYONE WHO MESSES WITH MY FRIENDS.
WOE TO THEM...

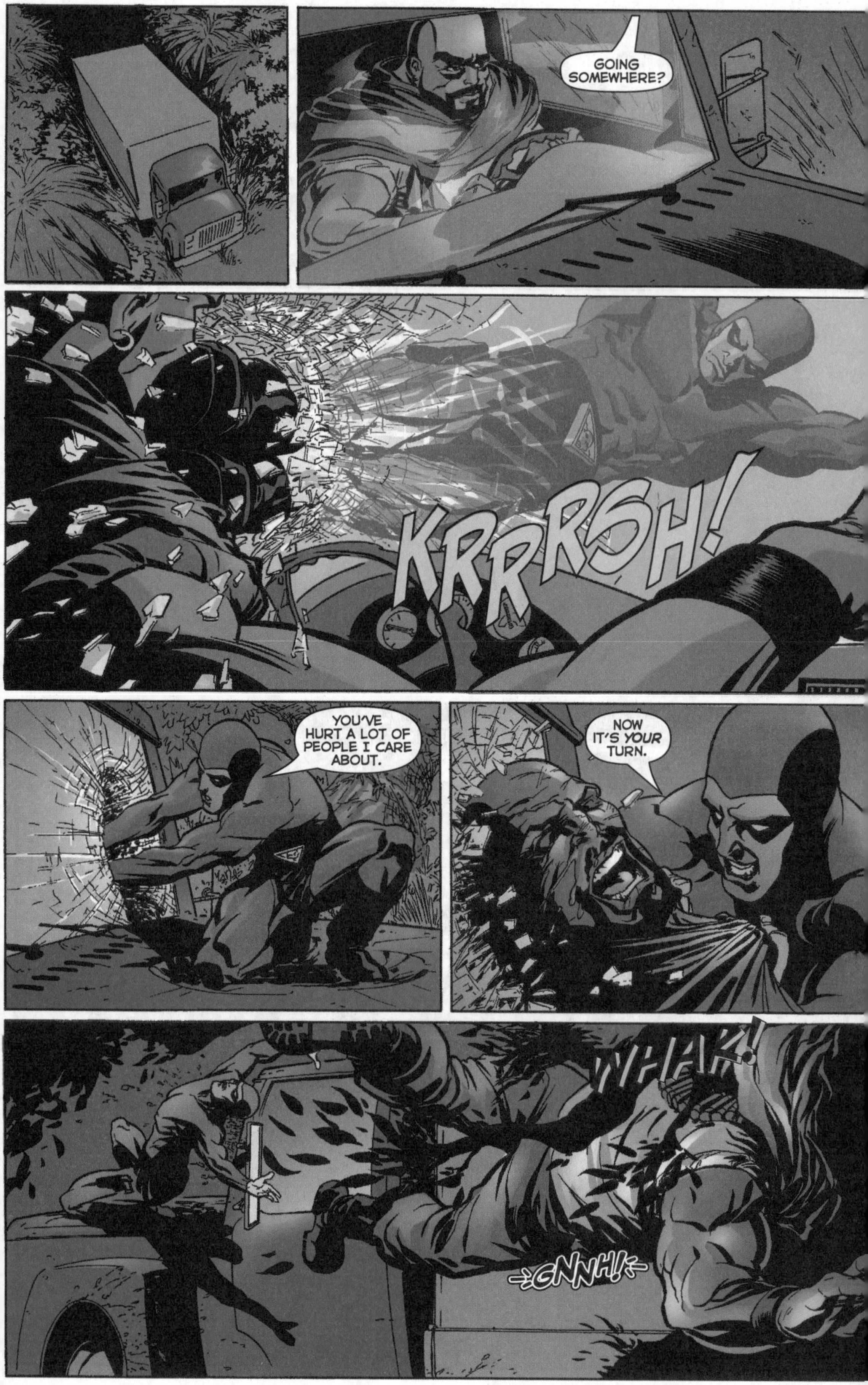
GOING SOMEWHERE?
KRRRSH!
YOU'VE HURT A LOT OF PEOPLE I CARE ABOUT.
NOW IT'S YOUR TURN.
WHAK!
GNNH!

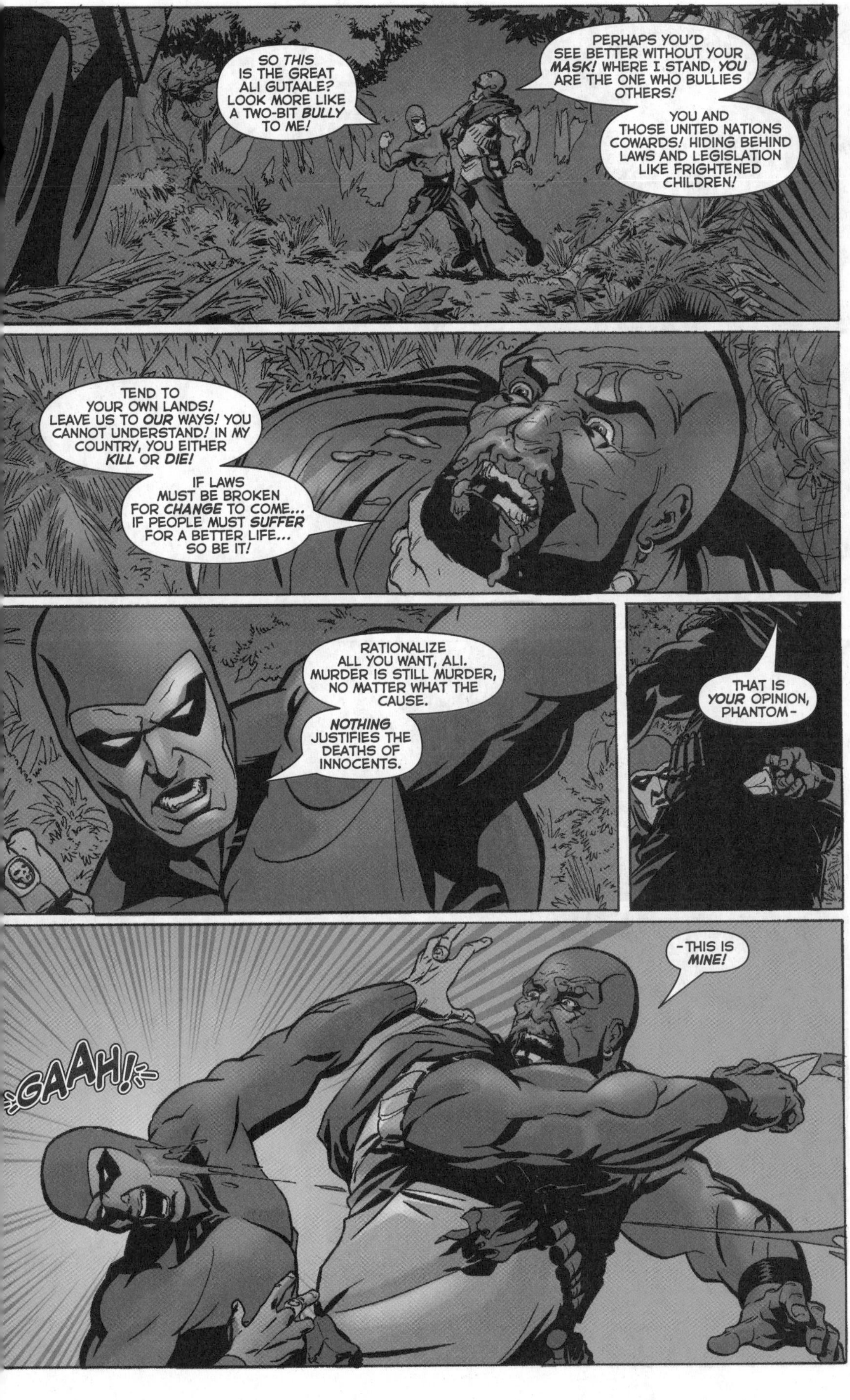

SO *THIS* IS THE GREAT ALI GUTAALE? LOOK MORE LIKE A TWO-BIT *BULLY* TO ME!
PERHAPS YOU'D SEE BETTER WITHOUT YOUR *MASK!* WHERE I STAND, *YOU* ARE THE ONE WHO BULLIES OTHERS!
YOU AND THOSE UNITED NATIONS COWARDS! HIDING BEHIND LAWS AND LEGISLATION LIKE FRIGHTENED CHILDREN!
TEND TO YOUR OWN LANDS! LEAVE US TO *OUR* WAYS! YOU CANNOT UNDERSTAND! IN MY COUNTRY, YOU EITHER *KILL* OR *DIE!*
IF LAWS MUST BE BROKEN FOR *CHANGE* TO COME... IF PEOPLE MUST *SUFFER* FOR A BETTER LIFE... SO BE IT!
RATIONALIZE ALL YOU WANT, ALI. MURDER IS STILL MURDER, NO MATTER WHAT THE CAUSE.
NOTHING JUSTIFIES THE DEATHS OF INNOCENTS.
THAT IS *YOUR* OPINION, PHANTOM-
-THIS IS *MINE!*
GAAH!

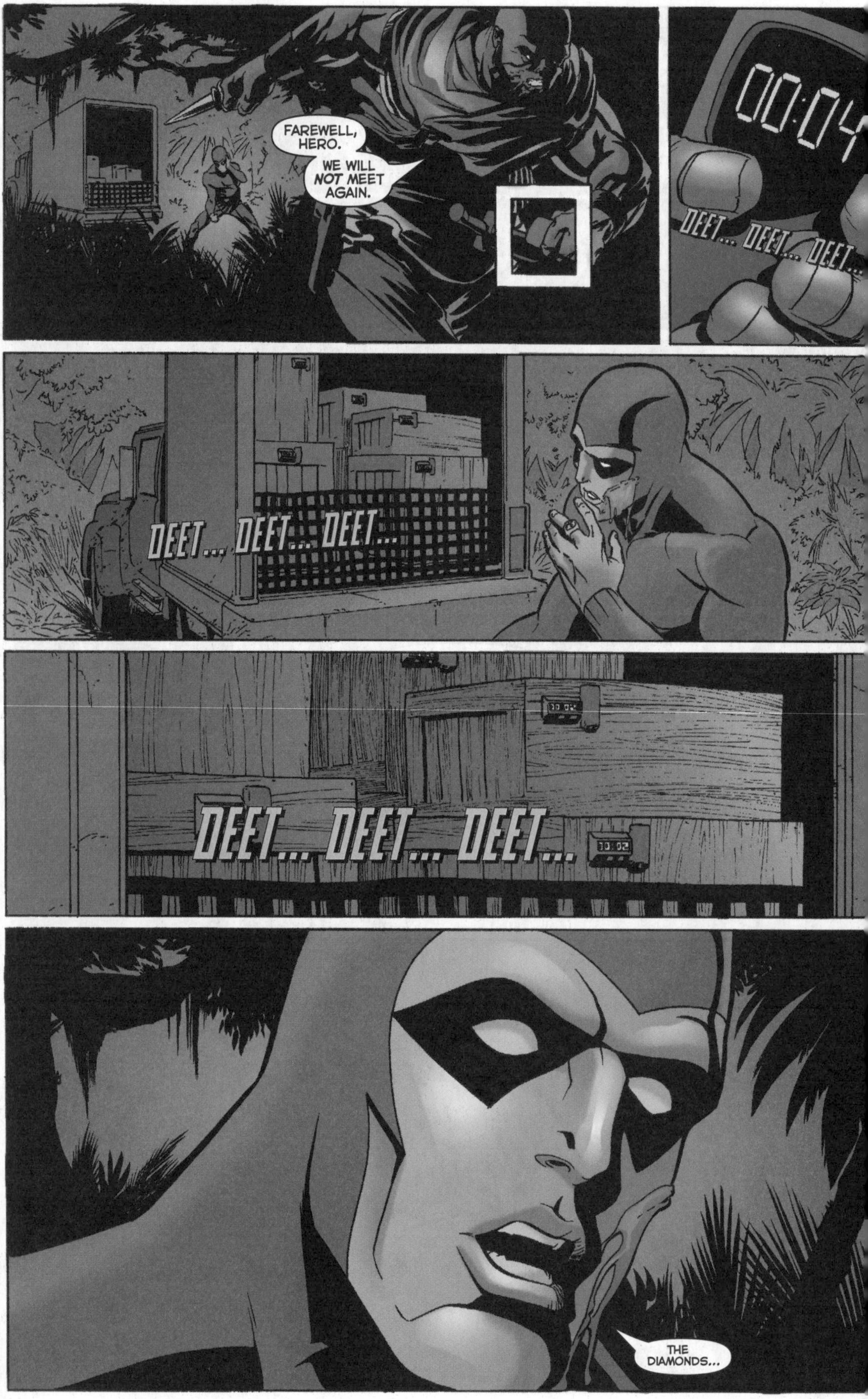

FAREWELL, HERO.
WE WILL *NOT* MEET AGAIN.
00:04
DEET... DEET... DEET...
DEET... DEET... DEET...
DEET... DEET... DEET...
THE DIAMONDS...

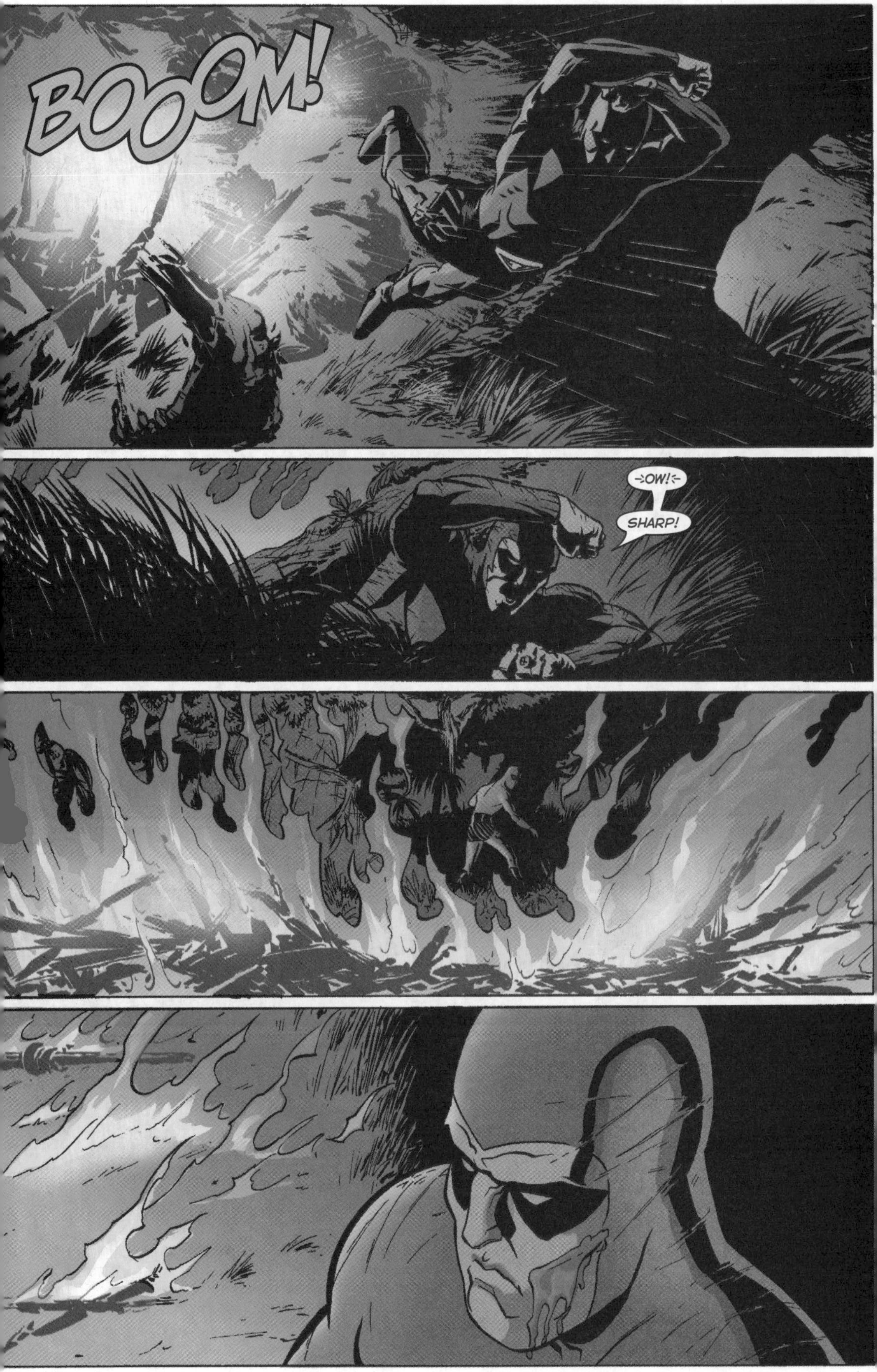
BOOOM!
OW!
SHARP!

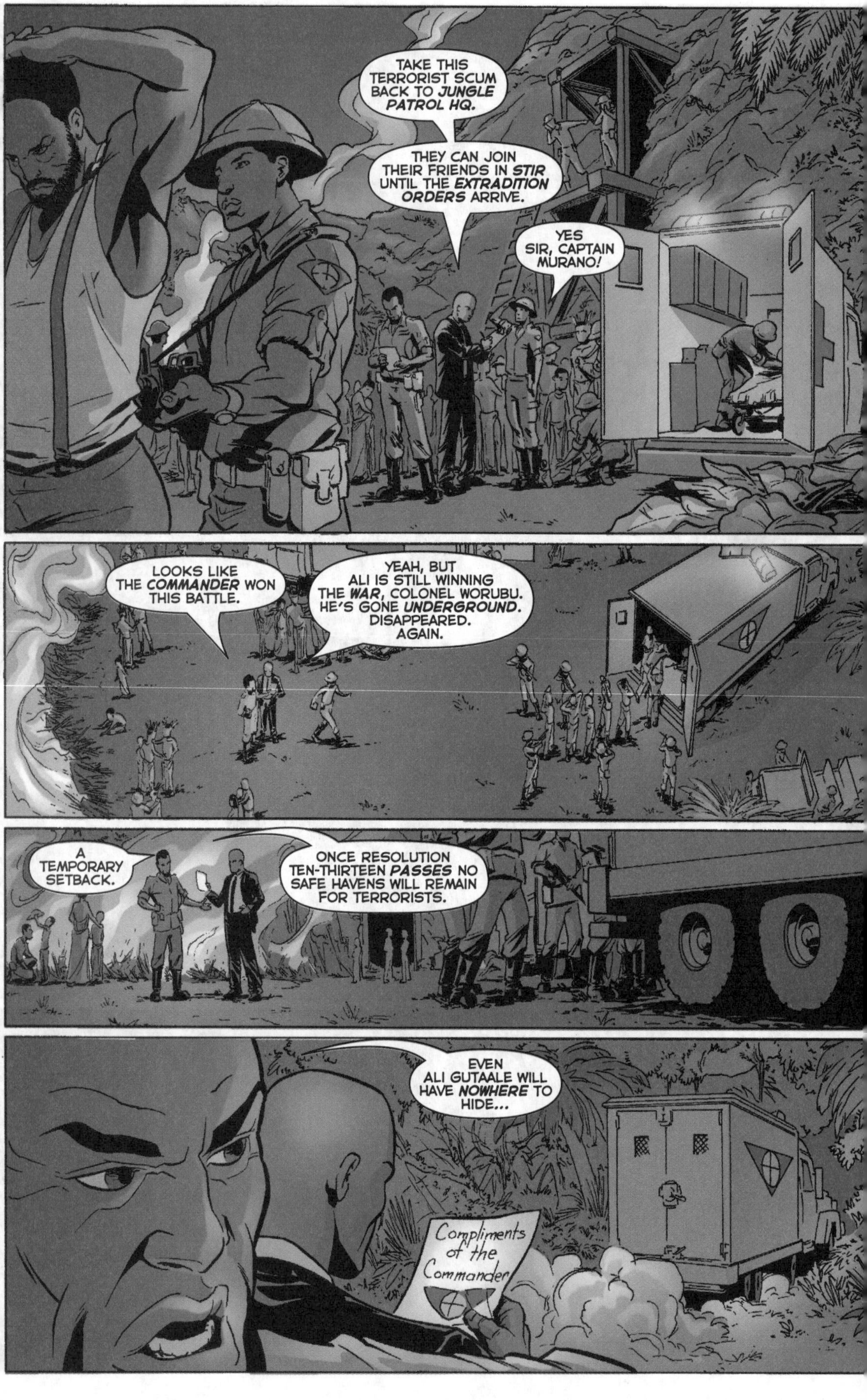
TAKE THIS TERRORIST SCUM BACK TO *JUNGLE PATROL HQ.*
THEY CAN JOIN THEIR FRIENDS IN *STIR* UNTIL THE *EXTRADITION ORDERS* ARRIVE.
YES SIR, CAPTAIN MURANO!
LOOKS LIKE THE *COMMANDER* WON THIS BATTLE.
YEAH, BUT ALI IS STILL WINNING THE *WAR*, COLONEL WORUBU. HE'S GONE *UNDERGROUND.* DISAPPEARED. AGAIN.
A TEMPORARY SETBACK.
ONCE RESOLUTION TEN-THIRTEEN *PASSES* NO SAFE HAVENS WILL REMAIN FOR TERRORISTS.
EVEN ALI GUTAALE WILL HAVE *NOWHERE* TO HIDE...
Compliments of the Commander

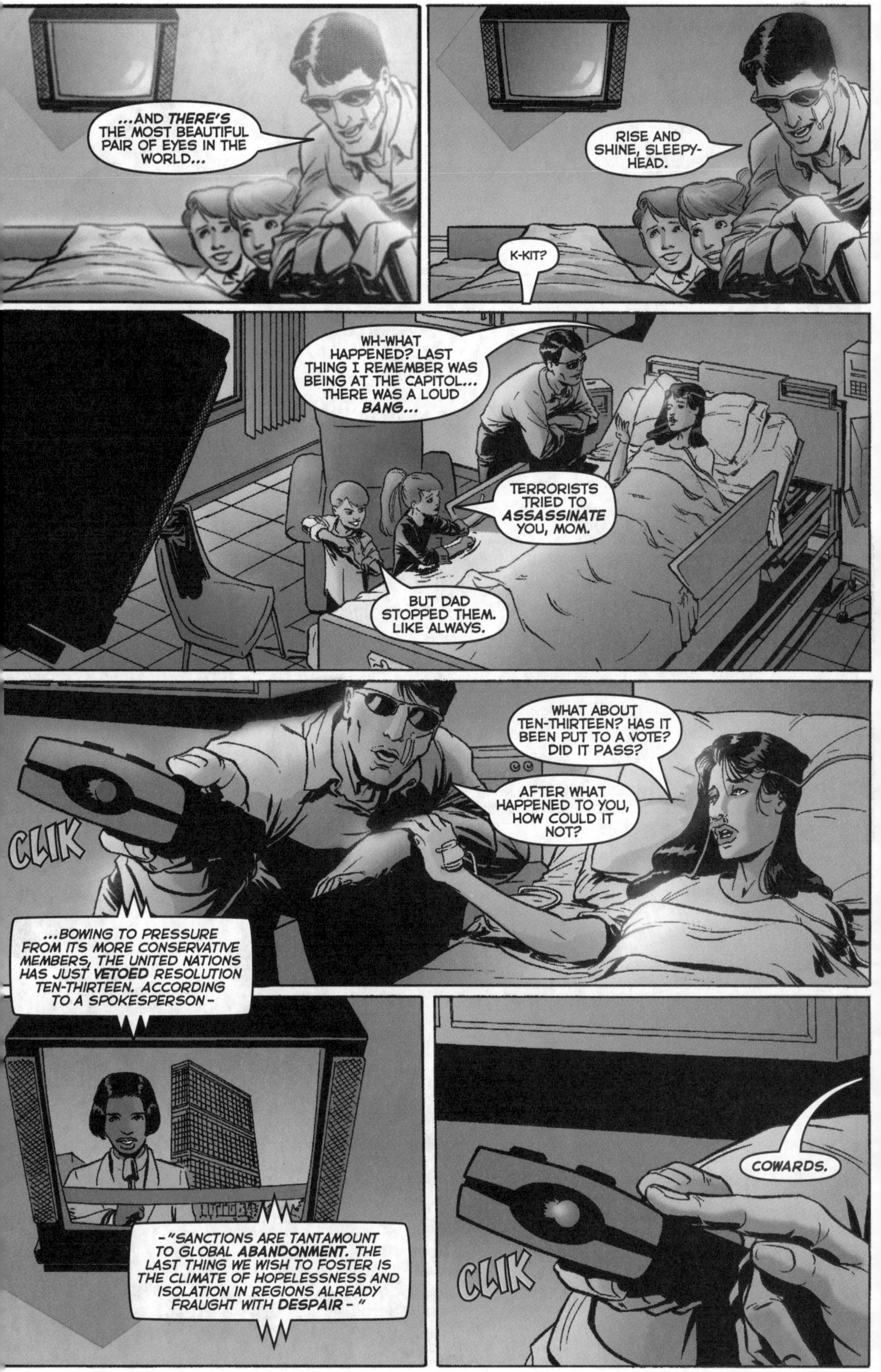
...AND THERE'S THE MOST BEAUTIFUL PAIR OF EYES IN THE WORLD...
RISE AND SHINE, SLEEPY-HEAD.
K-KIT?
WH-WHAT HAPPENED? LAST THING I REMEMBER WAS BEING AT THE CAPITOL... THERE WAS A LOUD BANG...
TERRORISTS TRIED TO ASSASSINATE YOU, MOM.
BUT DAD STOPPED THEM. LIKE ALWAYS.
WHAT ABOUT TEN-THIRTEEN? HAS IT BEEN PUT TO A VOTE? DID IT PASS?
AFTER WHAT HAPPENED TO YOU, HOW COULD IT NOT?
CLIK
...BOWING TO PRESSURE FROM ITS MORE CONSERVATIVE MEMBERS, THE UNITED NATIONS HAS JUST VETOED RESOLUTION TEN-THIRTEEN. ACCORDING TO A SPOKESPERSON -
-"SANCTIONS ARE TANTAMOUNT TO GLOBAL ABANDONMENT. THE LAST THING WE WISH TO FOSTER IS THE CLIMATE OF HOPELESSNESS AND ISOLATION IN REGIONS ALREADY FRAUGHT WITH DESPAIR - "
COWARDS.
CLIK

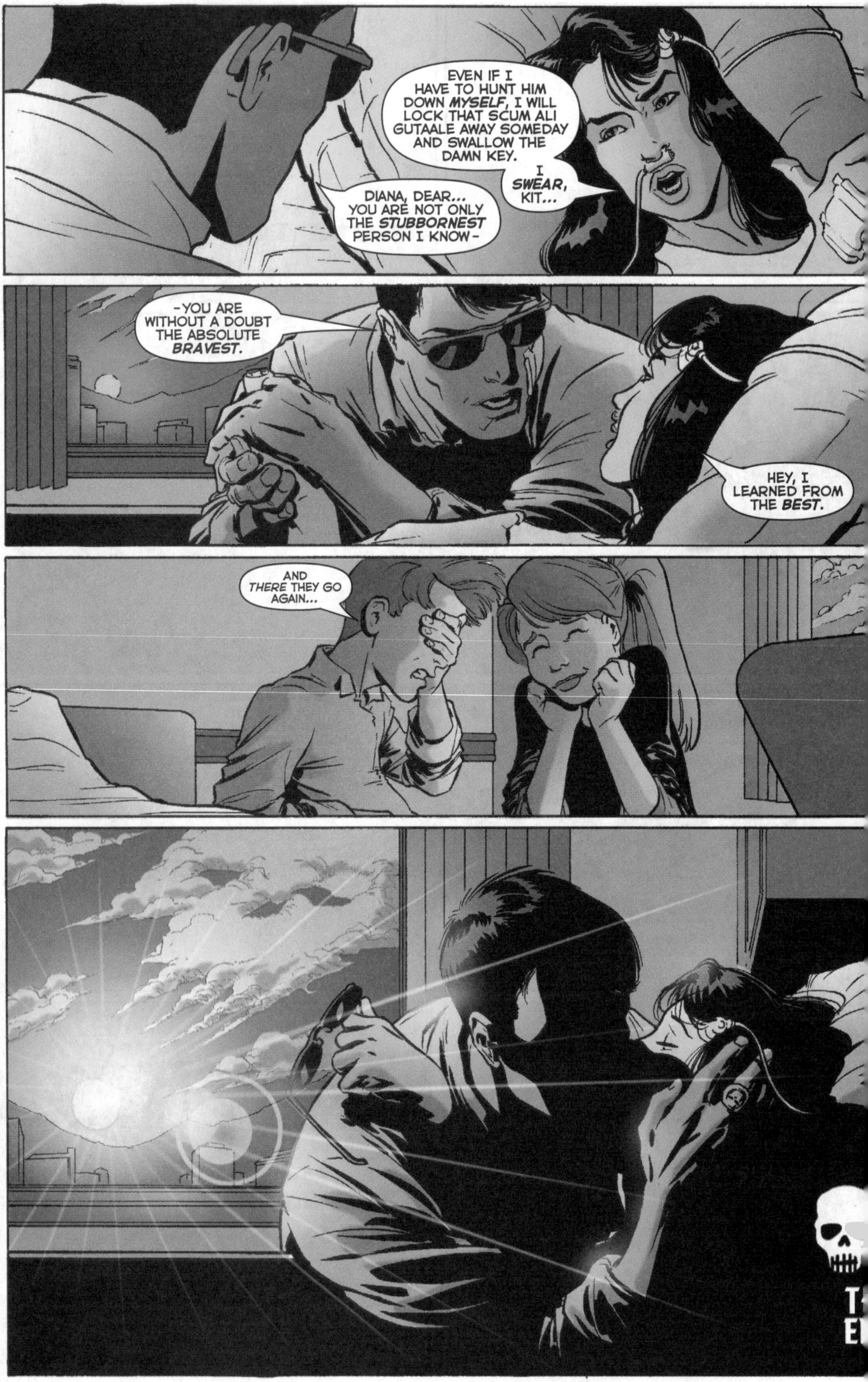
EVEN IF I HAVE TO HUNT HIM DOWN MYSELF, I WILL LOCK THAT SCUM ALI GUTAALE AWAY SOMEDAY AND SWALLOW THE DAMN KEY.
I SWEAR, KIT...
DIANA, DEAR... YOU ARE NOT ONLY THE STUBBORNEST PERSON I KNOW-
-YOU ARE WITHOUT A DOUBT THE ABSOLUTE BRAVEST.
HEY, I LEARNED FROM THE BEST.
AND THERE THEY GO AGAIN...

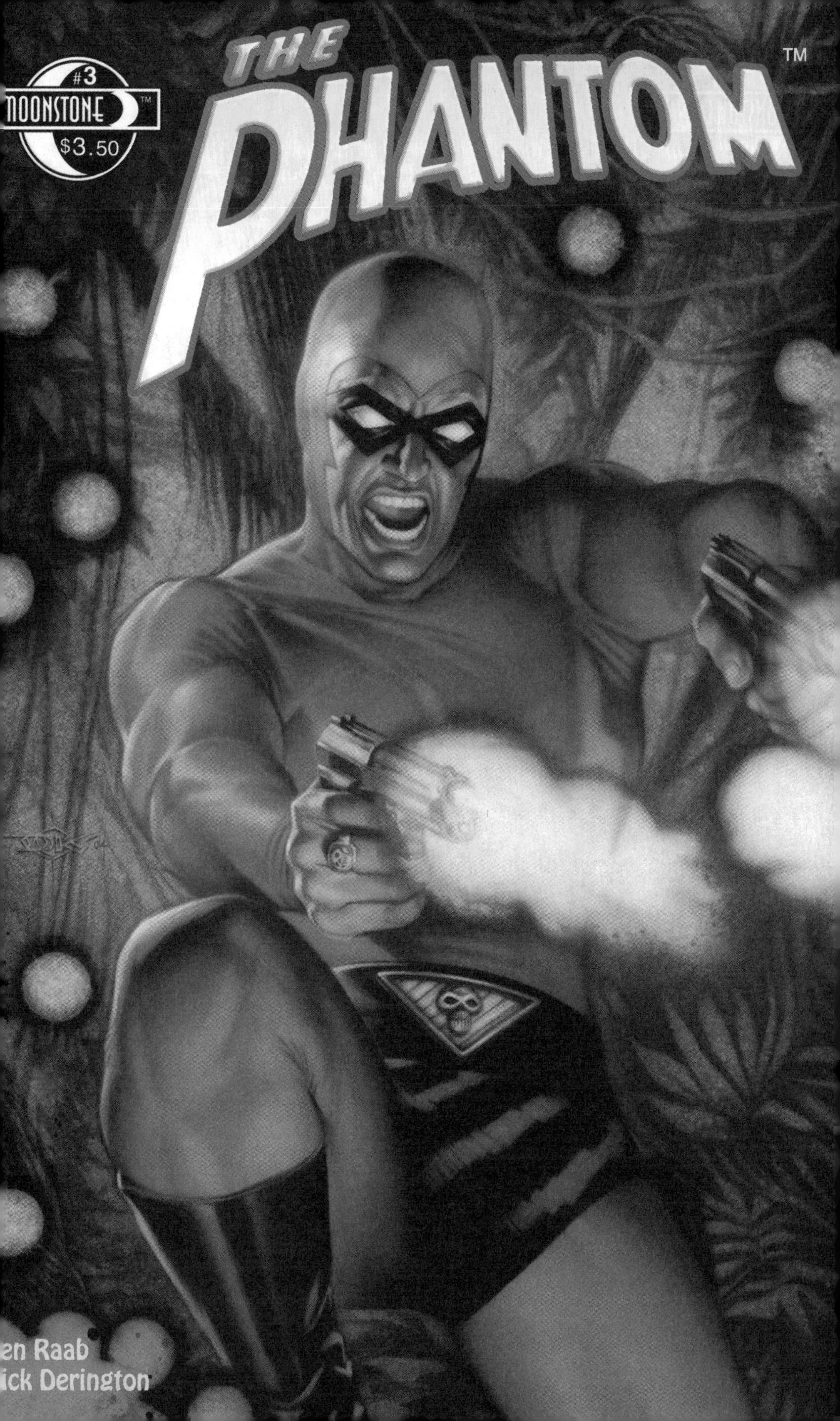

THE PHANTOM™
#3
MOONSTONE™
$3.50
en Raab
ick Derington

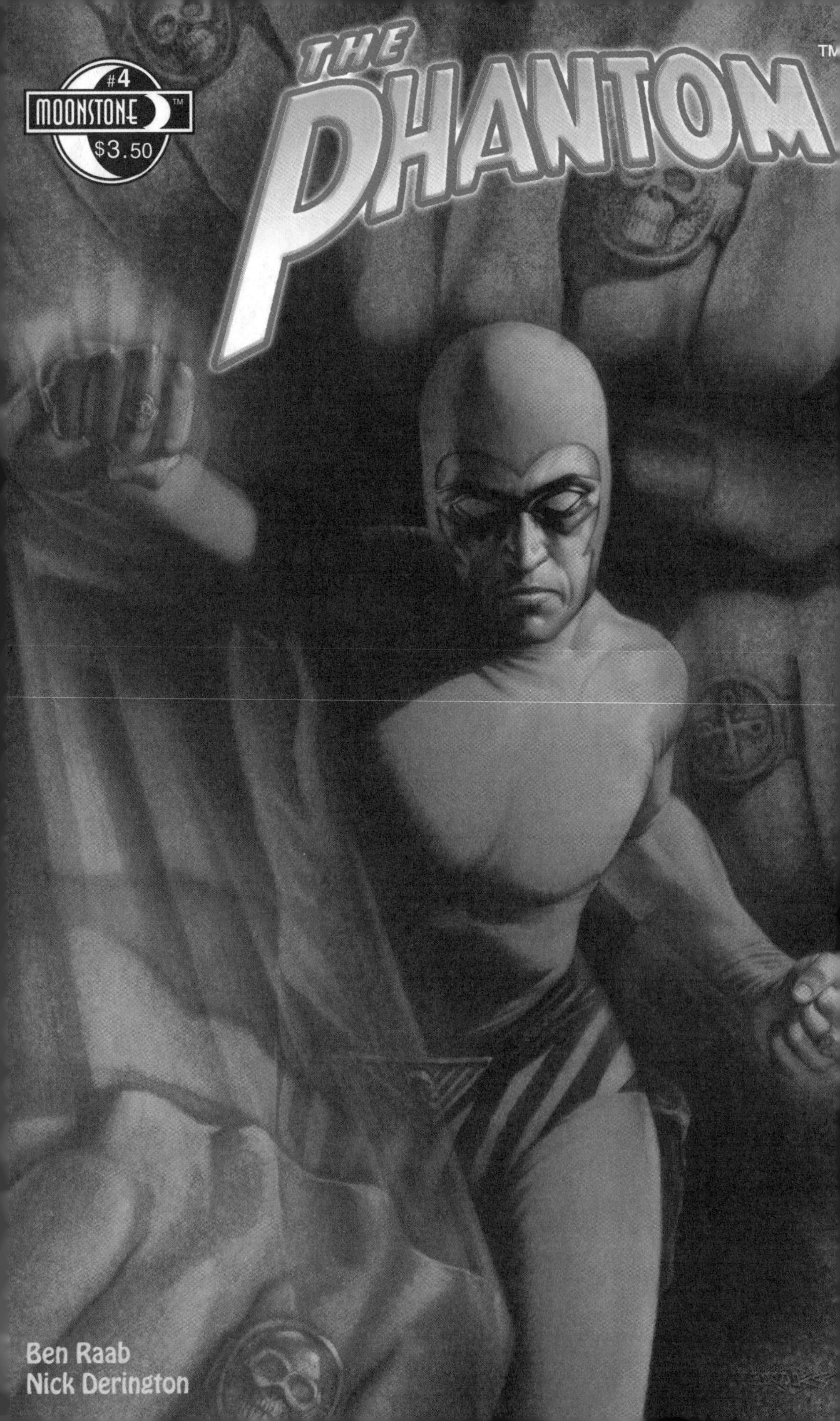
#4
MOONSTONE™
$3.50
THE PHANTOM™
Ben Raab
Nick Derington

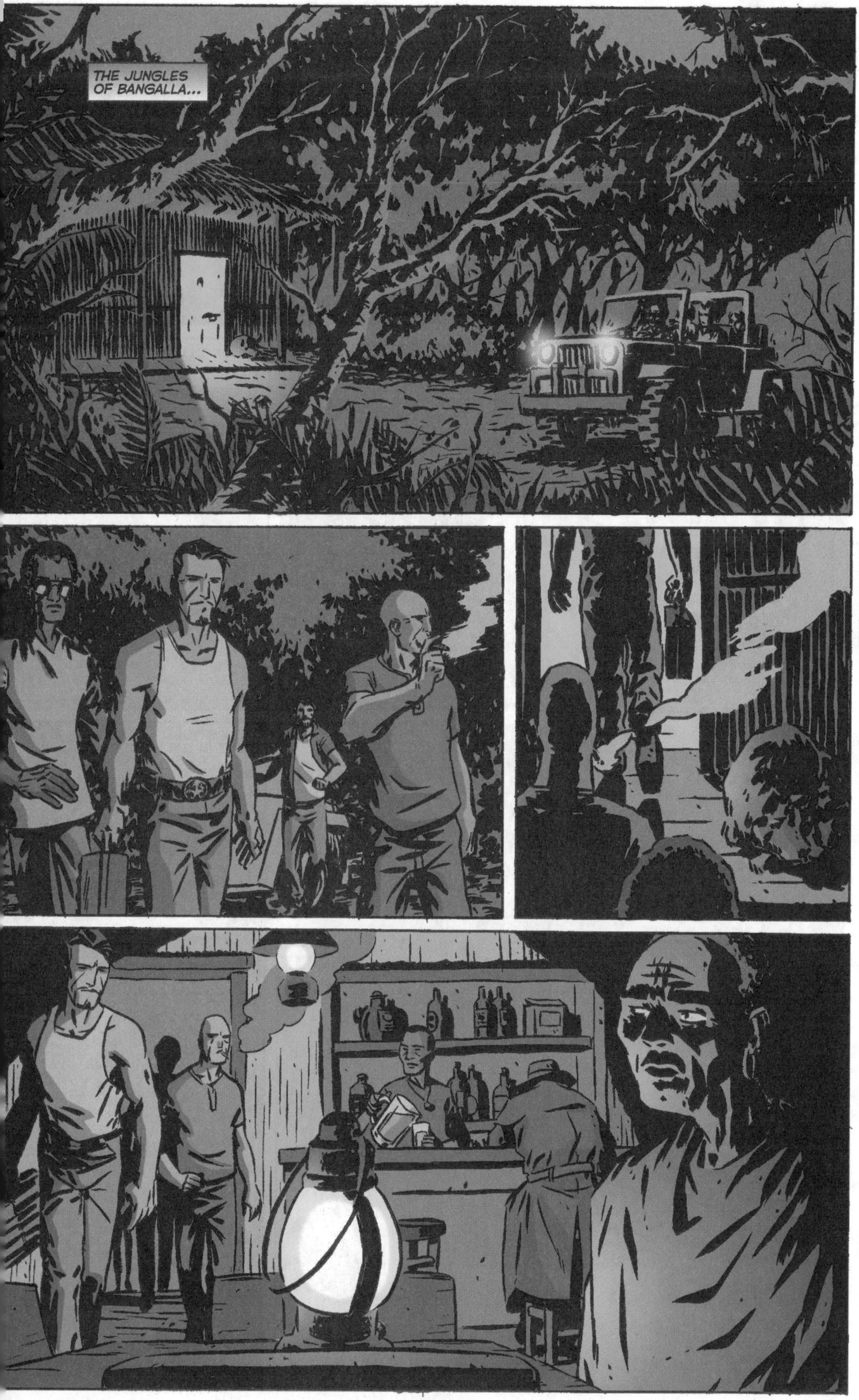
THE JUNGLES OF BANGALLA...

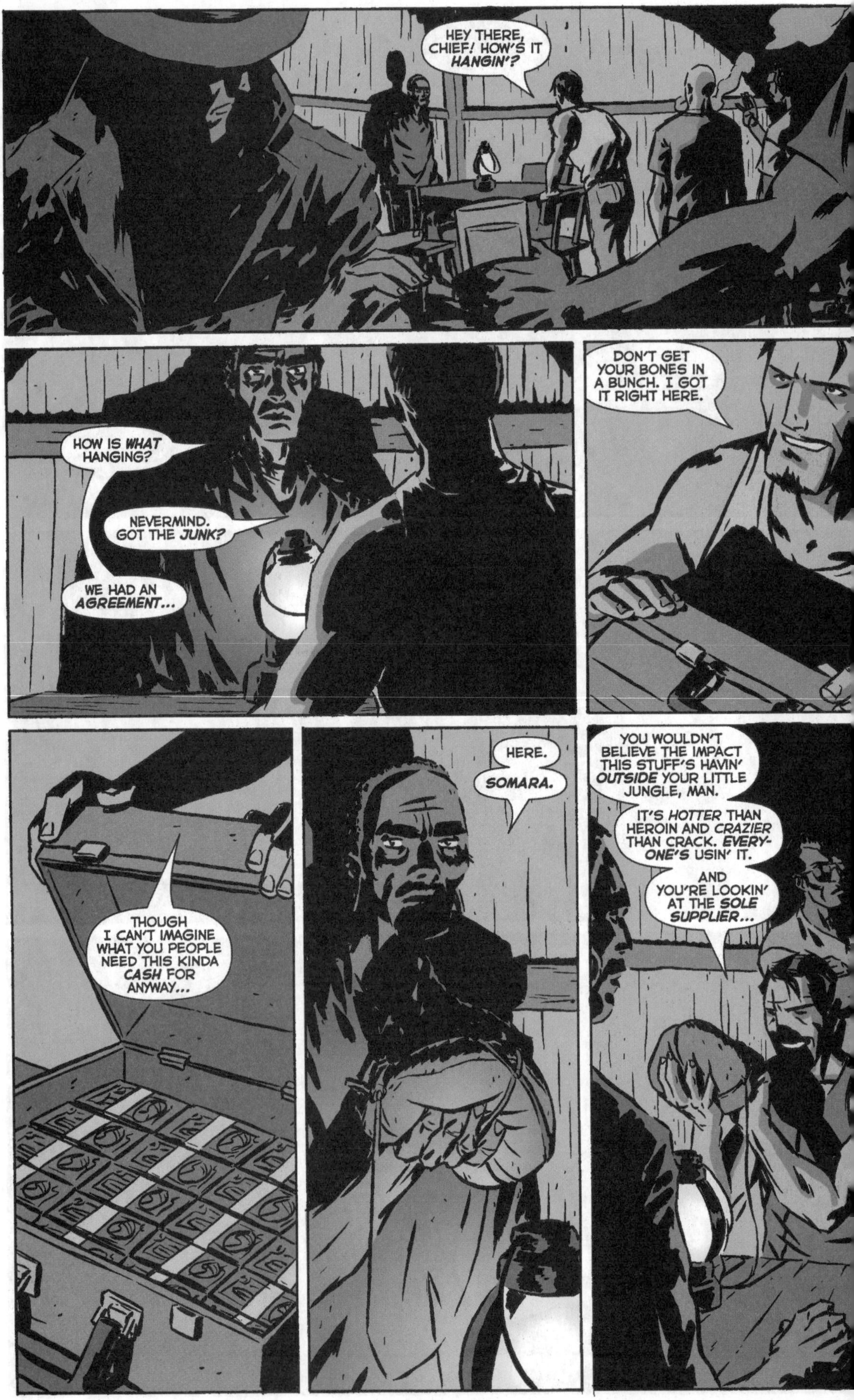
HEY THERE, CHIEF! HOW'S IT *HANGIN'?*
HOW IS *WHAT* HANGING?
NEVERMIND. GOT THE *JUNK?*
WE HAD AN *AGREEMENT...*
DON'T GET YOUR BONES IN A BUNCH. I GOT IT RIGHT HERE.
THOUGH I CAN'T IMAGINE WHAT YOU PEOPLE NEED THIS KINDA *CASH* FOR ANYWAY...
HERE.
SOMARA.
YOU WOULDN'T BELIEVE THE IMPACT THIS STUFF'S HAVIN' *OUTSIDE* YOUR LITTLE JUNGLE, MAN.
IT'S *HOTTER* THAN HEROIN AND *CRAZIER* THAN CRACK. *EVERYONE'S* USIN' IT.
AND YOU'RE LOOKIN' AT THE *SOLE SUPPLIER...*

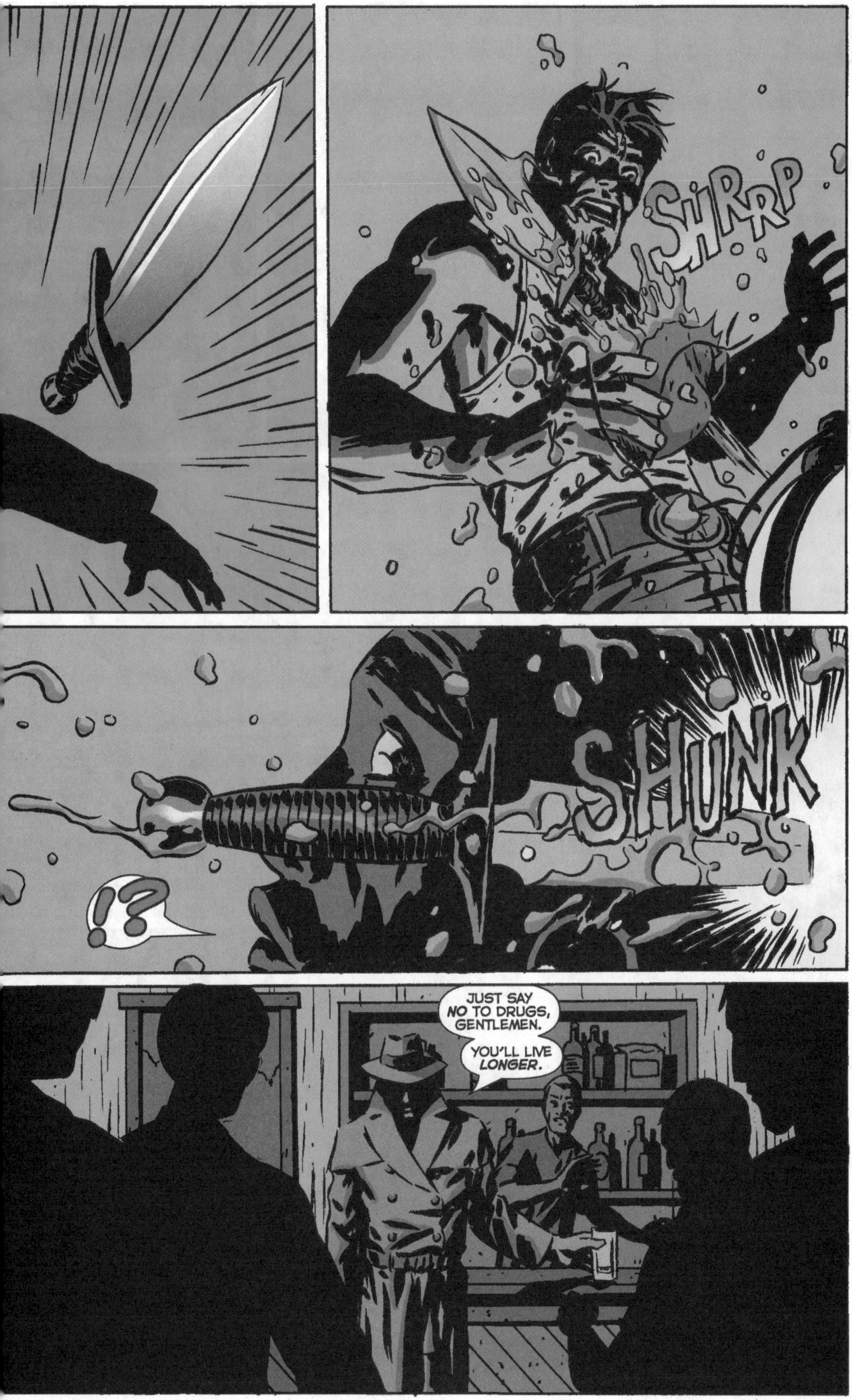
SHRRP
SHUNK
!?
JUST SAY NO TO DRUGS, GENTLEMEN.
YOU'LL LIVE LONGER.

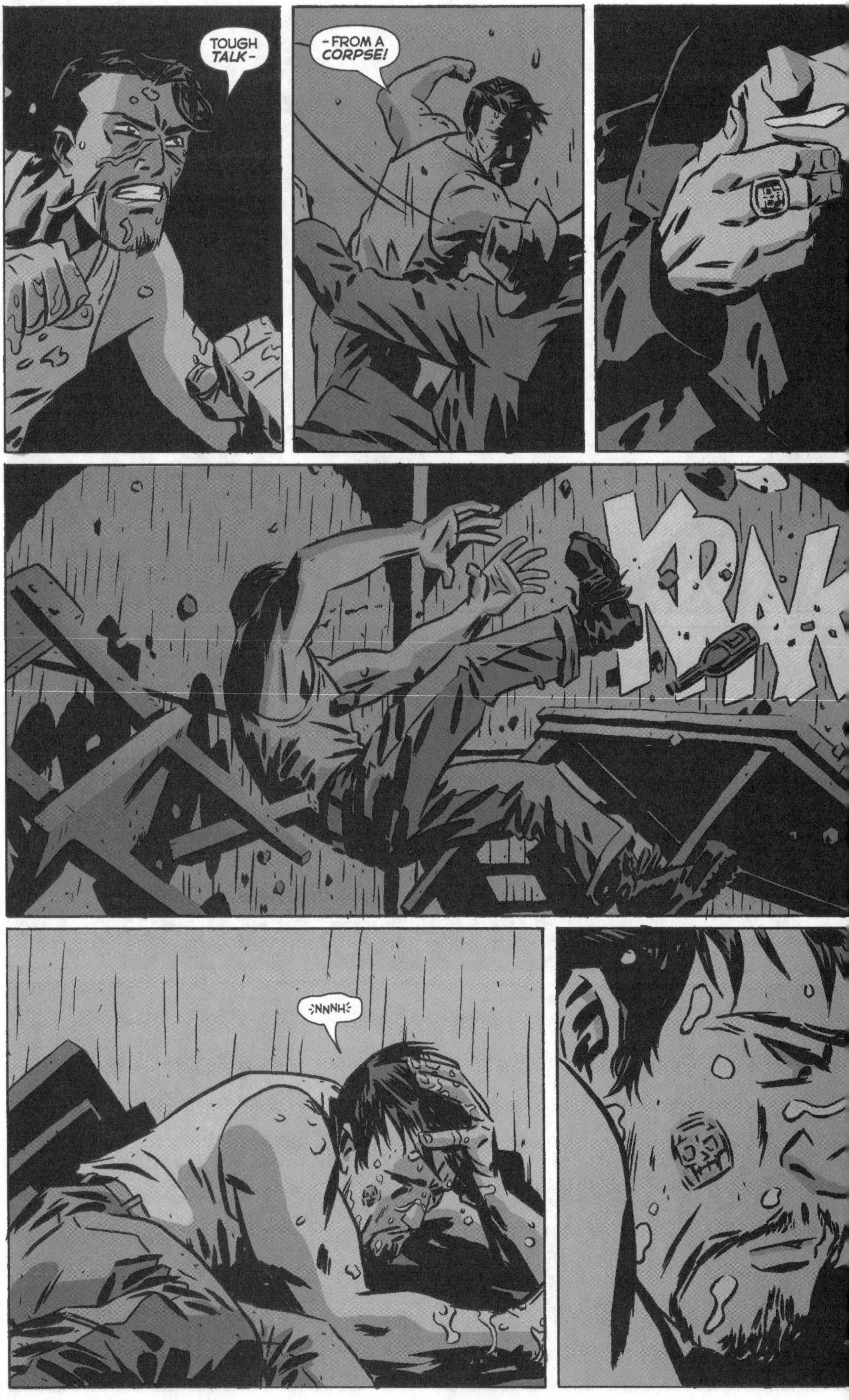
TOUGH TALK-
-FROM A CORPSE!
KRAK
NNNH

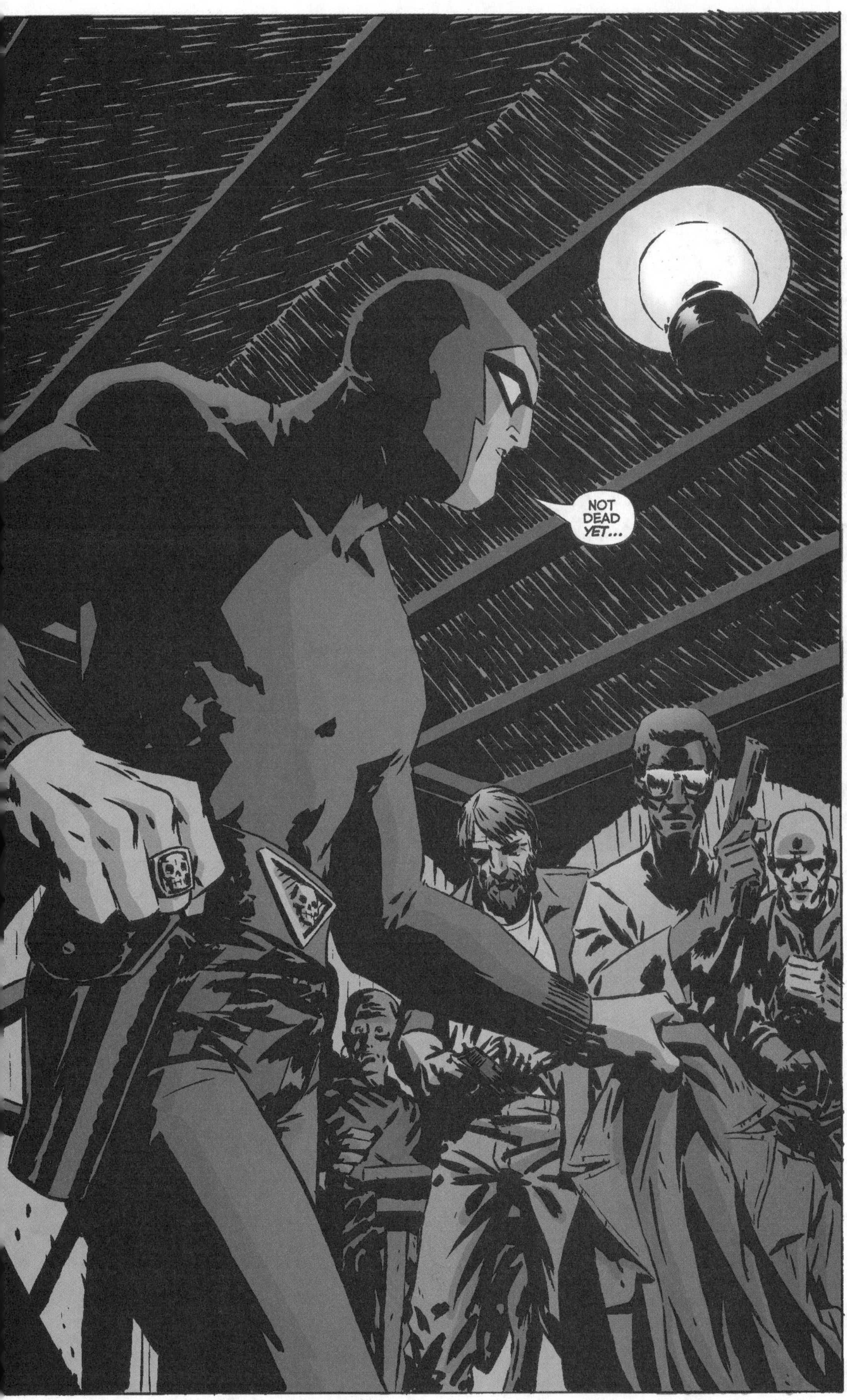
NOT DEAD YET...

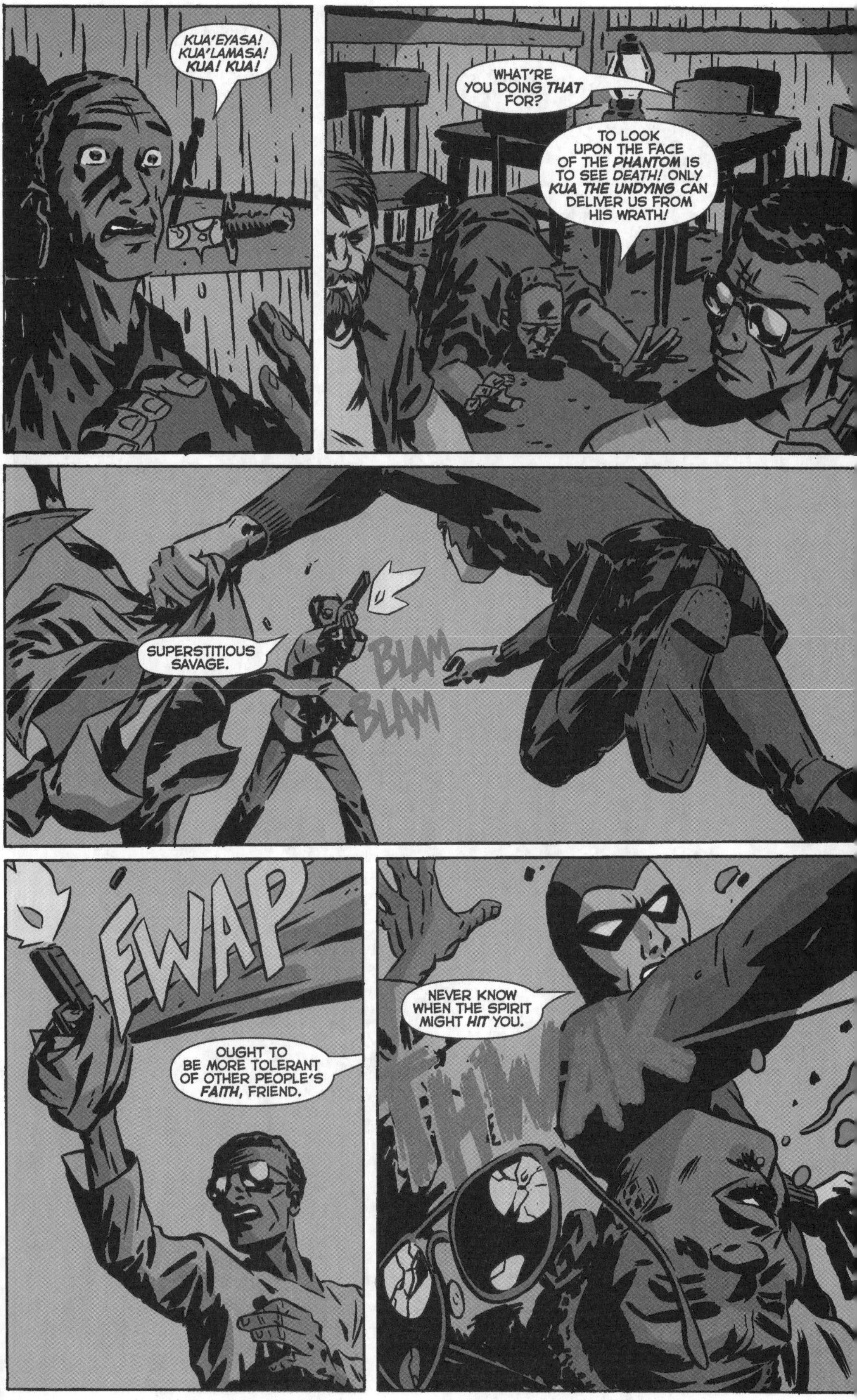
KUA'EYASA! KUA'LAMASA! KUA! KUA!
WHAT'RE YOU DOING *THAT* FOR?
TO LOOK UPON THE FACE OF THE *PHANTOM* IS TO SEE *DEATH!* ONLY *KUA THE UNDYING* CAN DELIVER US FROM HIS WRATH!
SUPERSTITIOUS SAVAGE.
BLAM
BLAM
FWAP
OUGHT TO BE MORE TOLERANT OF OTHER PEOPLE'S *FAITH*, FRIEND.
NEVER KNOW WHEN THE SPIRIT MIGHT *HIT* YOU.
THWAK

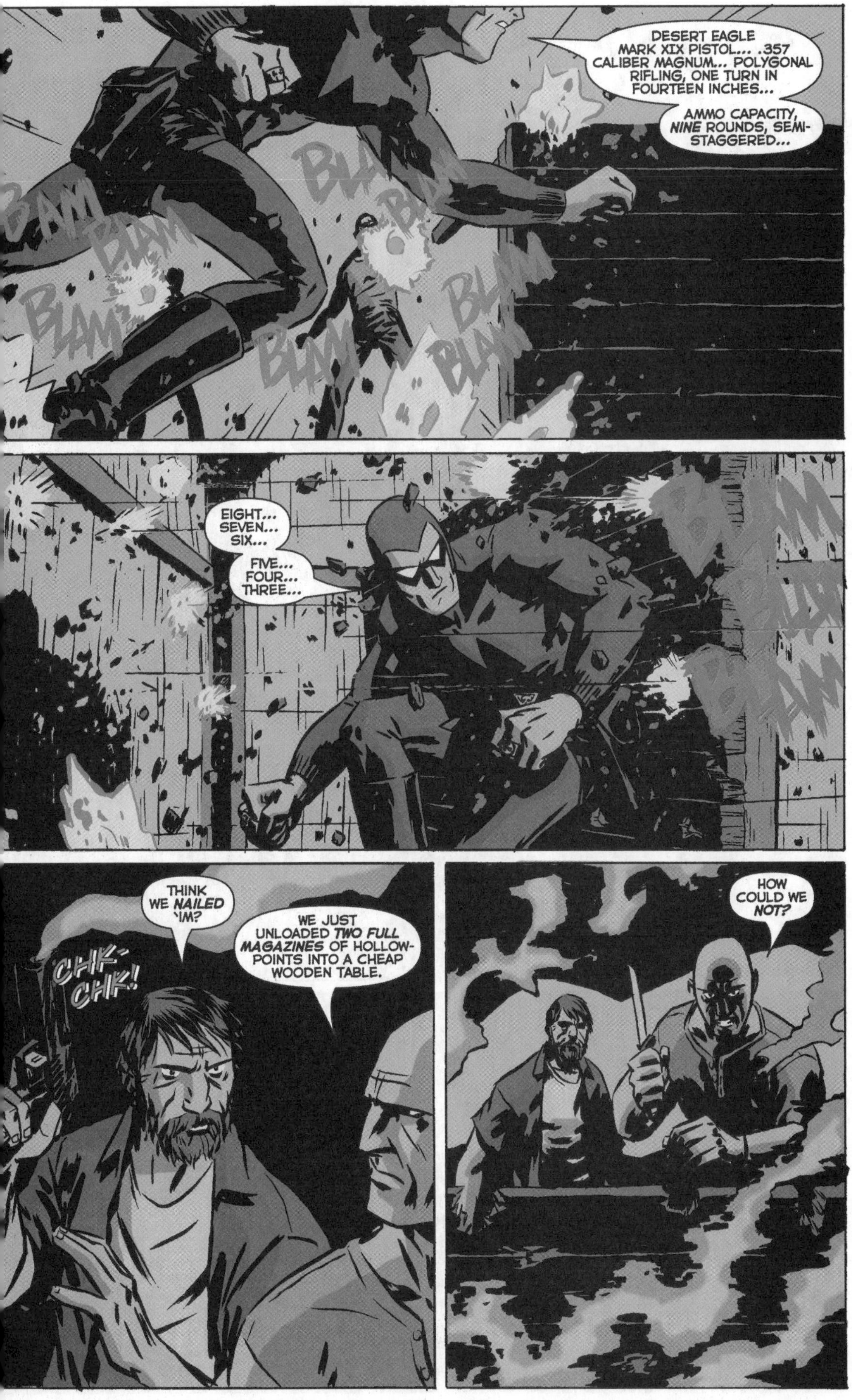
DESERT EAGLE MARK XIX PISTOL... .357 CALIBER MAGNUM... POLYGONAL RIFLING, ONE TURN IN FOURTEEN INCHES...
AMMO CAPACITY, NINE ROUNDS, SEMI-STAGGERED...
BAM BLAM BLAM BLAM
BLAM BLAM BLAM BLAM BLAM
EIGHT... SEVEN... SIX...
FIVE... FOUR... THREE...
BLAM
THINK WE NAILED 'IM?
CHK-CHK!
WE JUST UNLOADED TWO FULL MAGAZINES OF HOLLOW-POINTS INTO A CHEAP WOODEN TABLE.
HOW COULD WE NOT?

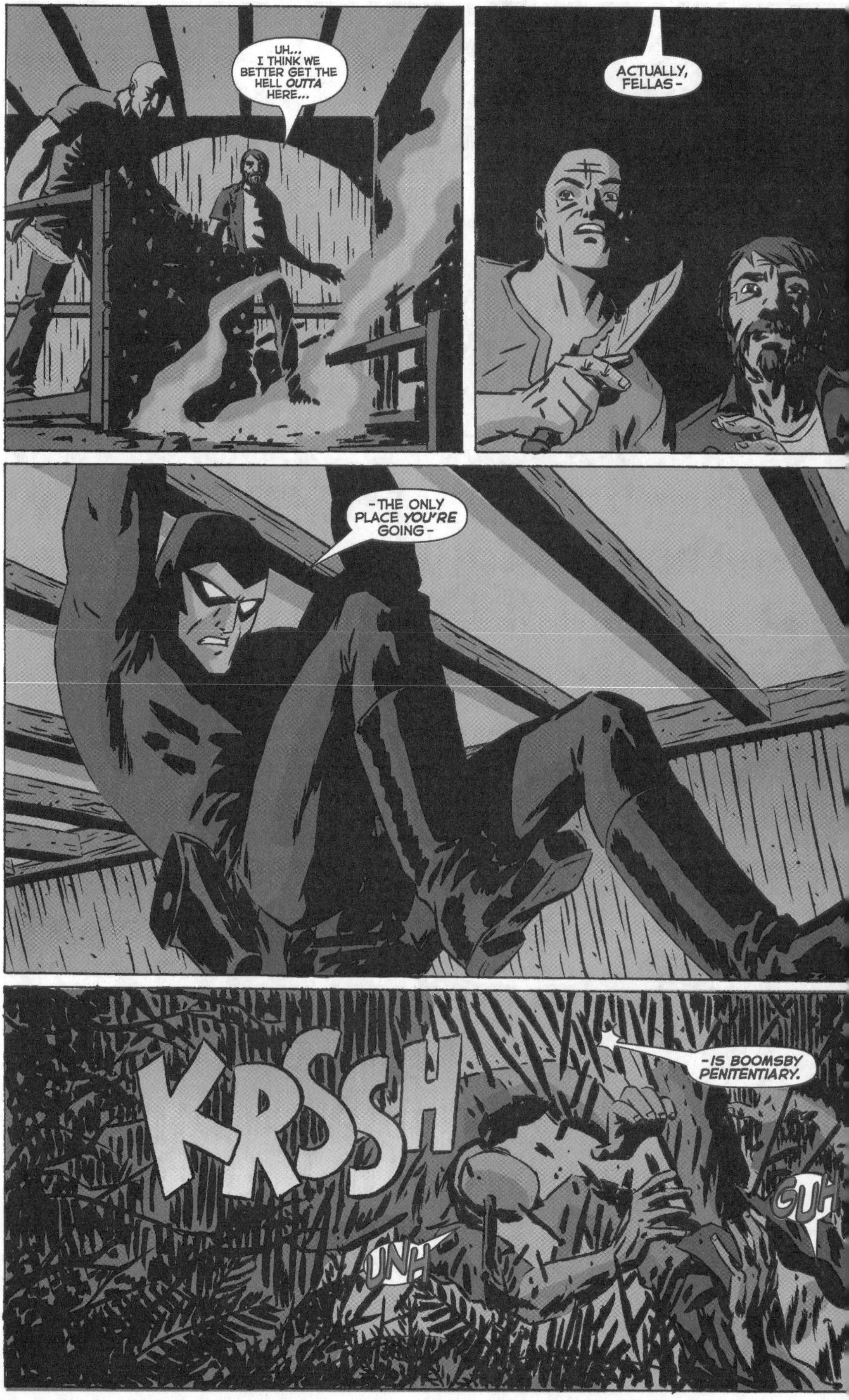
UH... I THINK WE BETTER GET THE HELL *OUTTA* HERE...
ACTUALLY, FELLAS-
-THE ONLY PLACE *YOU'RE* GOING-
KRSSH
-IS BOOMSBY PENITENTIARY.
UNH
GUH

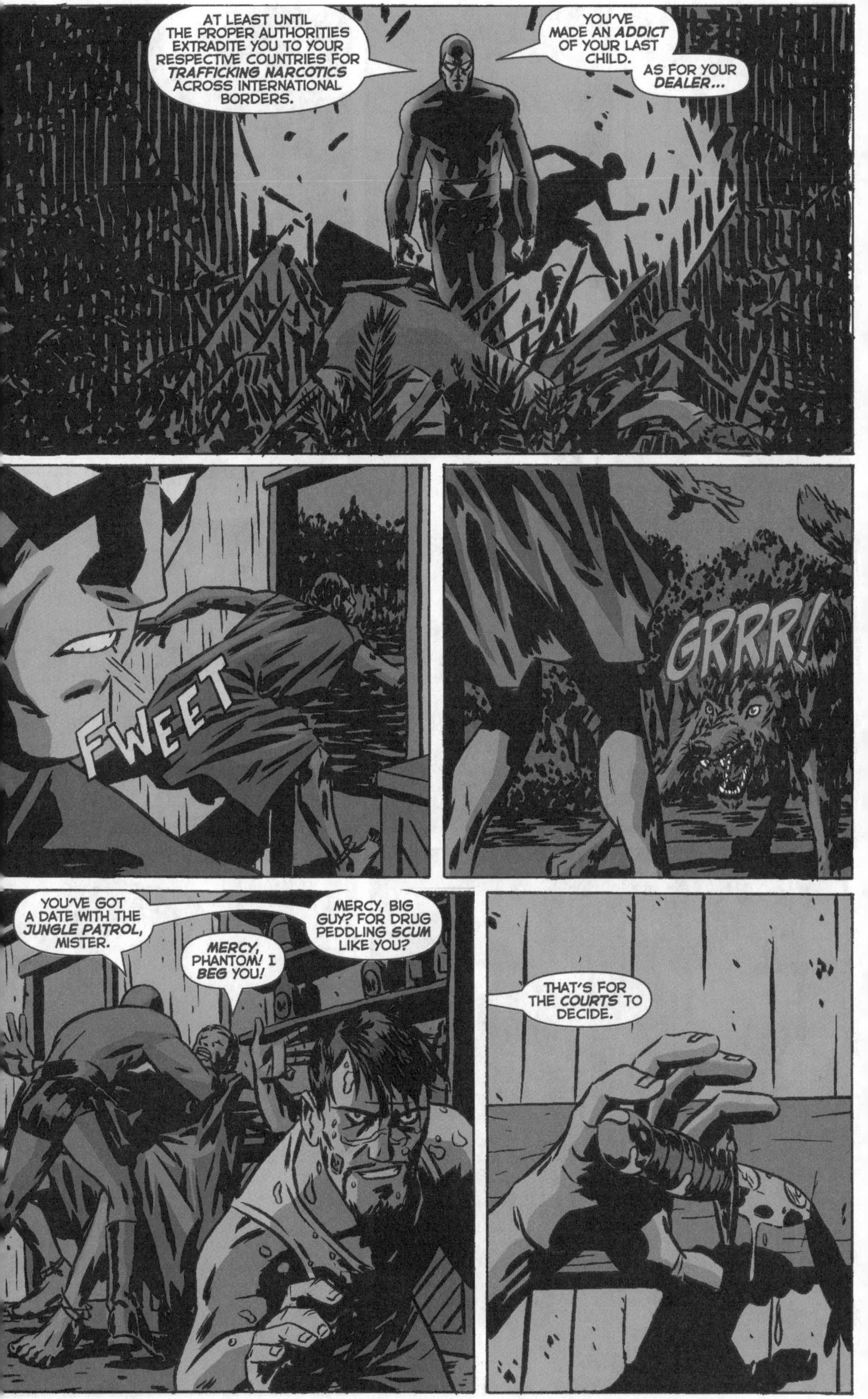
AT LEAST UNTIL THE PROPER AUTHORITIES EXTRADITE YOU TO YOUR RESPECTIVE COUNTRIES FOR *TRAFFICKING NARCOTICS* ACROSS INTERNATIONAL BORDERS.
YOU'VE MADE AN *ADDICT* OF YOUR LAST CHILD.
AS FOR YOUR *DEALER*...
FWEET
GRRR!
YOU'VE GOT A DATE WITH THE *JUNGLE PATROL*, MISTER.
MERCY, PHANTOM! I *BEG* YOU!
MERCY, BIG GUY? FOR DRUG PEDDLING *SCUM* LIKE YOU?
THAT'S FOR THE *COURTS* TO DECIDE.

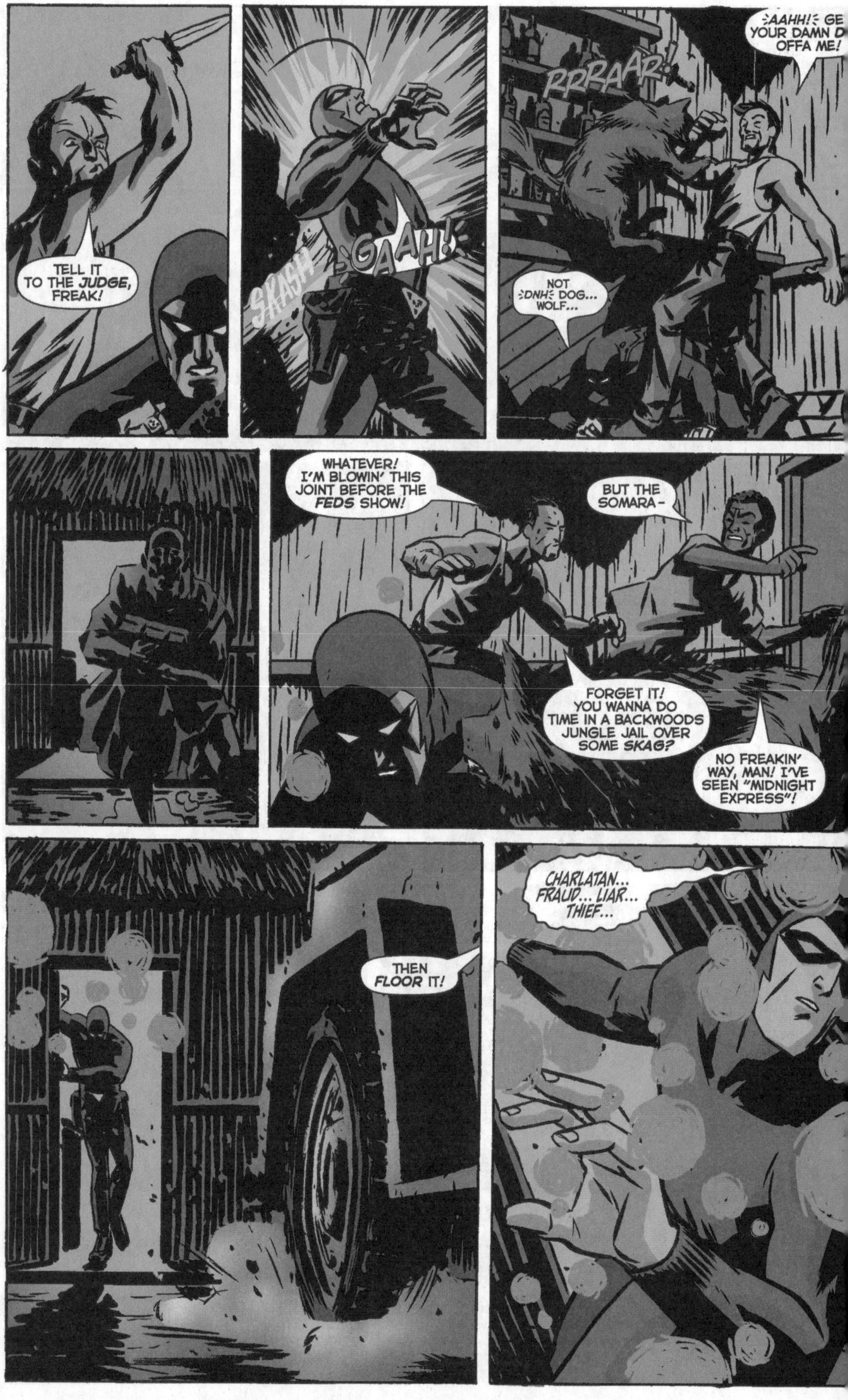
TELL IT TO THE JUDGE, FREAK!
SKASH
GAAH!
RRRAAR!
AAHH! GE YOUR DAMN D OFFA ME!
NOT DNH DOG... WOLF...
WHATEVER! I'M BLOWIN' THIS JOINT BEFORE THE FEDS SHOW!
BUT THE SOMARA-
FORGET IT! YOU WANNA DO TIME IN A BACKWOODS JUNGLE JAIL OVER SOME SKAG?
NO FREAKIN' WAY, MAN! I'VE SEEN "MIDNIGHT EXPRESS"!
THEN FLOOR IT!
CHARLATAN... FRAUD... LIAR... THIEF...

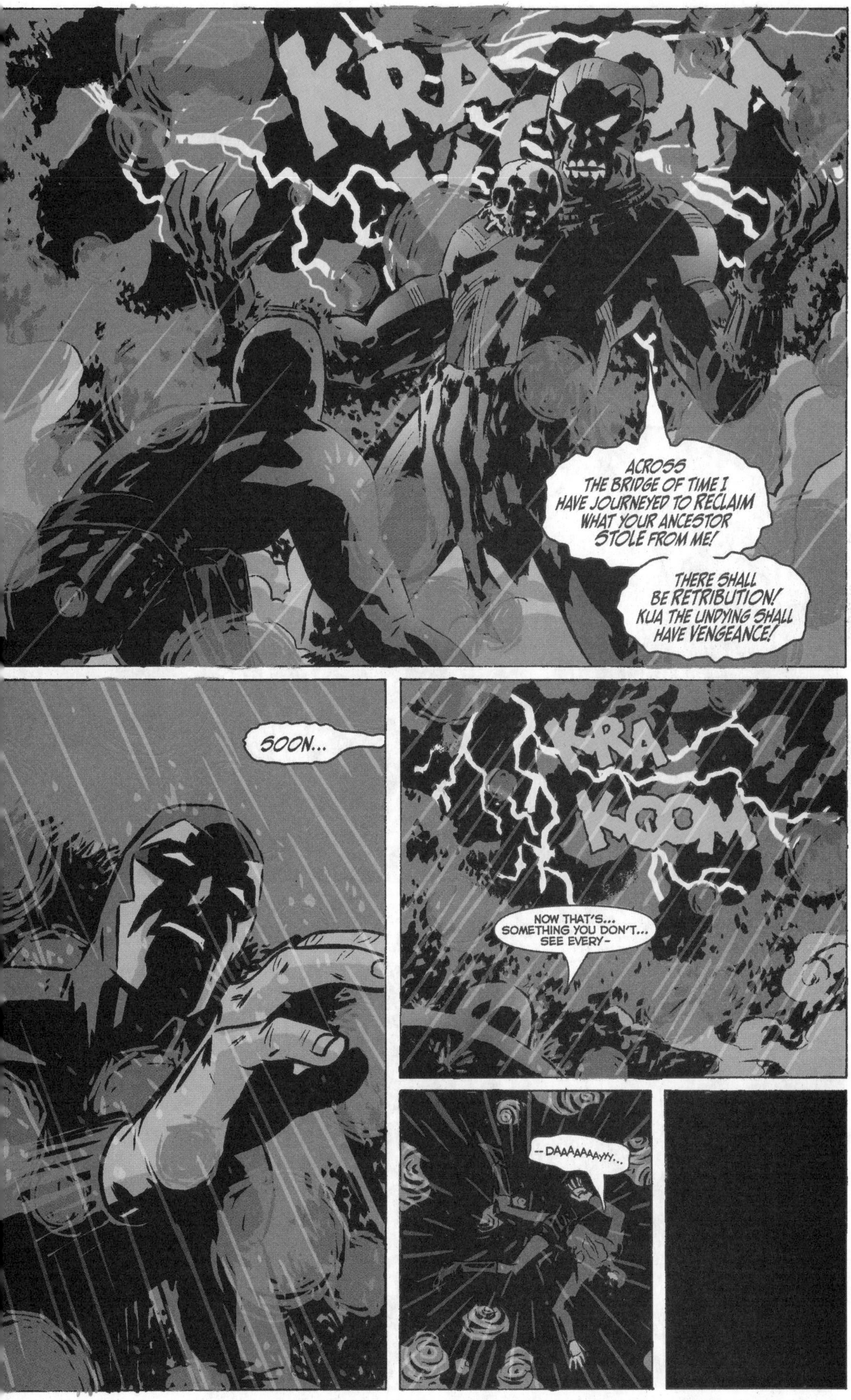
KRA-KOOM
ACROSS THE BRIDGE OF TIME I HAVE JOURNEYED TO RECLAIM WHAT YOUR ANCESTOR STOLE FROM ME!
THERE SHALL BE RETRIBUTION! KUA THE UNDYING SHALL HAVE VENGEANCE!
SOON...
KRA-KOOM
NOW THAT'S... SOMETHING YOU DON'T... SEE EVERY-
--DAAAAAAAyyy...

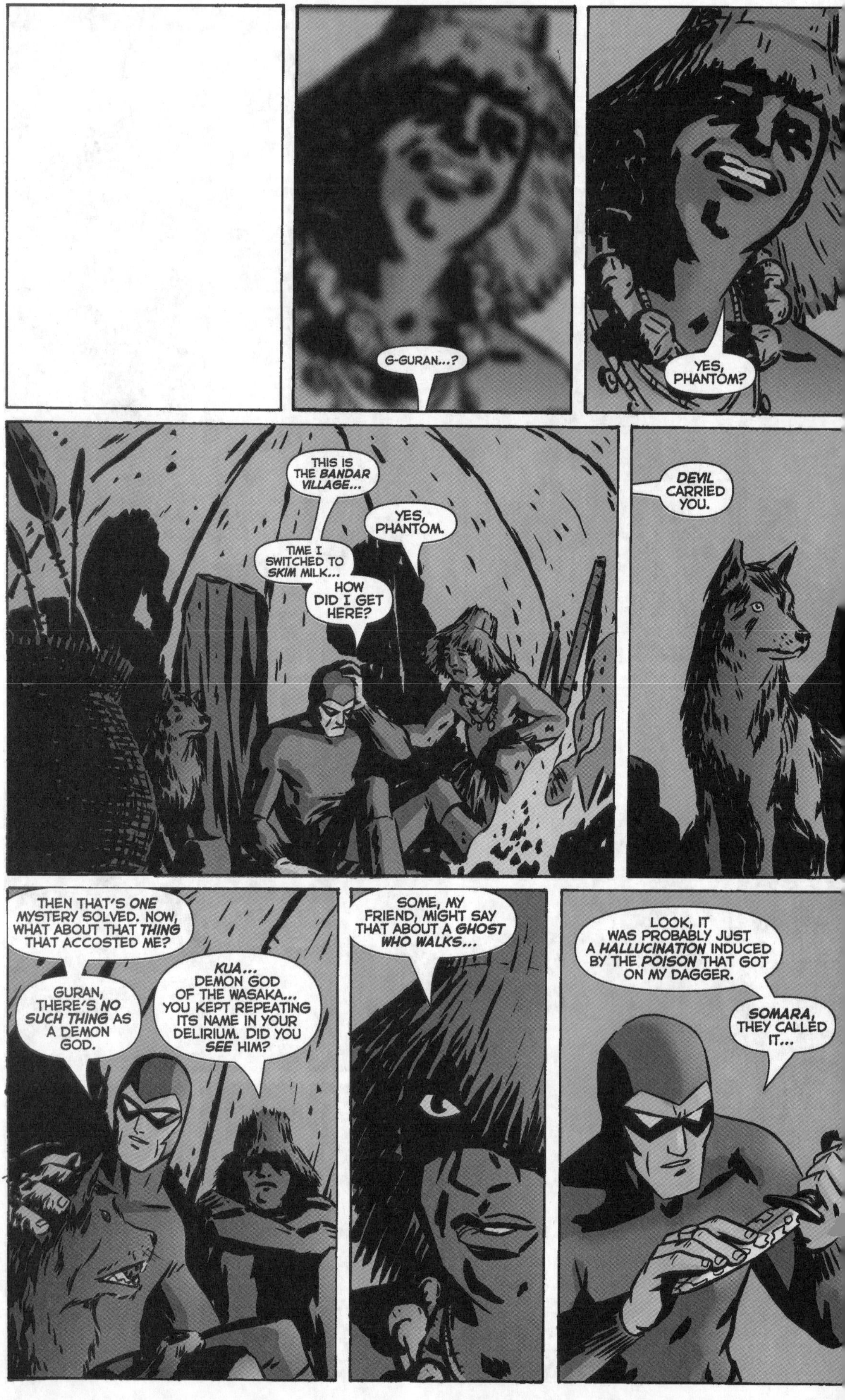
G-GURAN...?
YES, PHANTOM?
THIS IS THE BANDAR VILLAGE...
YES, PHANTOM.
TIME I SWITCHED TO SKIM MILK... HOW DID I GET HERE?
DEVIL CARRIED YOU.
THEN THAT'S ONE MYSTERY SOLVED. NOW, WHAT ABOUT THAT THING THAT ACCOSTED ME?
KUA... DEMON GOD OF THE WASAKA... YOU KEPT REPEATING ITS NAME IN YOUR DELIRIUM. DID YOU SEE HIM?
GURAN, THERE'S NO SUCH THING AS A DEMON GOD.
SOME, MY FRIEND, MIGHT SAY THAT ABOUT A GHOST WHO WALKS...
LOOK, IT WAS PROBABLY JUST A HALLUCINATION INDUCED BY THE POISON THAT GOT ON MY DAGGER.
SOMARA, THEY CALLED IT...

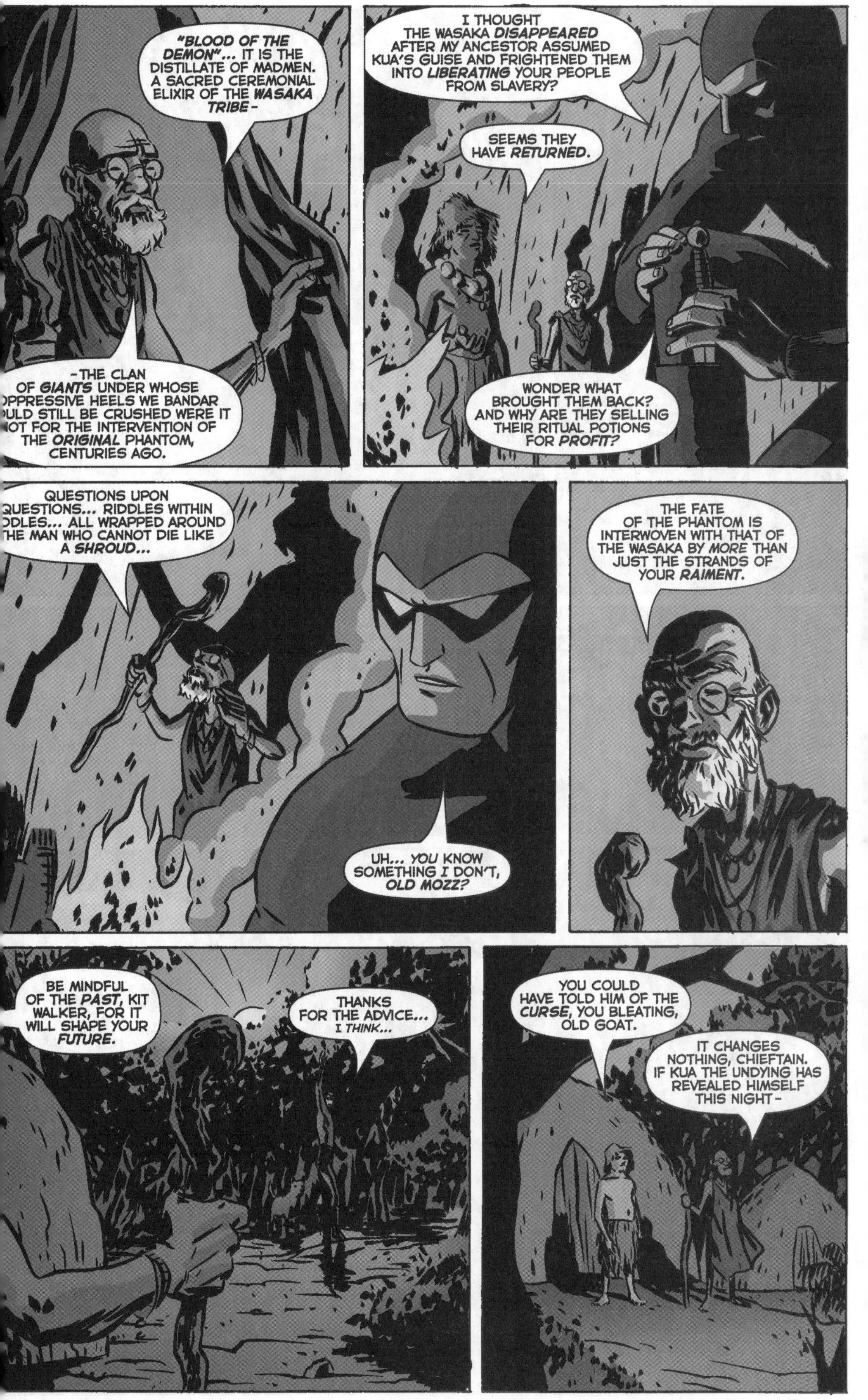
"BLOOD OF THE DEMON"... IT IS THE DISTILLATE OF MADMEN. A SACRED CEREMONIAL ELIXIR OF THE WASAKA TRIBE-
-THE CLAN OF GIANTS UNDER WHOSE PPRESSIVE HEELS WE BANDAR ULD STILL BE CRUSHED WERE IT OT FOR THE INTERVENTION OF THE ORIGINAL PHANTOM, CENTURIES AGO.
I THOUGHT THE WASAKA DISAPPEARED AFTER MY ANCESTOR ASSUMED KUA'S GUISE AND FRIGHTENED THEM INTO LIBERATING YOUR PEOPLE FROM SLAVERY?
SEEMS THEY HAVE RETURNED.
WONDER WHAT BROUGHT THEM BACK? AND WHY ARE THEY SELLING THEIR RITUAL POTIONS FOR PROFIT?
QUESTIONS UPON UESTIONS... RIDDLES WITHIN DDLES... ALL WRAPPED AROUND THE MAN WHO CANNOT DIE LIKE A SHROUD...
UH... YOU KNOW SOMETHING I DON'T, OLD MOZZ?
THE FATE OF THE PHANTOM IS INTERWOVEN WITH THAT OF THE WASAKA BY MORE THAN JUST THE STRANDS OF YOUR RAIMENT.
BE MINDFUL OF THE PAST, KIT WALKER, FOR IT WILL SHAPE YOUR FUTURE.
THANKS FOR THE ADVICE... I THINK...
YOU COULD HAVE TOLD HIM OF THE CURSE, YOU BLEATING, OLD GOAT.
IT CHANGES NOTHING, CHIEFTAIN. IF KUA THE UNDYING HAS REVEALED HIMSELF THIS NIGHT-

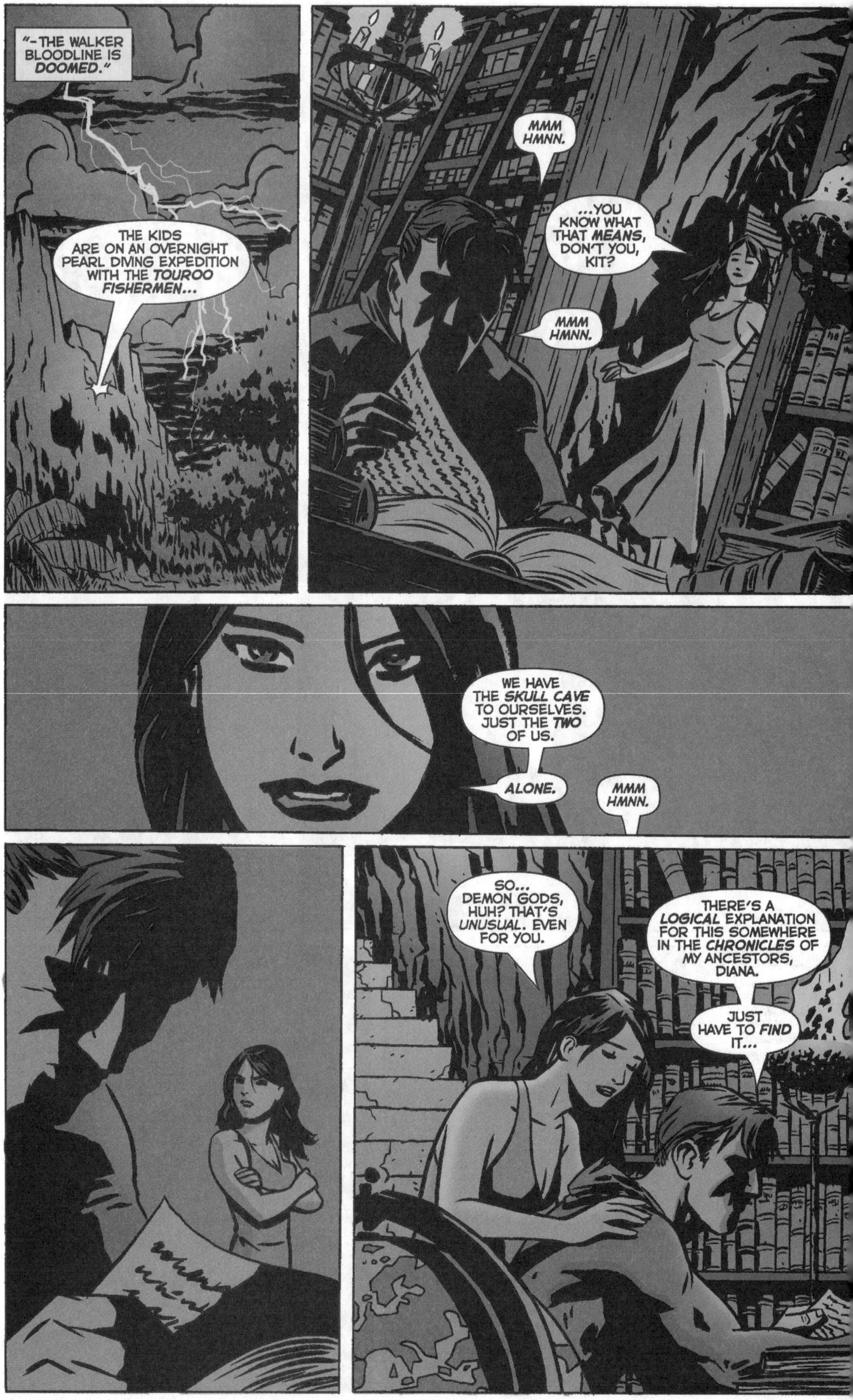
"-THE WALKER BLOODLINE IS DOOMED."
THE KIDS ARE ON AN OVERNIGHT PEARL DIVING EXPEDITION WITH THE TOUROO FISHERMEN...
MMM HMNN.
...YOU KNOW WHAT THAT MEANS, DON'T YOU, KIT?
MMM HMNN.
WE HAVE THE SKULL CAVE TO OURSELVES. JUST THE TWO OF US.
ALONE.
MMM HMNN.
SO... DEMON GODS, HUH? THAT'S UNUSUAL. EVEN FOR YOU.
THERE'S A LOGICAL EXPLANATION FOR THIS SOMEWHERE IN THE CHRONICLES OF MY ANCESTORS, DIANA.
JUST HAVE TO FIND IT...

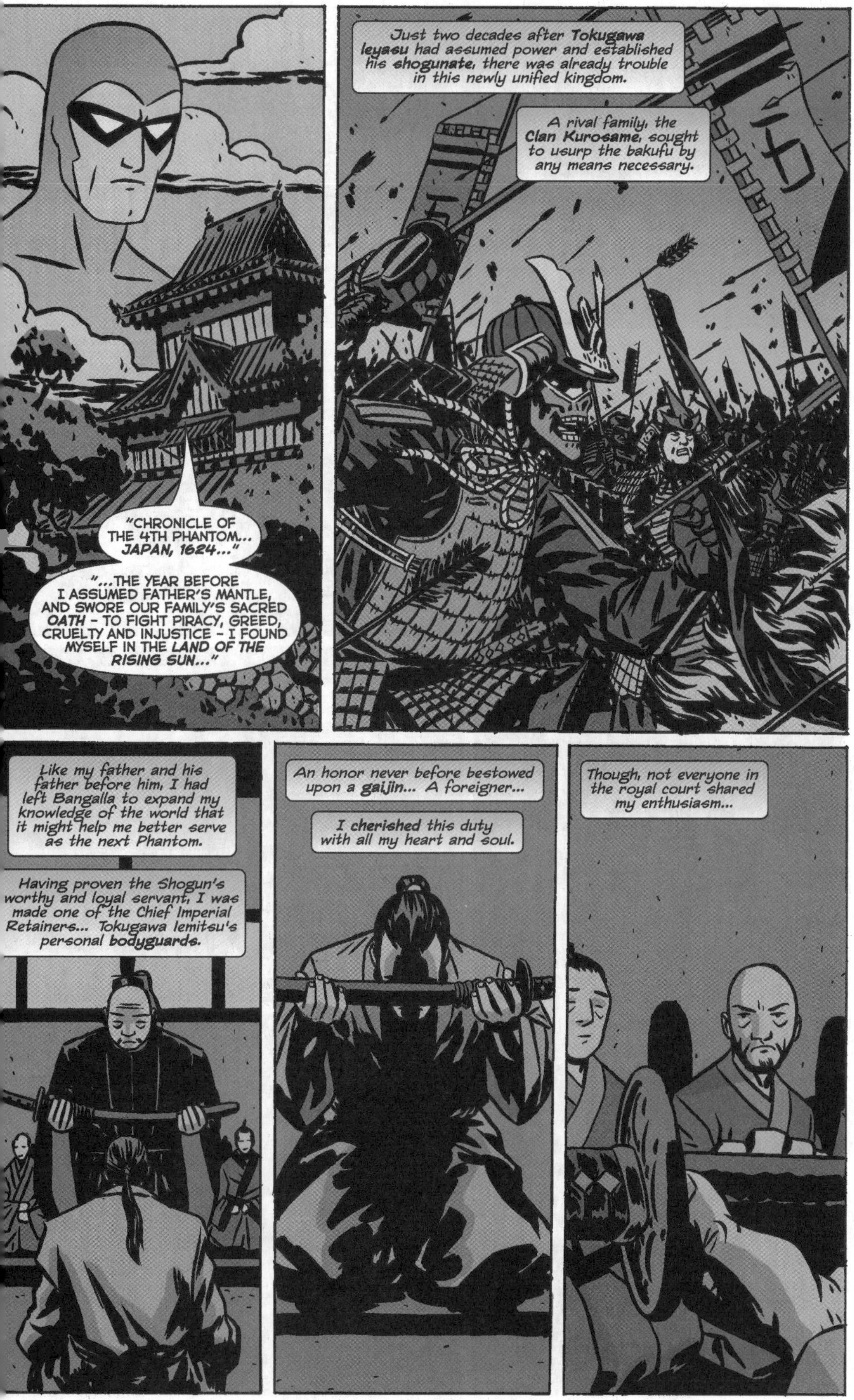
"CHRONICLE OF THE 4TH PHANTOM... JAPAN, 1624..."
"...THE YEAR BEFORE I ASSUMED FATHER'S MANTLE, AND SWORE OUR FAMILY'S SACRED OATH - TO FIGHT PIRACY, GREED, CRUELTY AND INJUSTICE - I FOUND MYSELF IN THE LAND OF THE RISING SUN..."
Just two decades after Tokugawa Ieyasu had assumed power and established his shogunate, there was already trouble in this newly unified kingdom.
A rival family, the Clan Kurosame, sought to usurp the bakufu by any means necessary.
Like my father and his father before him, I had left Bangalla to expand my knowledge of the world that it might help me better serve as the next Phantom.
Having proven the Shogun's worthy and loyal servant, I was made one of the Chief Imperial Retainers... Tokugawa Iemitsu's personal bodyguards.
An honor never before bestowed upon a gaijin... A foreigner...
I cherished this duty with all my heart and soul.
Though, not everyone in the royal court shared my enthusiasm...

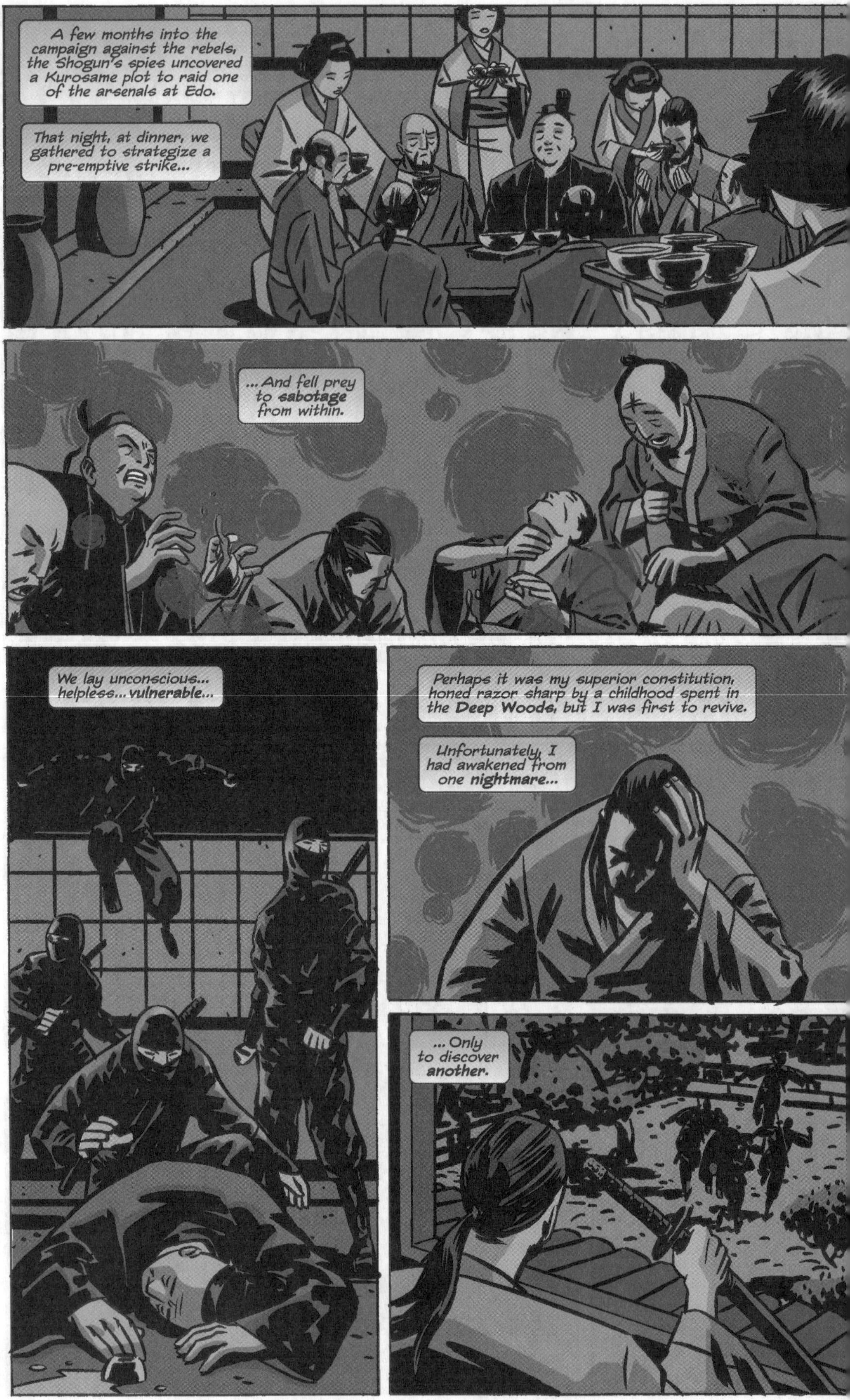
A few months into the campaign against the rebels, the Shogun's spies uncovered a Kurosame plot to raid one of the arsenals at Edo.
That night, at dinner, we gathered to strategize a pre-emptive strike...
...And fell prey to sabotage from within.
We lay unconscious... helpless... vulnerable...
Perhaps it was my superior constitution, honed razor sharp by a childhood spent in the Deep Woods, but I was first to revive.
Unfortunately, I had awakened from one nightmare...
...Only to discover another.

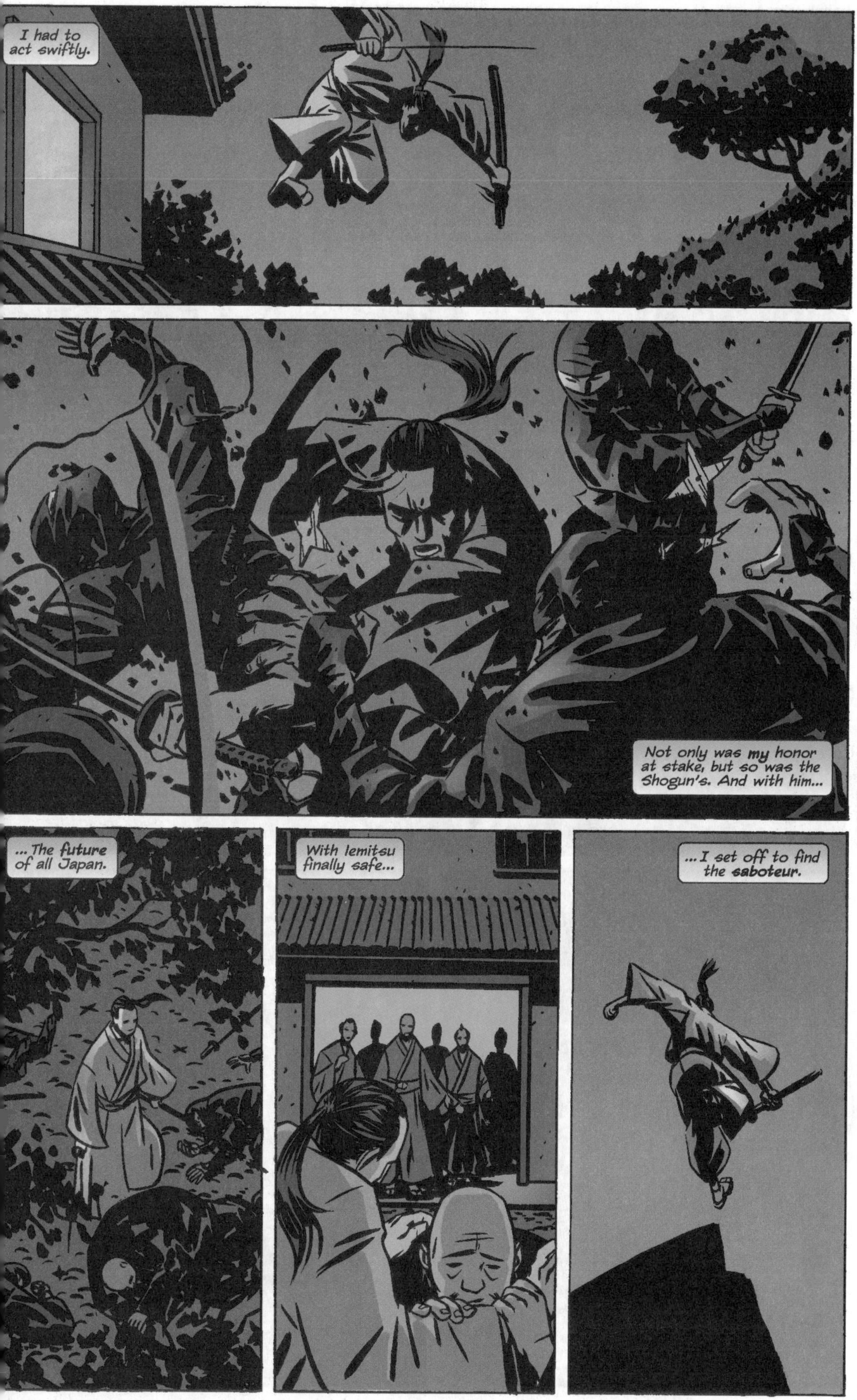
I had to act swiftly.
Not only was my honor at stake, but so was the Shogun's. And with him...
...The future of all Japan.
With Iemitsu finally safe...
...I set off to find the saboteur.

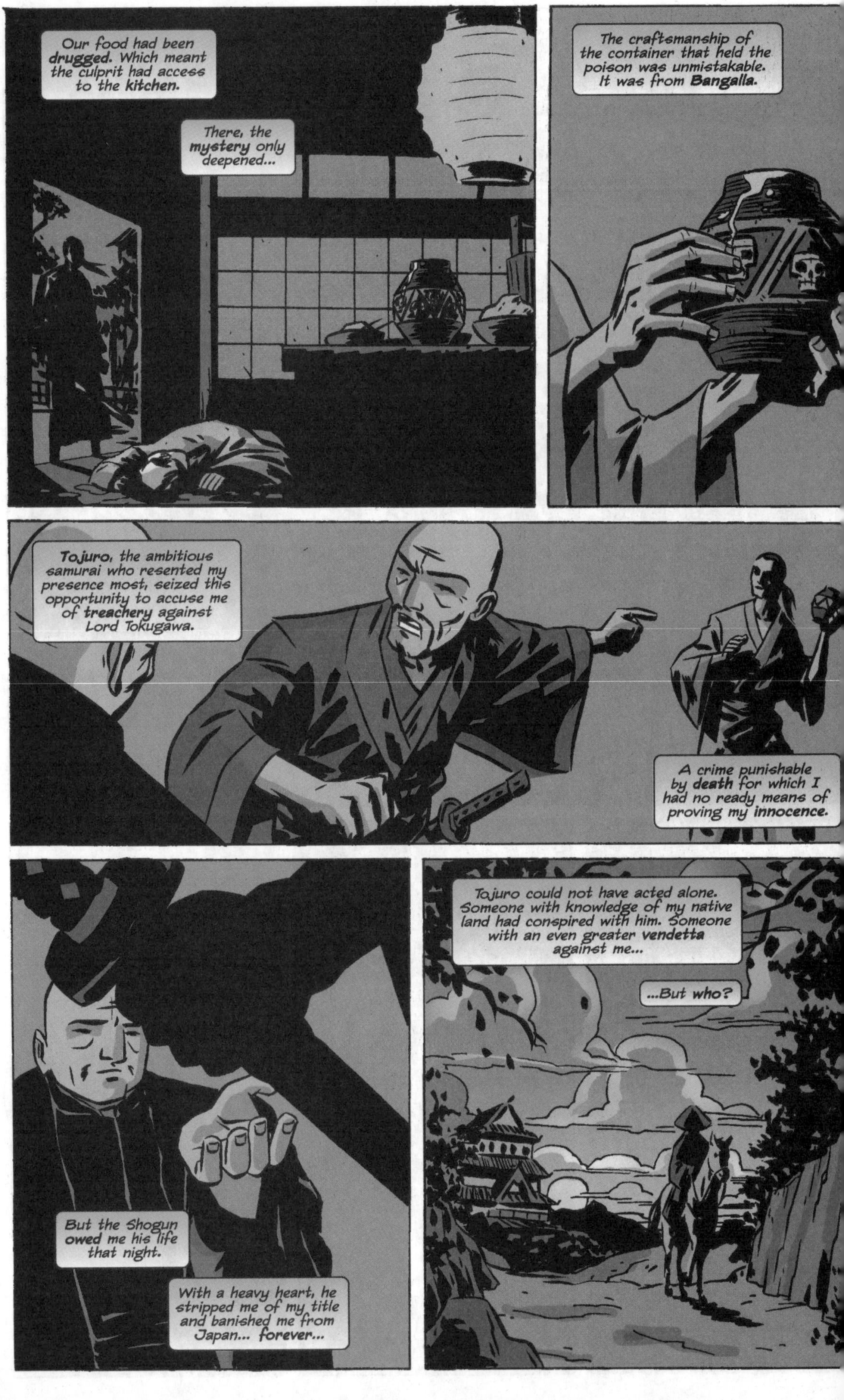
Our food had been drugged. Which meant the culprit had access to the kitchen.
There, the mystery only deepened...
The craftsmanship of the container that held the poison was unmistakable. It was from Bangalla.
Tojuro, the ambitious samurai who resented my presence most, seized this opportunity to accuse me of treachery against Lord Tokugawa.
A crime punishable by death for which I had no ready means of proving my innocence.
But the Shogun owed me his life that night.
With a heavy heart, he stripped me of my title and banished me from Japan... forever...
Tojuro could not have acted alone. Someone with knowledge of my native land had conspired with him. Someone with an even greater vendetta against me...
...But who?

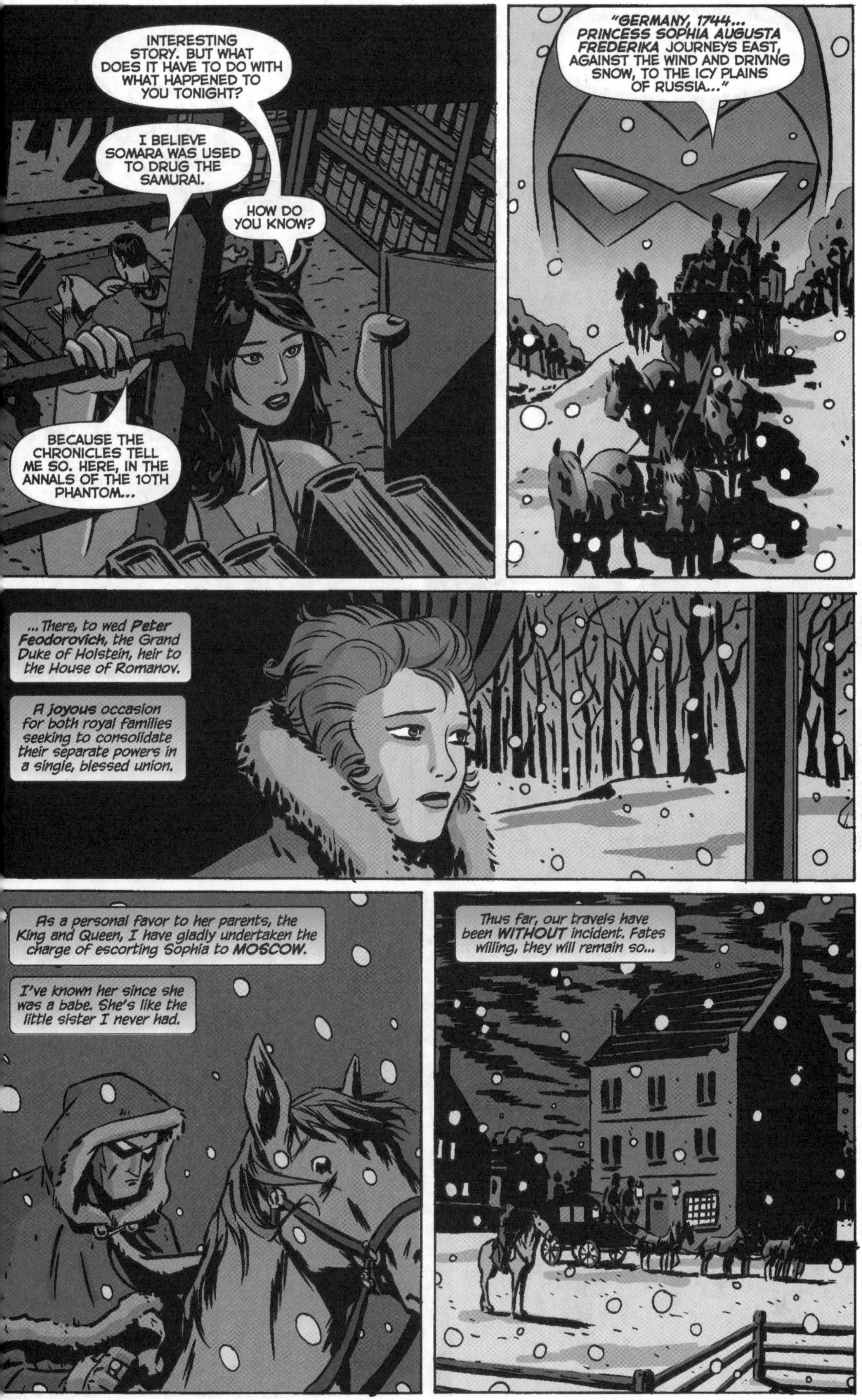

INTERESTING STORY. BUT WHAT DOES IT HAVE TO DO WITH WHAT HAPPENED TO YOU TONIGHT?
I BELIEVE SOMARA WAS USED TO DRUG THE SAMURAI.
HOW DO YOU KNOW?
BECAUSE THE CHRONICLES TELL ME SO. HERE, IN THE ANNALS OF THE 10TH PHANTOM...
"GERMANY, 1744... PRINCESS SOPHIA AUGUSTA FREDERIKA JOURNEYS EAST, AGAINST THE WIND AND DRIVING SNOW, TO THE ICY PLAINS OF RUSSIA..."
...There, to wed Peter Feodorovich, the Grand Duke of Holstein, heir to the House of Romanov.
A joyous occasion for both royal families seeking to consolidate their separate powers in a single, blessed union.
As a personal favor to her parents, the King and Queen, I have gladly undertaken the charge of escorting Sophia to MOSCOW.
I've known her since she was a babe. She's like the little sister I never had.
Thus far, our travels have been WITHOUT incident. Fates willing, they will remain so...

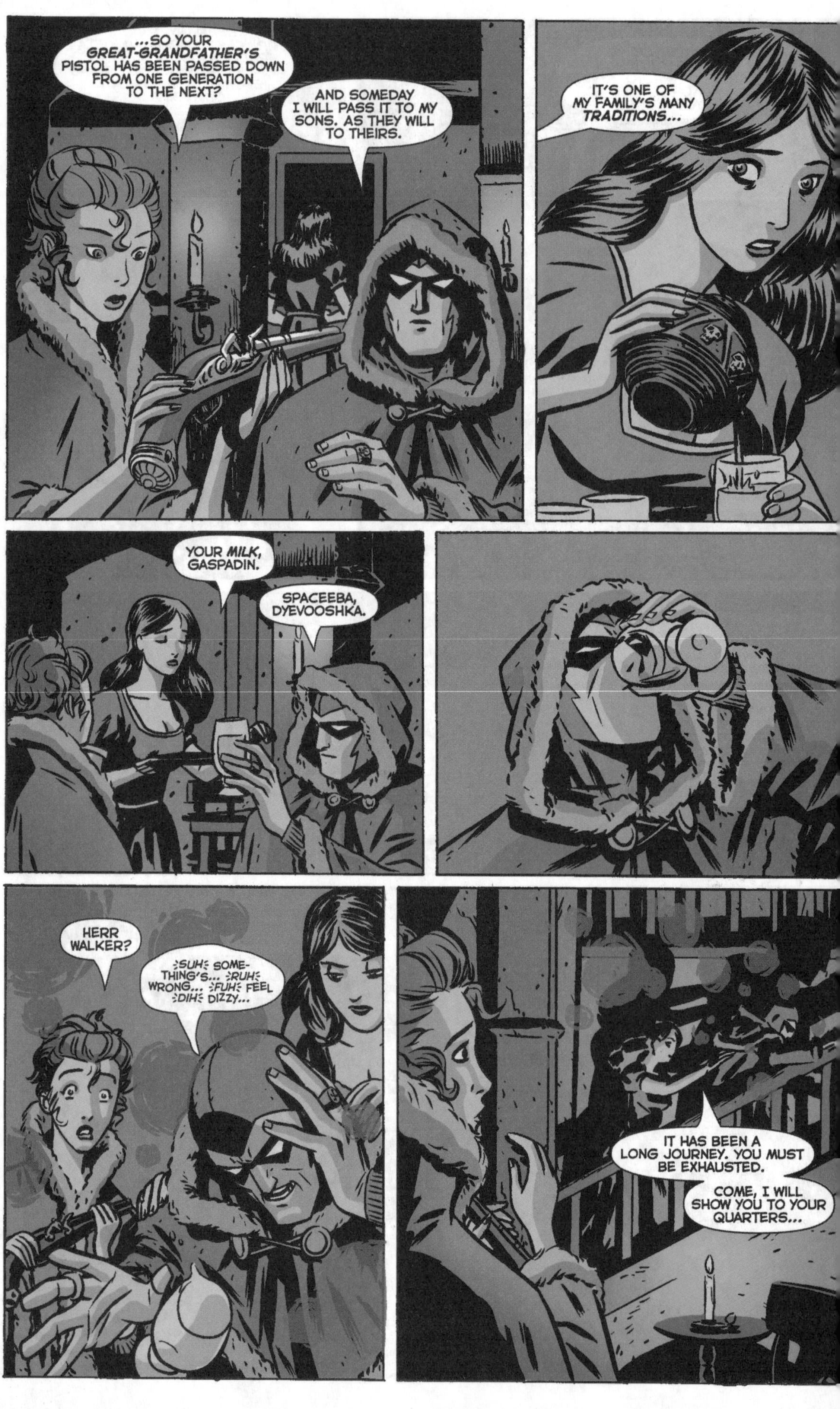
...SO YOUR GREAT-GRANDFATHER'S PISTOL HAS BEEN PASSED DOWN FROM ONE GENERATION TO THE NEXT?
AND SOMEDAY I WILL PASS IT TO MY SONS. AS THEY WILL TO THEIRS.
IT'S ONE OF MY FAMILY'S MANY TRADITIONS...
YOUR MILK, GASPADIN.
SPACEEBA, DYEVOOSHKA.
HERR WALKER?
SUH SOME-THING'S... RUH WRONG... FUH FEEL DIH DIZZY...
IT HAS BEEN A LONG JOURNEY. YOU MUST BE EXHAUSTED.
COME, I WILL SHOW YOU TO YOUR QUARTERS...

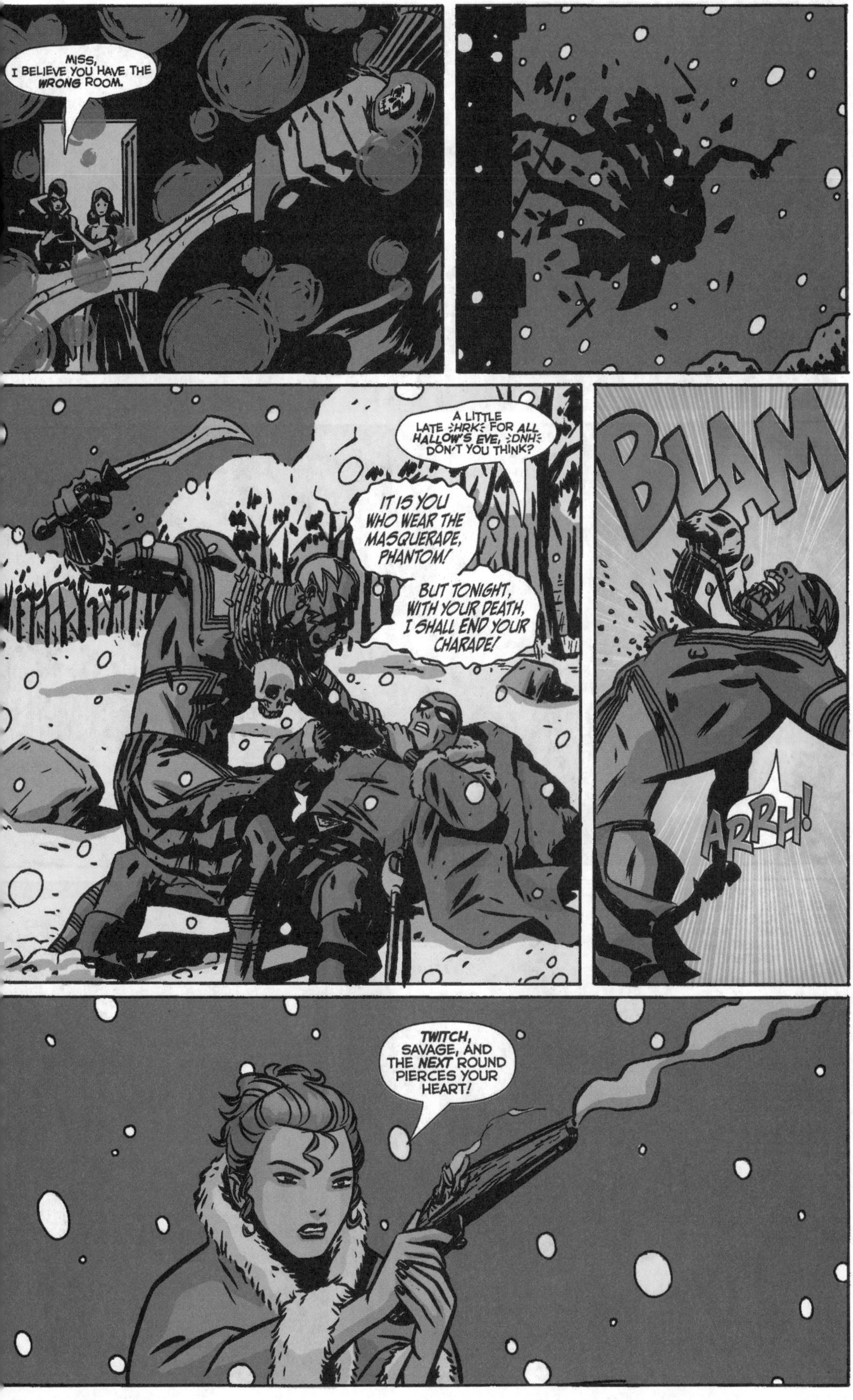
MISS, I BELIEVE YOU HAVE THE WRONG ROOM.
A LITTLE LATE HRK FOR ALL HALLOW'S EVE, DNH DON'T YOU THINK?
IT IS YOU WHO WEAR THE MASQUERADE, PHANTOM!
BUT TONIGHT, WITH YOUR DEATH, I SHALL END YOUR CHARADE!
BLAM
ARRH!
TWITCH, SAVAGE, AND THE NEXT ROUND PIERCES YOUR HEART!

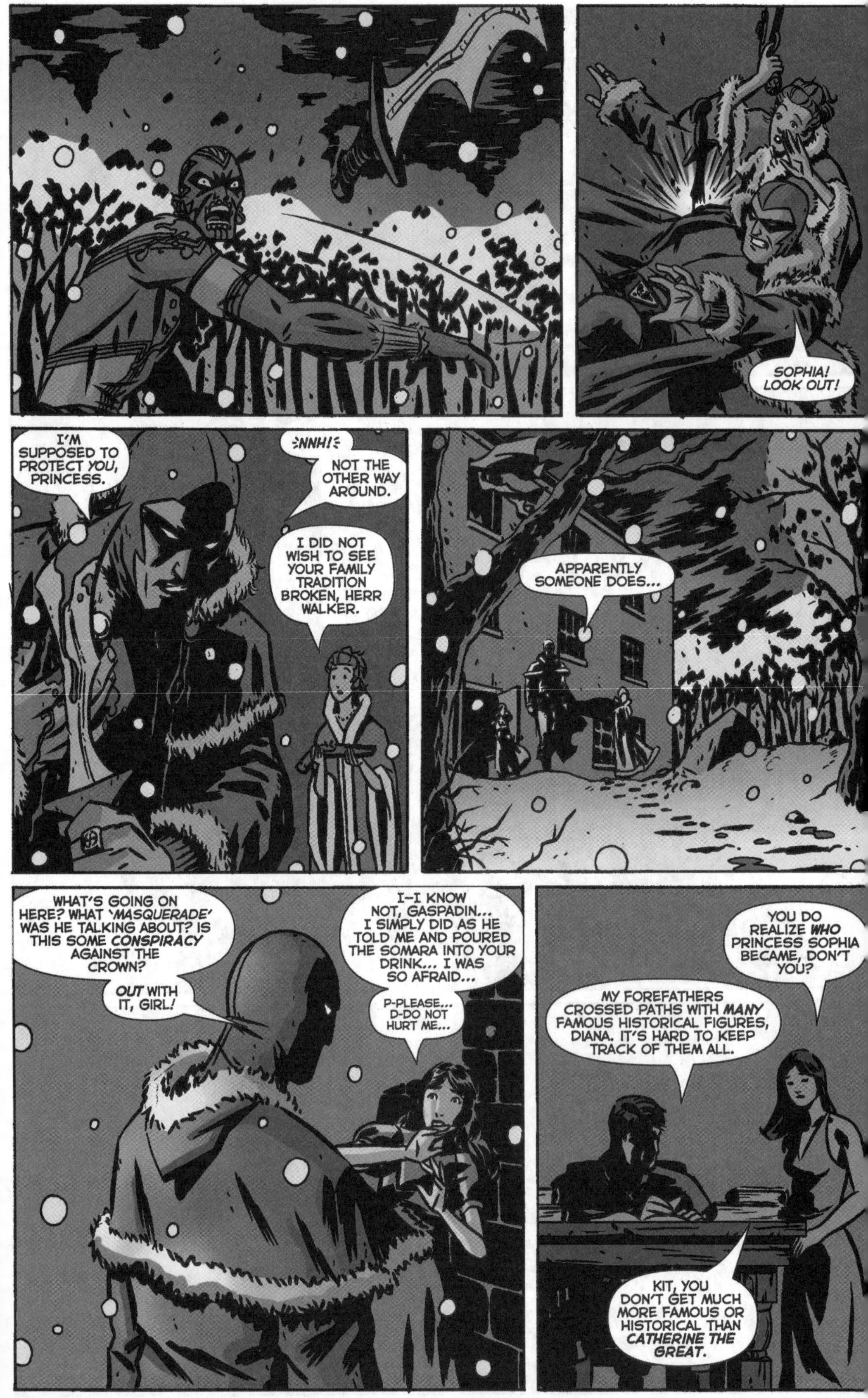
SOPHIA! LOOK OUT!
I'M SUPPOSED TO PROTECT YOU, PRINCESS.
NNH!
NOT THE OTHER WAY AROUND.
I DID NOT WISH TO SEE YOUR FAMILY TRADITION BROKEN, HERR WALKER.
APPARENTLY SOMEONE DOES...
WHAT'S GOING ON HERE? WHAT 'MASQUERADE' WAS HE TALKING ABOUT? IS THIS SOME CONSPIRACY AGAINST THE CROWN?
OUT WITH IT, GIRL!
I-I KNOW NOT, GASPADIN... I SIMPLY DID AS HE TOLD ME AND POURED THE SOMARA INTO YOUR DRINK... I WAS SO AFRAID...
P-PLEASE... D-DO NOT HURT ME...
YOU DO REALIZE WHO PRINCESS SOPHIA BECAME, DON'T YOU?
MY FOREFATHERS CROSSED PATHS WITH MANY FAMOUS HISTORICAL FIGURES, DIANA. IT'S HARD TO KEEP TRACK OF THEM ALL.
KIT, YOU DON'T GET MUCH MORE FAMOUS OR HISTORICAL THAN CATHERINE THE GREAT.

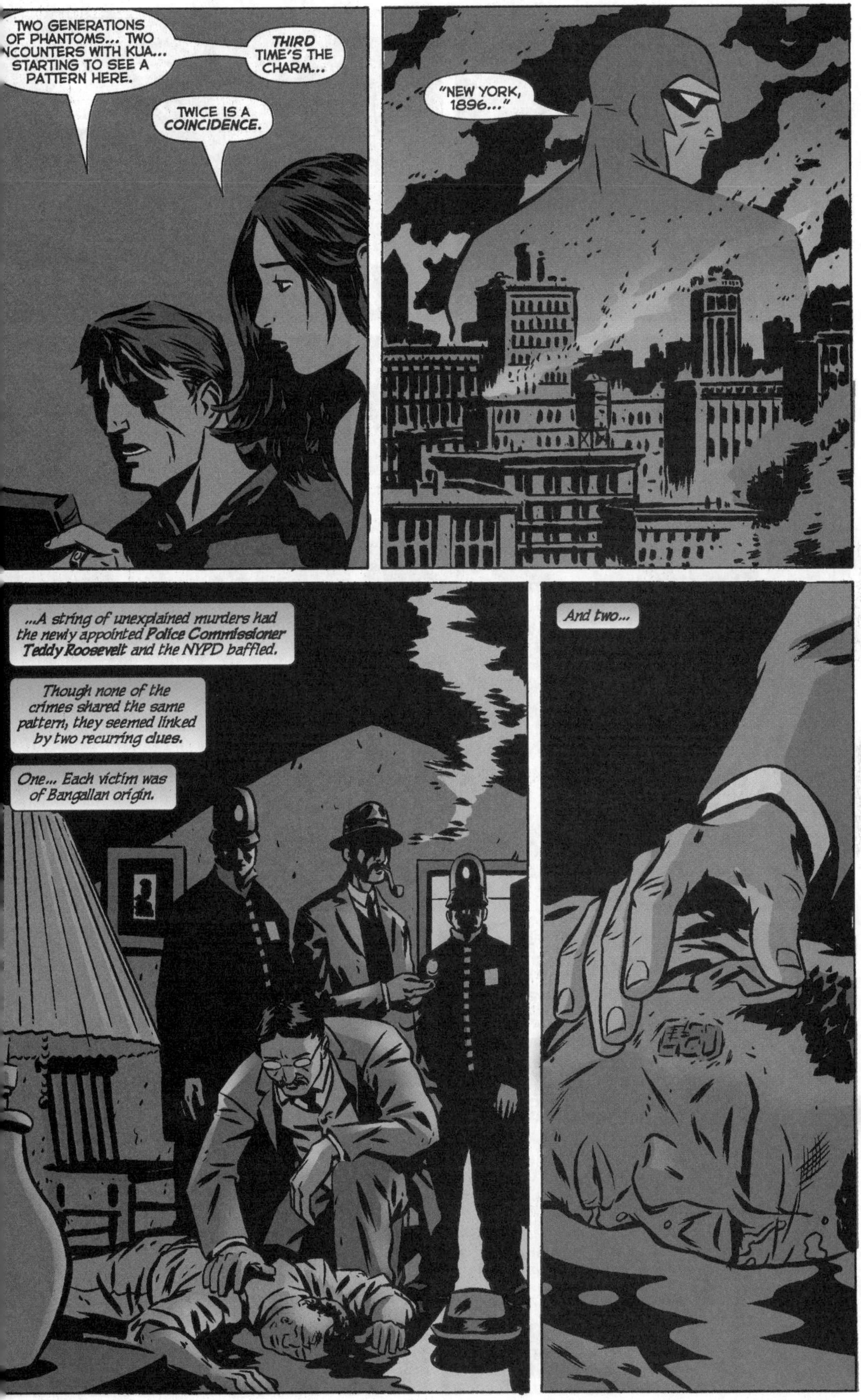
TWO GENERATIONS OF PHANTOMS... TWO ENCOUNTERS WITH KUA... STARTING TO SEE A PATTERN HERE.
TWICE IS A *COINCIDENCE.*
THIRD TIME'S THE CHARM...
"NEW YORK, 1896..."
...A string of unexplained murders had the newly appointed ***Police Commissioner Teddy Roosevelt*** *and the NYPD baffled.*
Though none of the crimes shared the same pattern, they seemed linked by two recurring clues.
One... Each victim was of Bangallan origin.
And two...

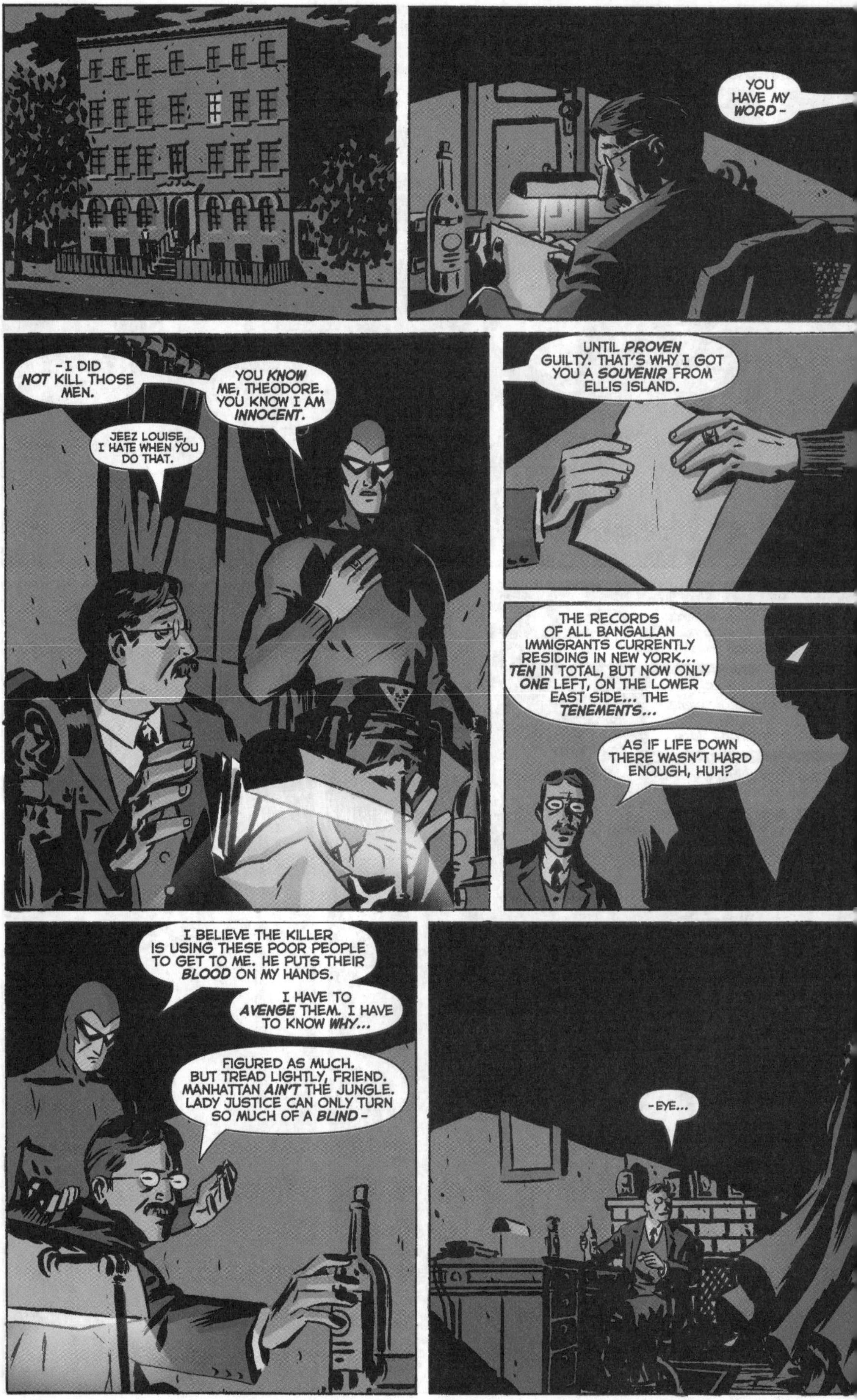

YOU HAVE MY WORD -
- I DID NOT KILL THOSE MEN.
YOU KNOW ME, THEODORE. YOU KNOW I AM INNOCENT.
JEEZ LOUISE, I HATE WHEN YOU DO THAT.
UNTIL PROVEN GUILTY. THAT'S WHY I GOT YOU A SOUVENIR FROM ELLIS ISLAND.
THE RECORDS OF ALL BANGALLAN IMMIGRANTS CURRENTLY RESIDING IN NEW YORK... TEN IN TOTAL, BUT NOW ONLY ONE LEFT, ON THE LOWER EAST SIDE... THE TENEMENTS...
AS IF LIFE DOWN THERE WASN'T HARD ENOUGH, HUH?
I BELIEVE THE KILLER IS USING THESE POOR PEOPLE TO GET TO ME. HE PUTS THEIR BLOOD ON MY HANDS.
I HAVE TO AVENGE THEM. I HAVE TO KNOW WHY...
FIGURED AS MUCH. BUT TREAD LIGHTLY, FRIEND. MANHATTAN AIN'T THE JUNGLE. LADY JUSTICE CAN ONLY TURN SO MUCH OF A BLIND -
- EYE...

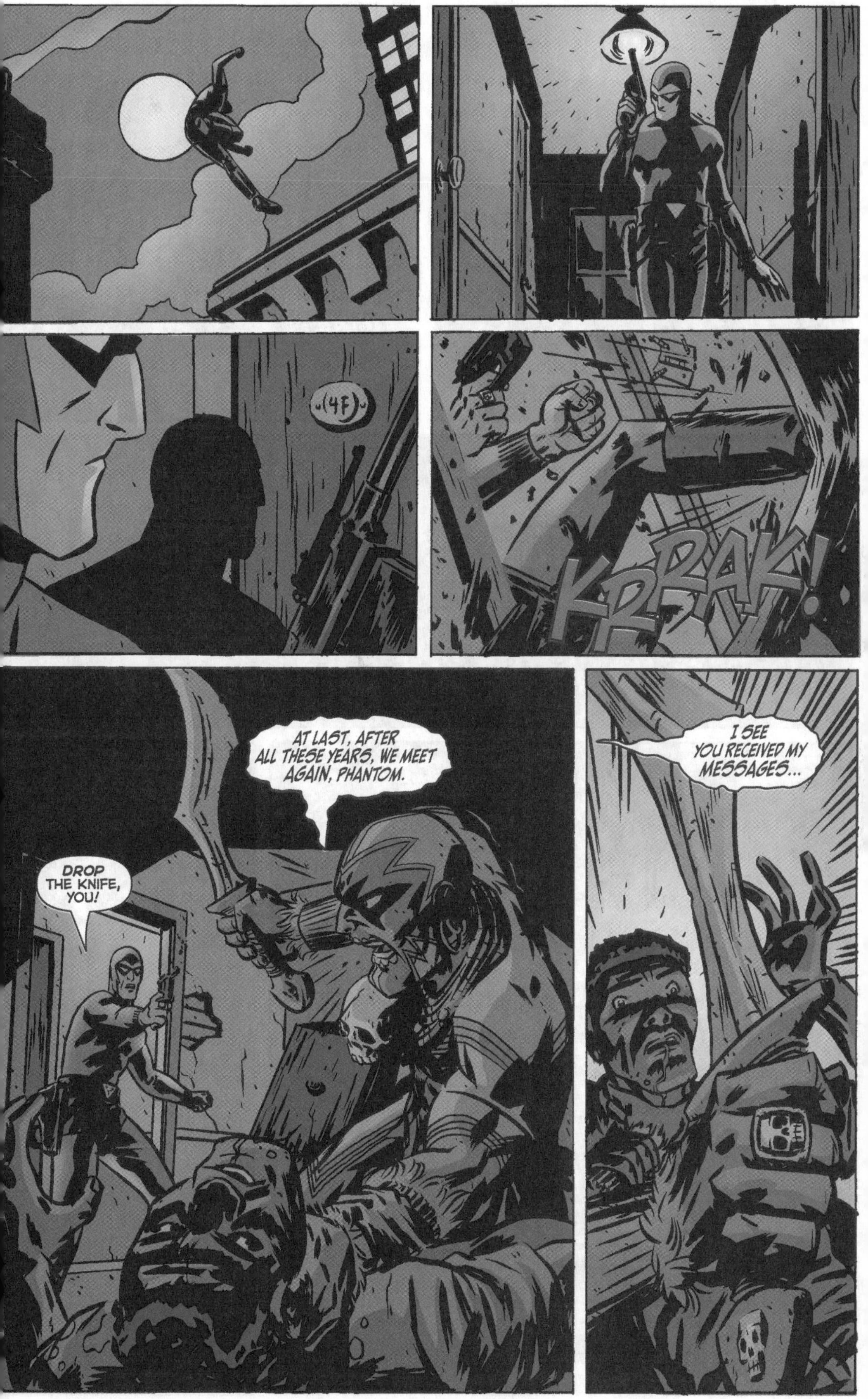
4F
KRRAK!
AT LAST, AFTER ALL THESE YEARS, WE MEET AGAIN, PHANTOM.
DROP THE KNIFE, YOU!
I SEE YOU RECEIVED MY MESSAGES...

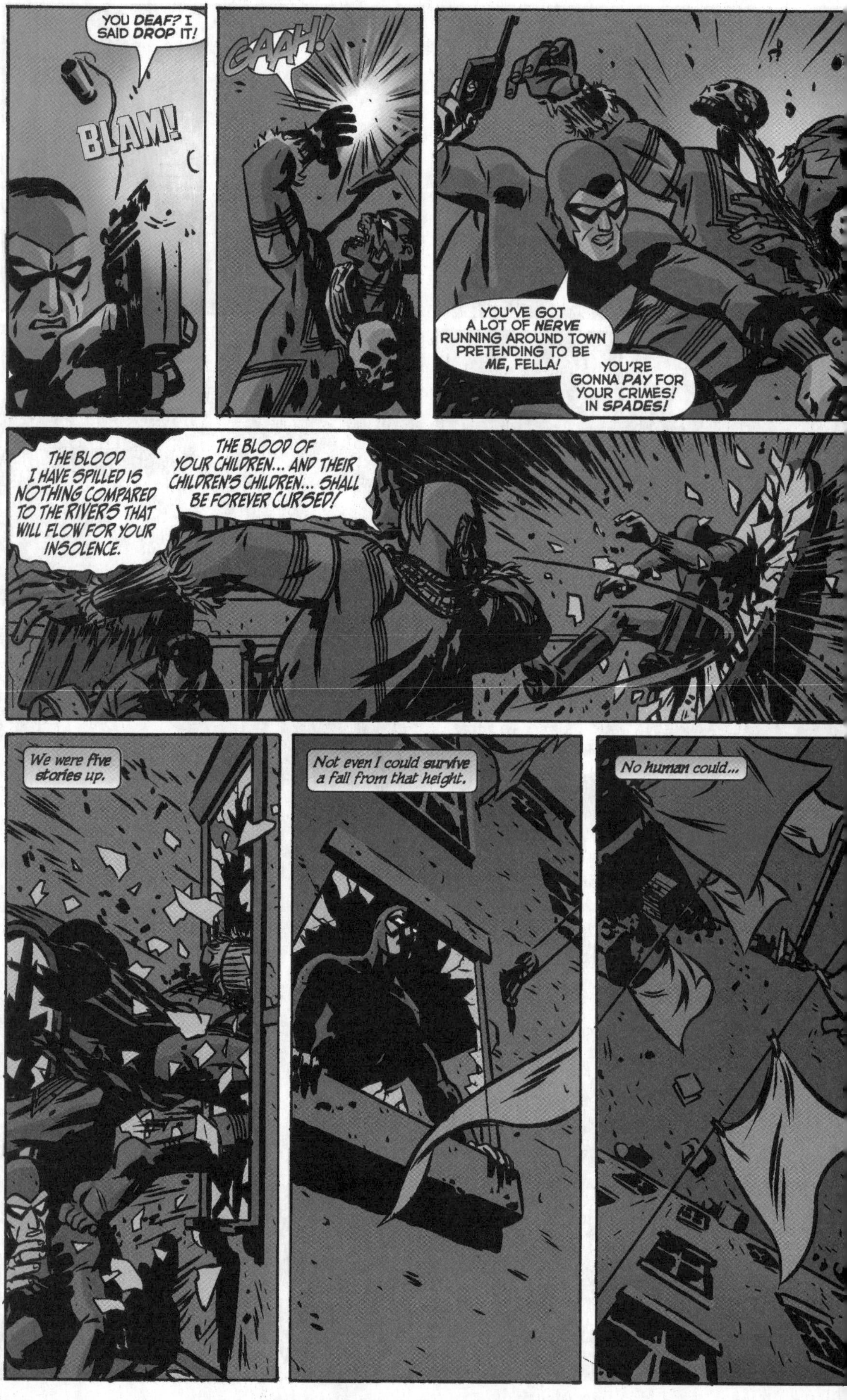
YOU DEAF? I SAID DROP IT!
BLAM!
GAAH!
YOU'VE GOT A LOT OF NERVE RUNNING AROUND TOWN PRETENDING TO BE ME, FELLA!
YOU'RE GONNA PAY FOR YOUR CRIMES! IN SPADES!
THE BLOOD I HAVE SPILLED IS NOTHING COMPARED TO THE RIVERS THAT WILL FLOW FOR YOUR INSOLENCE.
THE BLOOD OF YOUR CHILDREN... AND THEIR CHILDREN'S CHILDREN... SHALL BE FOREVER CURSED!
We were five stories up.
Not even I could survive a fall from that height.
No human could...

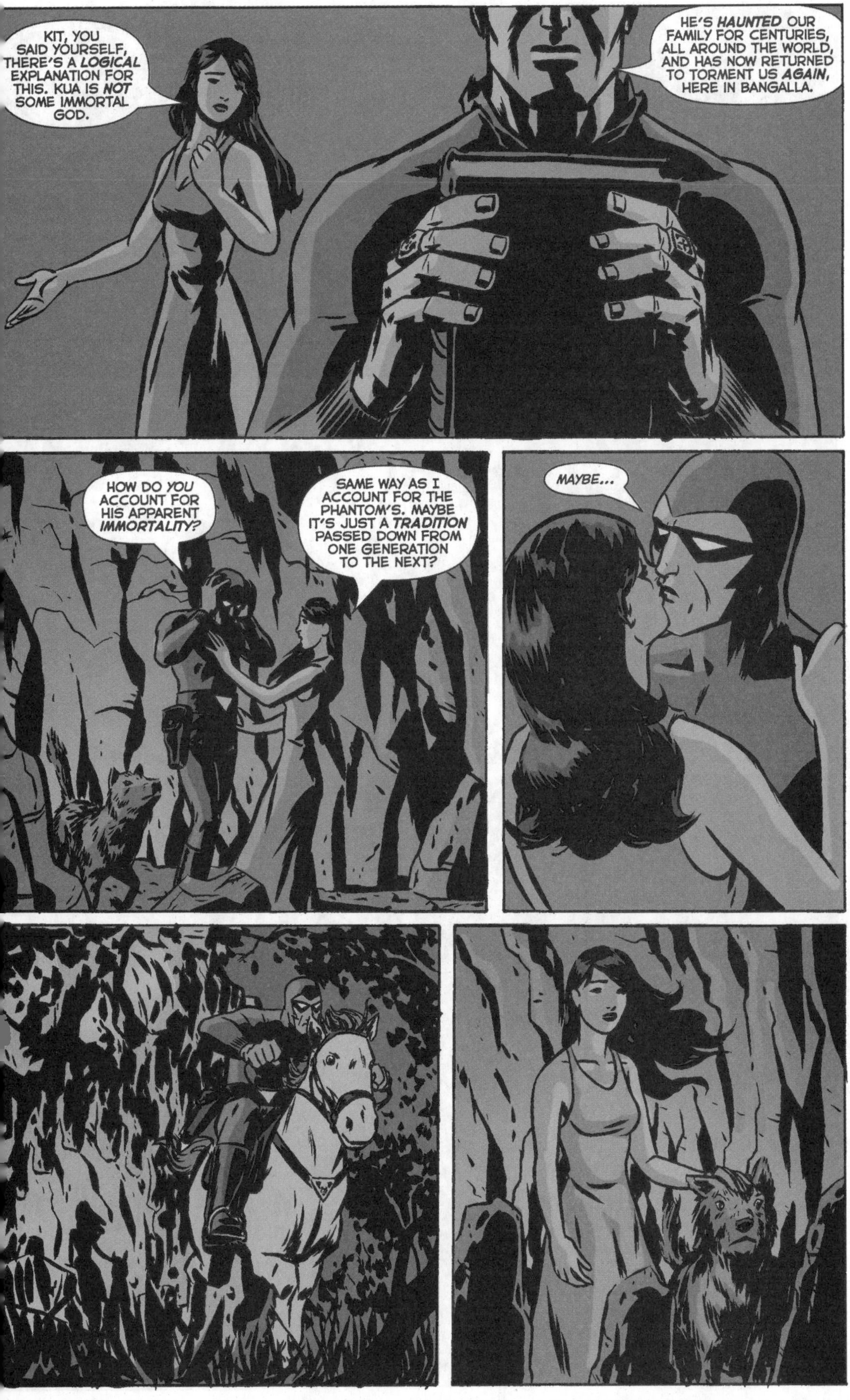

KIT, YOU SAID YOURSELF, THERE'S A *LOGICAL* EXPLANATION FOR THIS. KUA IS *NOT* SOME IMMORTAL GOD.
HE'S *HAUNTED* OUR FAMILY FOR CENTURIES, ALL AROUND THE WORLD, AND HAS NOW RETURNED TO TORMENT US *AGAIN*, HERE IN BANGALLA.
HOW DO *YOU* ACCOUNT FOR HIS APPARENT *IMMORTALITY?*
SAME WAY AS I ACCOUNT FOR THE PHANTOM'S. MAYBE IT'S JUST A *TRADITION* PASSED DOWN FROM ONE GENERATION TO THE NEXT?
MAYBE...

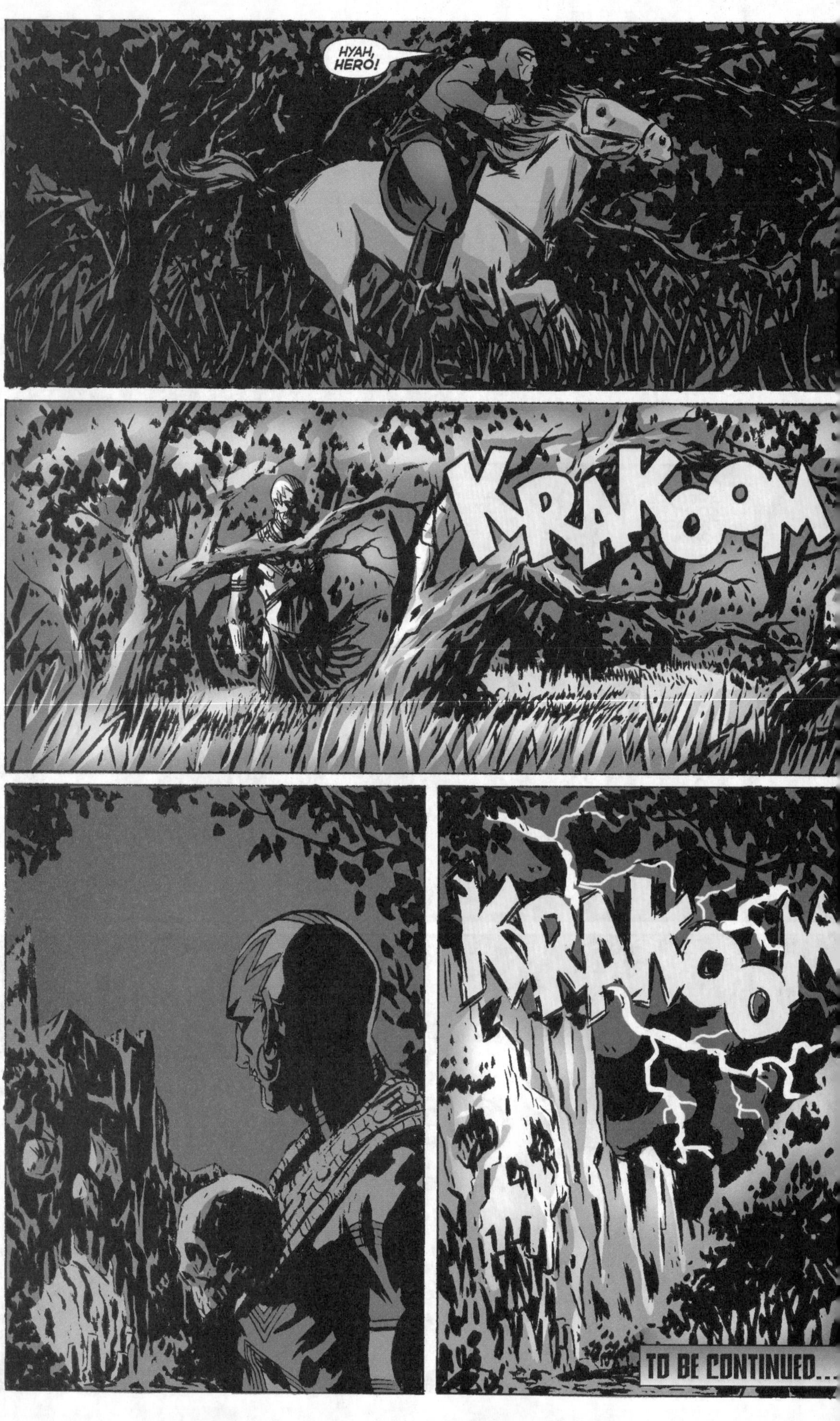
HYAH, HERO!
KRAKOOM
KRAKOOM
TO BE CONTINUED...

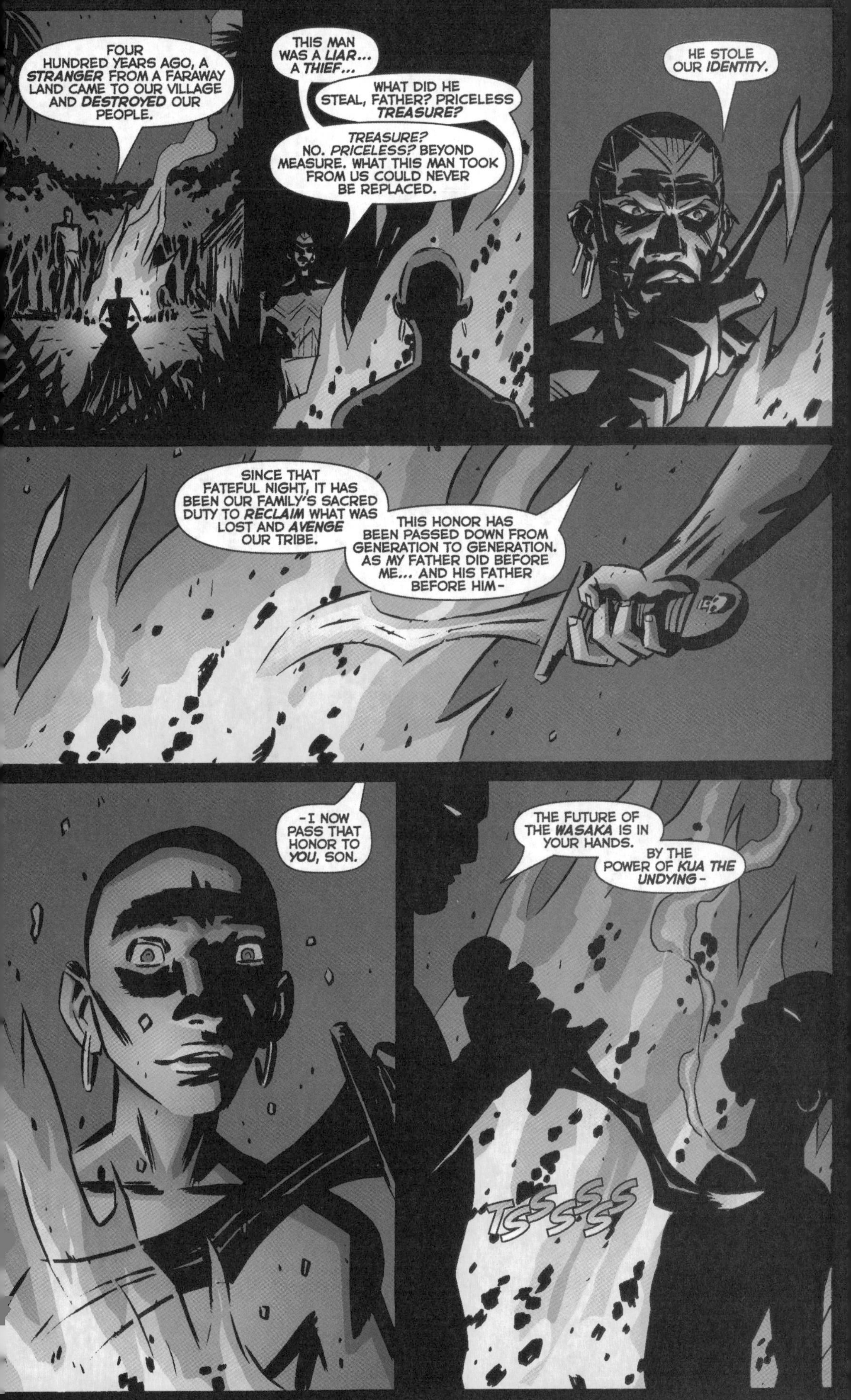
FOUR HUNDRED YEARS AGO, A STRANGER FROM A FARAWAY LAND CAME TO OUR VILLAGE AND DESTROYED OUR PEOPLE.
THIS MAN WAS A LIAR... A THIEF...
WHAT DID HE STEAL, FATHER? PRICELESS TREASURE?
TREASURE? NO. PRICELESS? BEYOND MEASURE. WHAT THIS MAN TOOK FROM US COULD NEVER BE REPLACED.
HE STOLE OUR IDENTITY.
SINCE THAT FATEFUL NIGHT, IT HAS BEEN OUR FAMILY'S SACRED DUTY TO RECLAIM WHAT WAS LOST AND AVENGE OUR TRIBE.
THIS HONOR HAS BEEN PASSED DOWN FROM GENERATION TO GENERATION. AS MY FATHER DID BEFORE ME... AND HIS FATHER BEFORE HIM-
-I NOW PASS THAT HONOR TO YOU, SON.
THE FUTURE OF THE WASAKA IS IN YOUR HANDS.
BY THE POWER OF KUA THE UNDYING-
TSSSSS

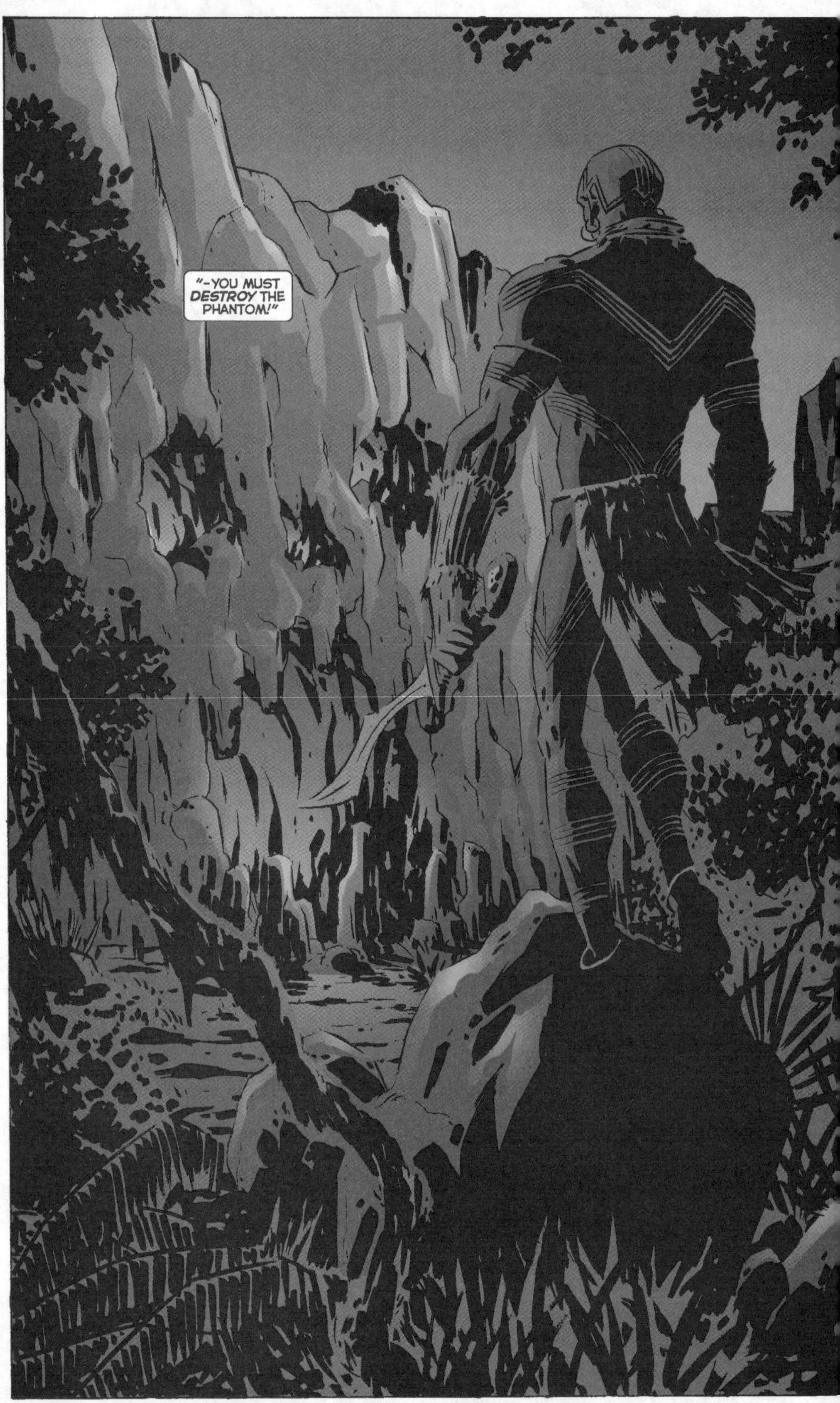
"-YOU MUST DESTROY THE PHANTOM!"

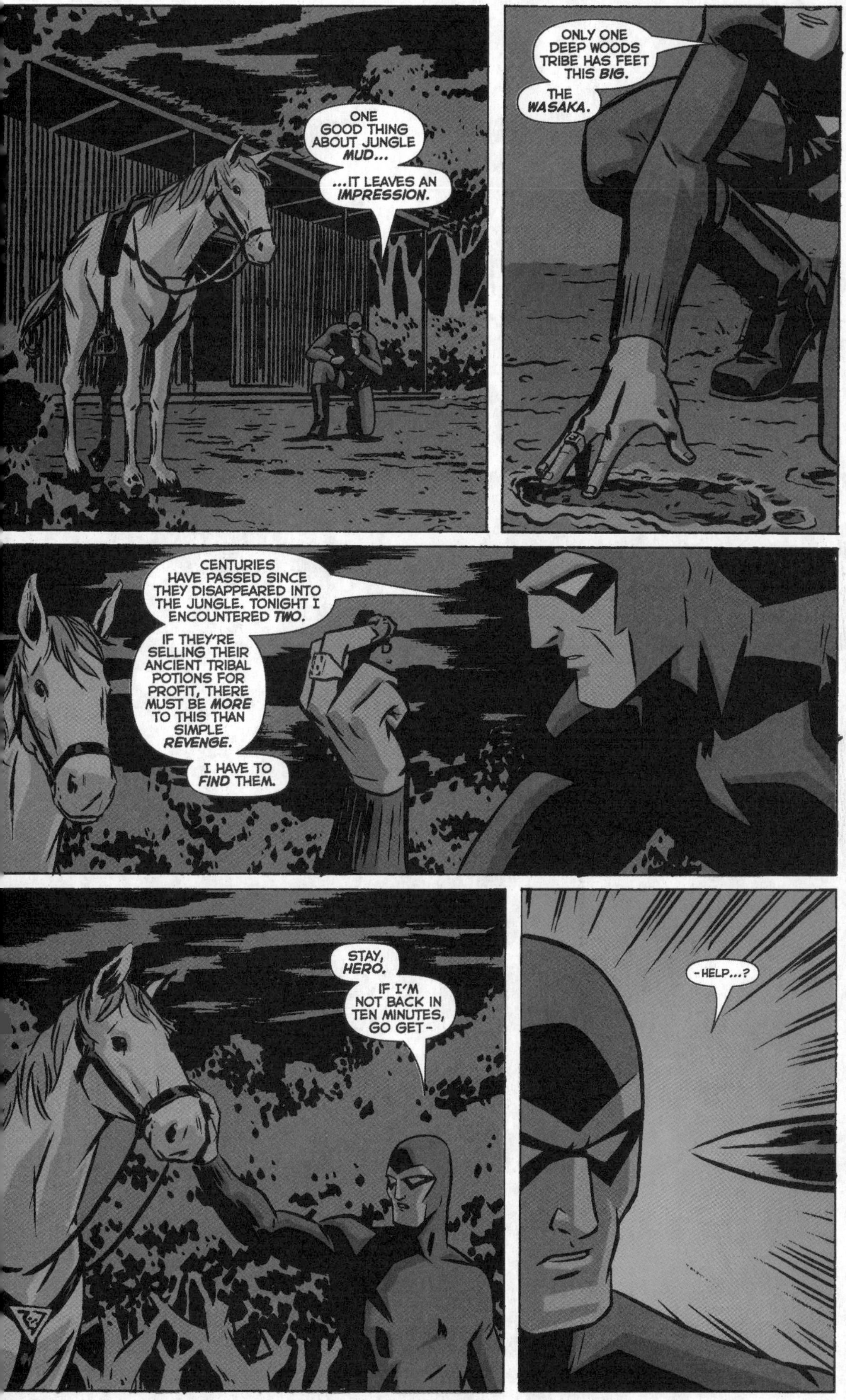
ONE GOOD THING ABOUT JUNGLE MUD...
...IT LEAVES AN IMPRESSION.
ONLY ONE DEEP WOODS TRIBE HAS FEET THIS BIG.
THE WASAKA.
CENTURIES HAVE PASSED SINCE THEY DISAPPEARED INTO THE JUNGLE. TONIGHT I ENCOUNTERED TWO.
IF THEY'RE SELLING THEIR ANCIENT TRIBAL POTIONS FOR PROFIT, THERE MUST BE MORE TO THIS THAN SIMPLE REVENGE.
I HAVE TO FIND THEM.
STAY, HERO.
IF I'M NOT BACK IN TEN MINUTES, GO GET-
-HELP...?

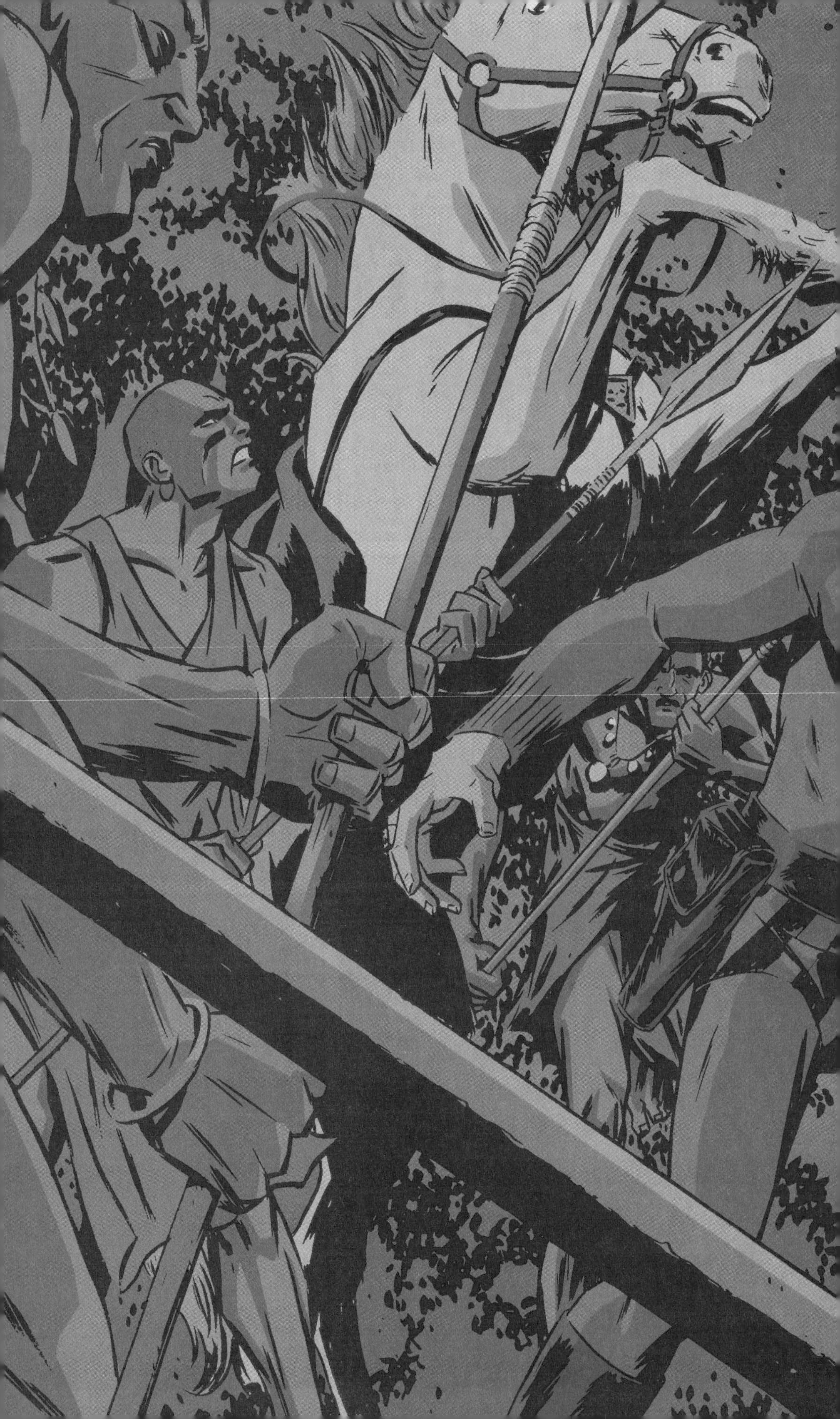

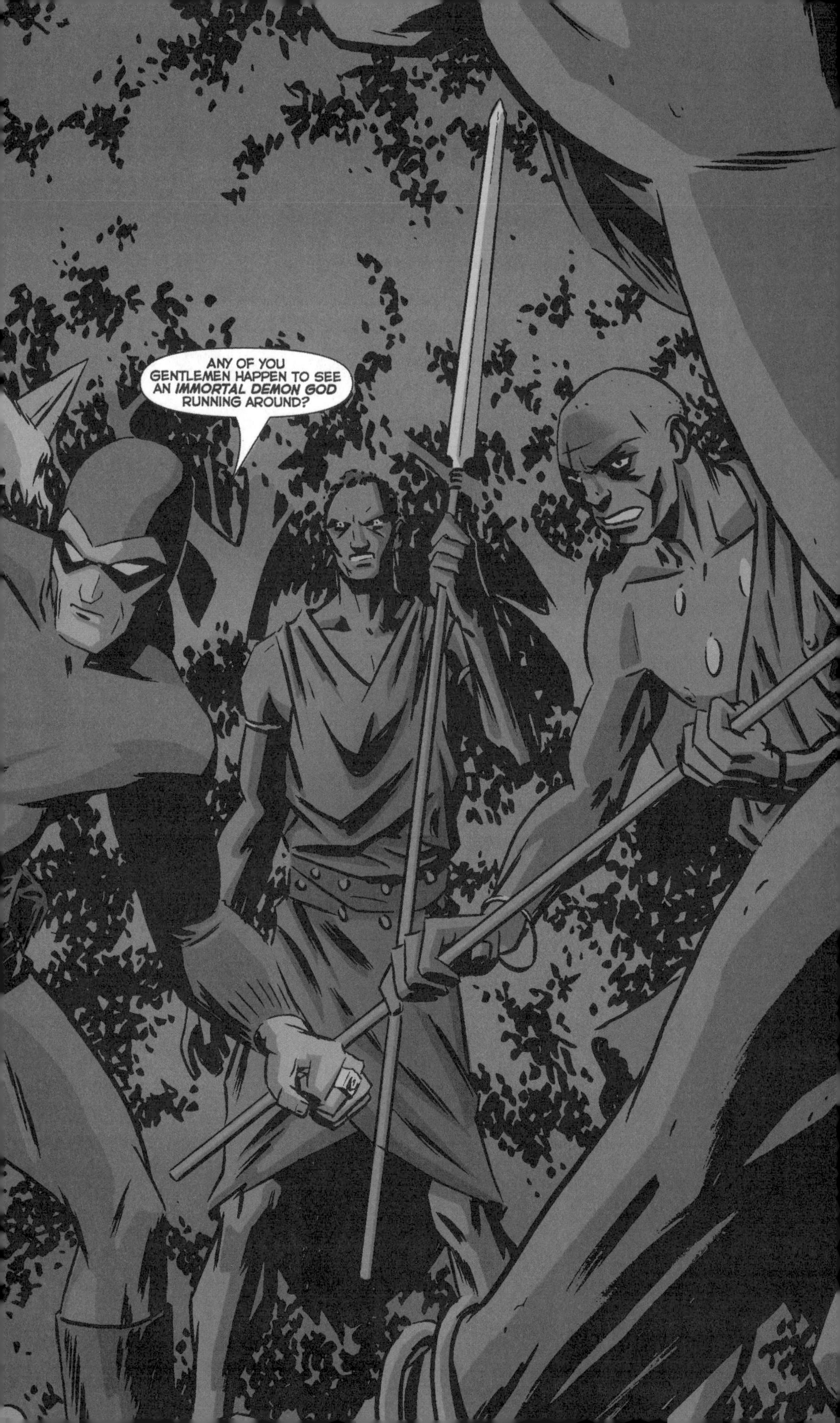
ANY OF YOU GENTLEMEN HAPPEN TO SEE AN *IMMORTAL DEMON GOD* RUNNING AROUND?

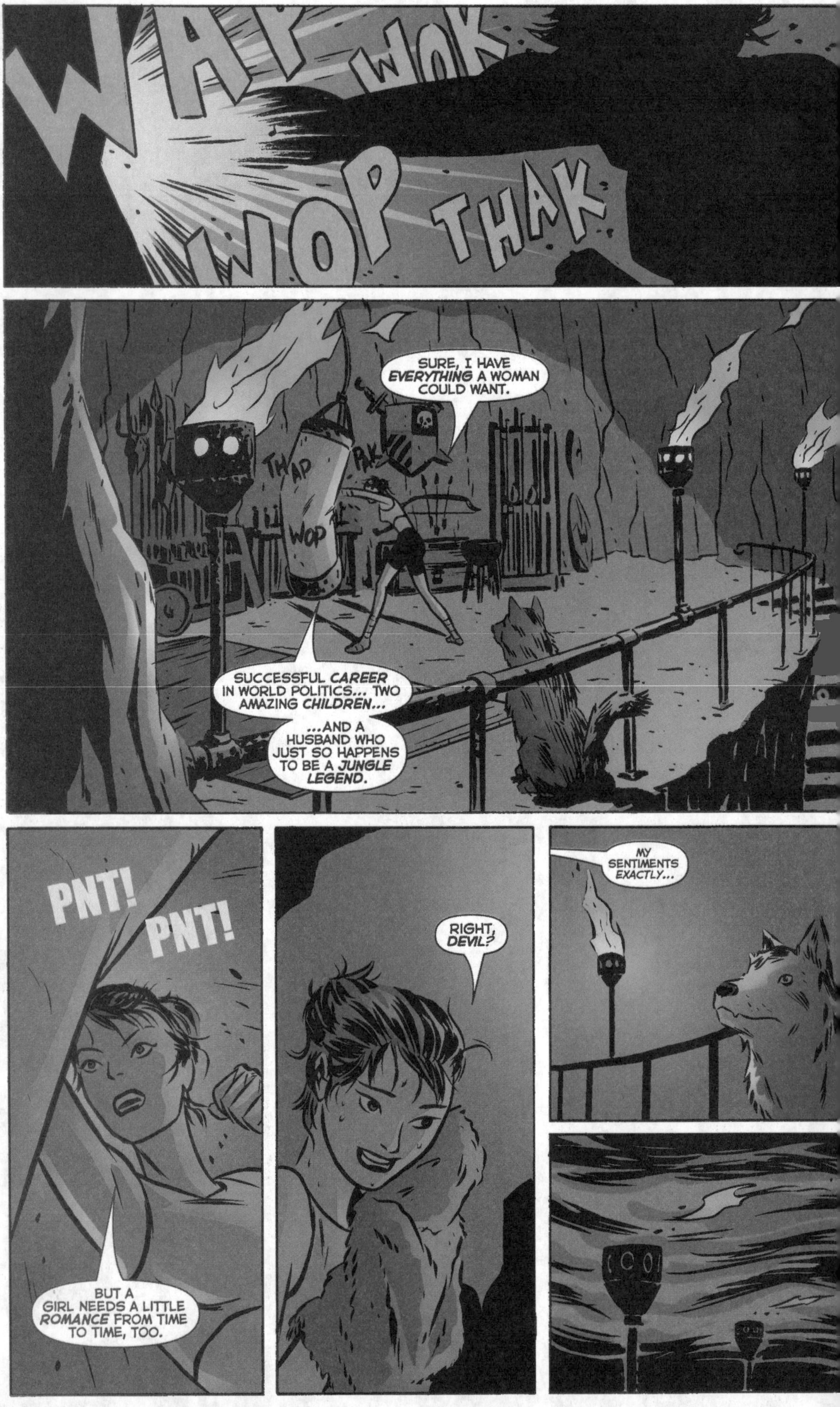
WAP
WOK
WOP
THAK
SURE, I HAVE EVERYTHING A WOMAN COULD WANT.
THAP
PAK
WOP
SUCCESSFUL CAREER IN WORLD POLITICS... TWO AMAZING CHILDREN...
...AND A HUSBAND WHO JUST SO HAPPENS TO BE A JUNGLE LEGEND.
PNT!
PNT!
BUT A GIRL NEEDS A LITTLE ROMANCE FROM TIME TO TIME, TOO.
RIGHT, DEVIL?
MY SENTIMENTS EXACTLY...

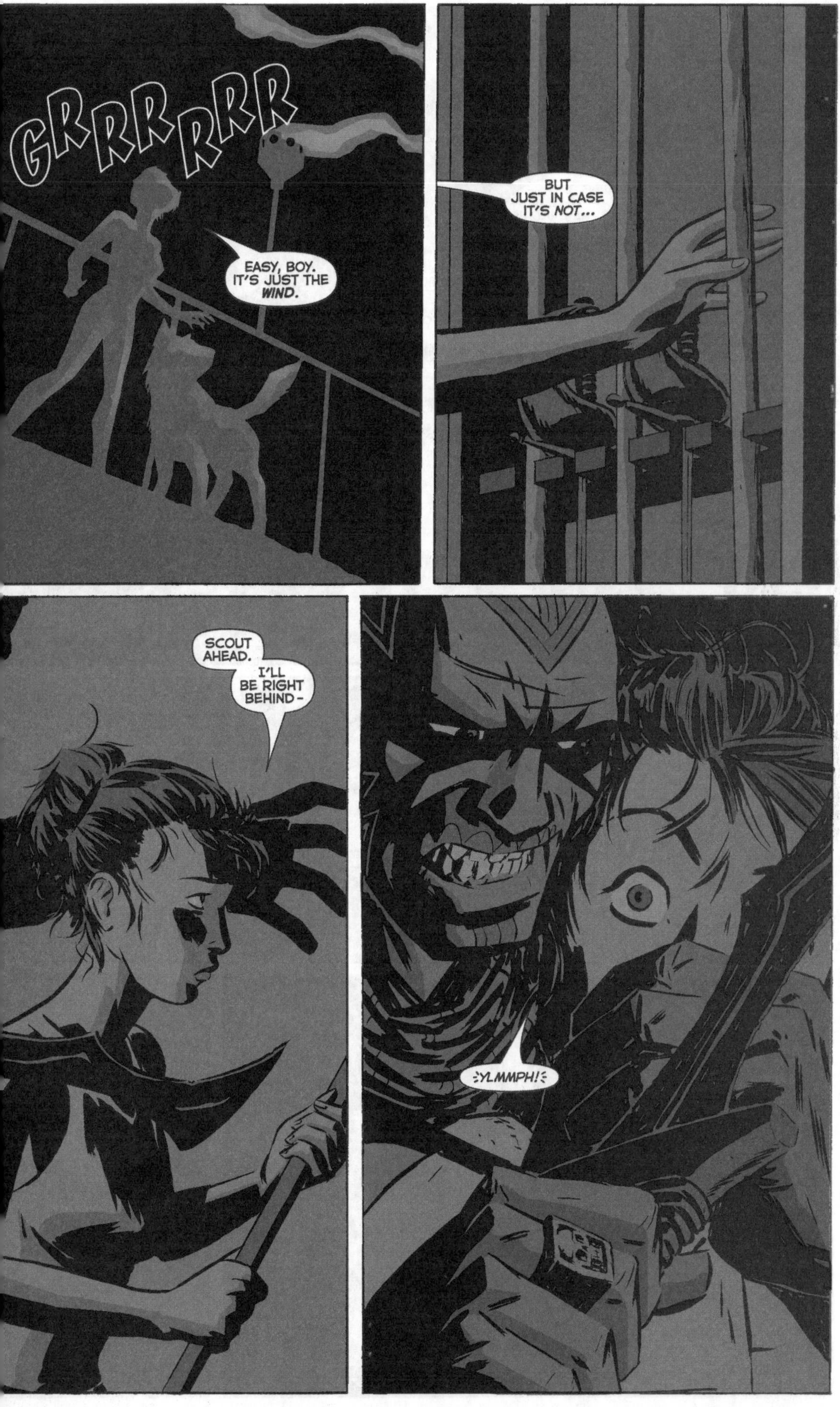
GRRRRRR
EASY, BOY. IT'S JUST THE *WIND*.
BUT JUST IN CASE IT'S *NOT*...
SCOUT AHEAD. I'LL BE RIGHT BEHIND–
YLMMPH!

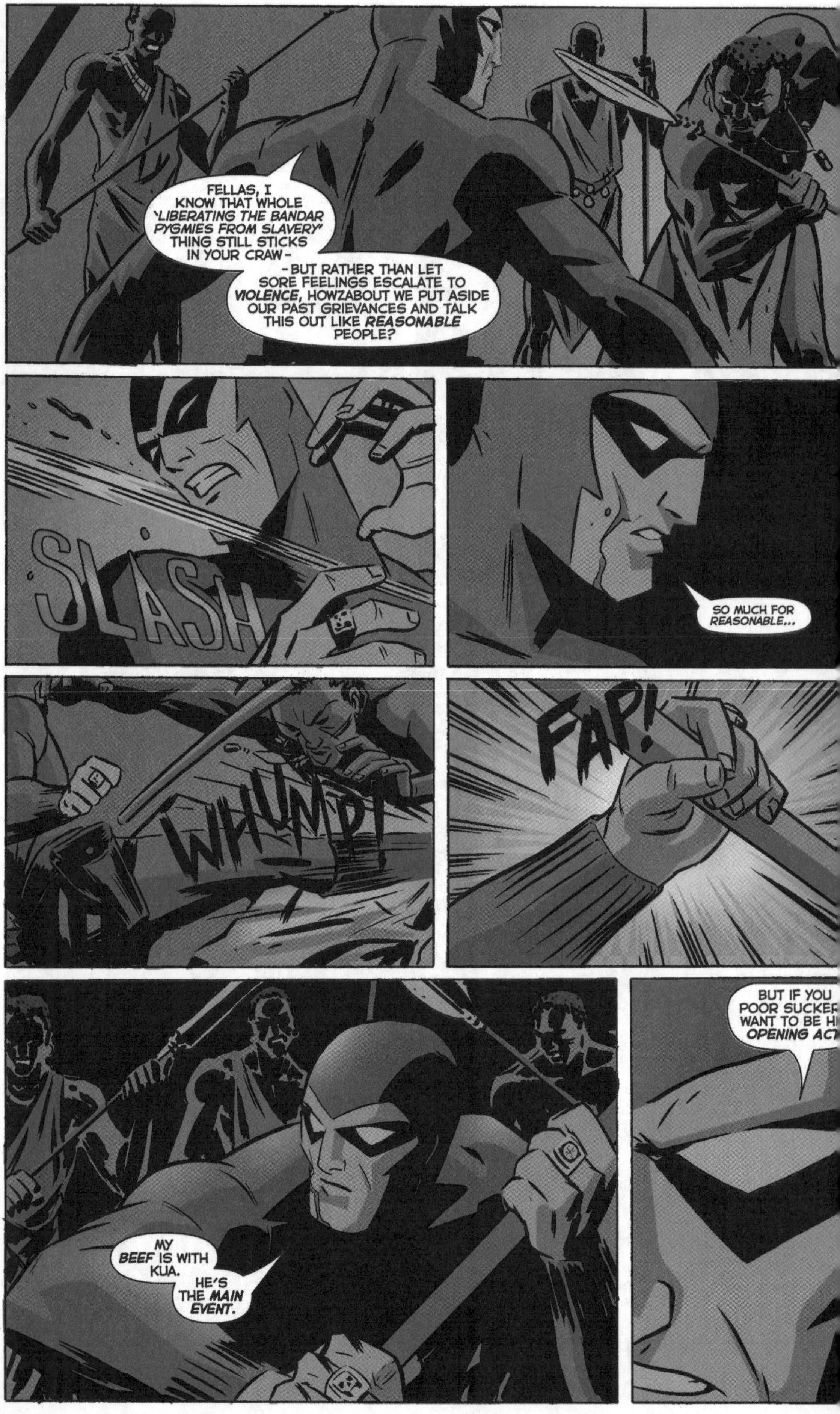
FELLAS, I KNOW THAT WHOLE *'LIBERATING THE BANDAR PYGMIES FROM SLAVERY'* THING STILL STICKS IN YOUR CRAW-
-BUT RATHER THAN LET SORE FEELINGS ESCALATE TO *VIOLENCE*, HOWZABOUT WE PUT ASIDE OUR PAST GRIEVANCES AND TALK THIS OUT LIKE *REASONABLE* PEOPLE?
SLASH
SO MUCH FOR *REASONABLE...*
WHUMP!
FAP!
MY *BEEF* IS WITH KUA.
HE'S THE *MAIN EVENT*.
BUT IF YOU POOR SUCKER WANT TO BE HI *OPENING ACT*

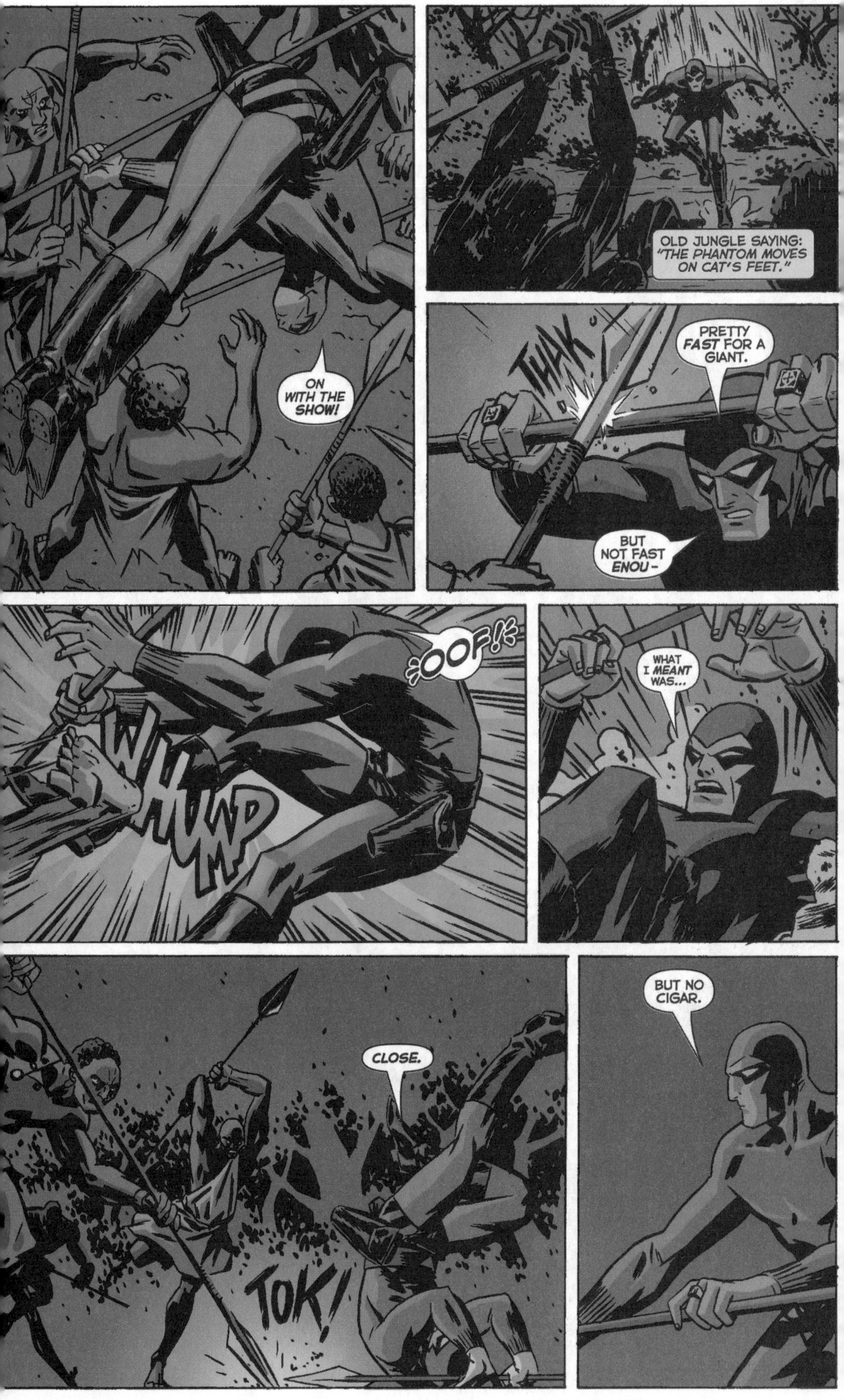
ON WITH THE SHOW!
OLD JUNGLE SAYING: "THE PHANTOM MOVES ON CAT'S FEET."
THAK
PRETTY FAST FOR A GIANT.
BUT NOT FAST ENOU-
OOF!
WHUMP
WHAT I MEANT WAS...
CLOSE.
TOK!
BUT NO CIGAR.

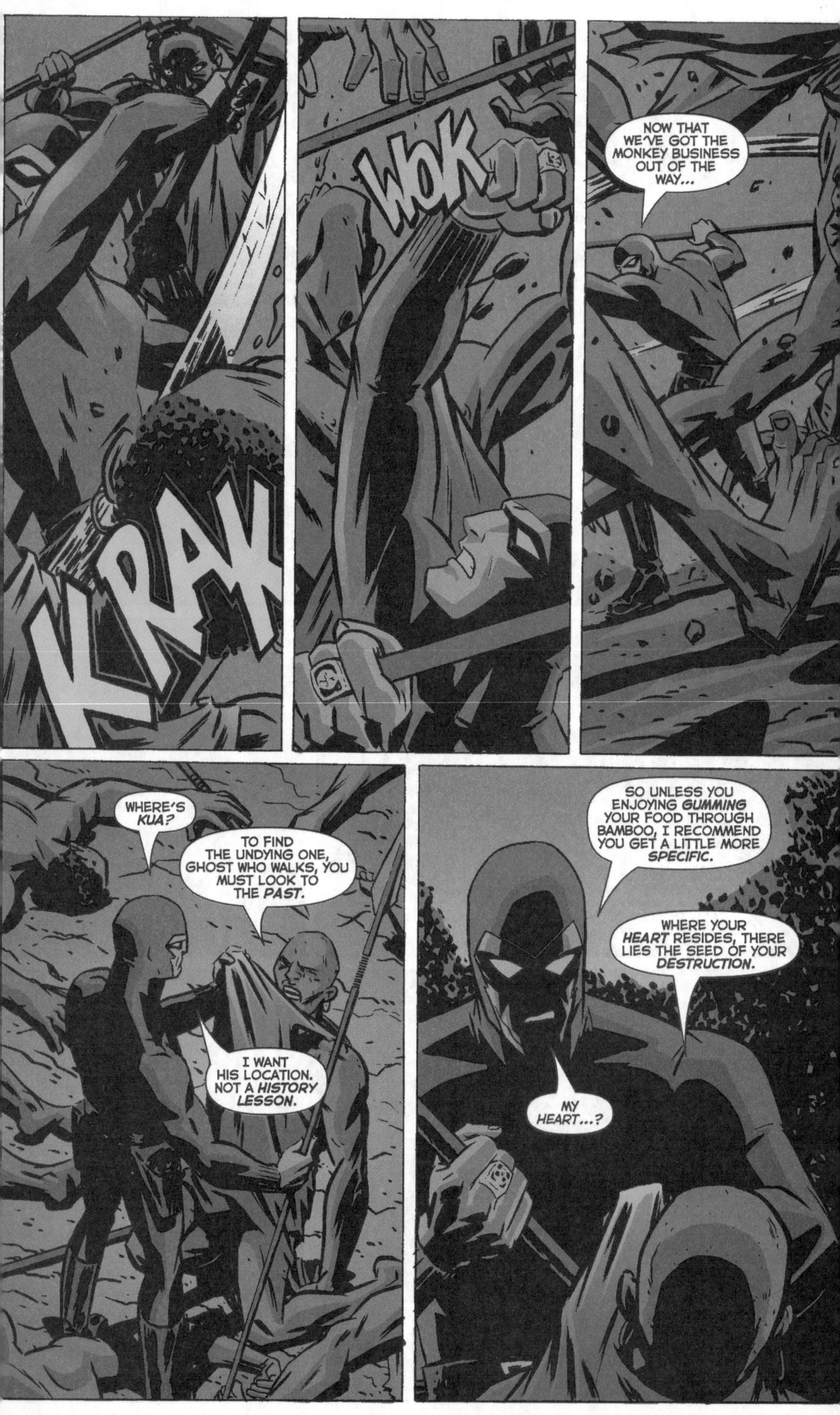
KRAK
WOK
NOW THAT WE'VE GOT THE MONKEY BUSINESS OUT OF THE WAY...
WHERE'S KUA?
TO FIND THE UNDYING ONE, GHOST WHO WALKS, YOU MUST LOOK TO THE PAST.
I WANT HIS LOCATION. NOT A HISTORY LESSON.
SO UNLESS YOU ENJOYING GUMMING YOUR FOOD THROUGH BAMBOO, I RECOMMEND YOU GET A LITTLE MORE SPECIFIC.
WHERE YOUR HEART RESIDES, THERE LIES THE SEED OF YOUR DESTRUCTION.
MY HEART...?

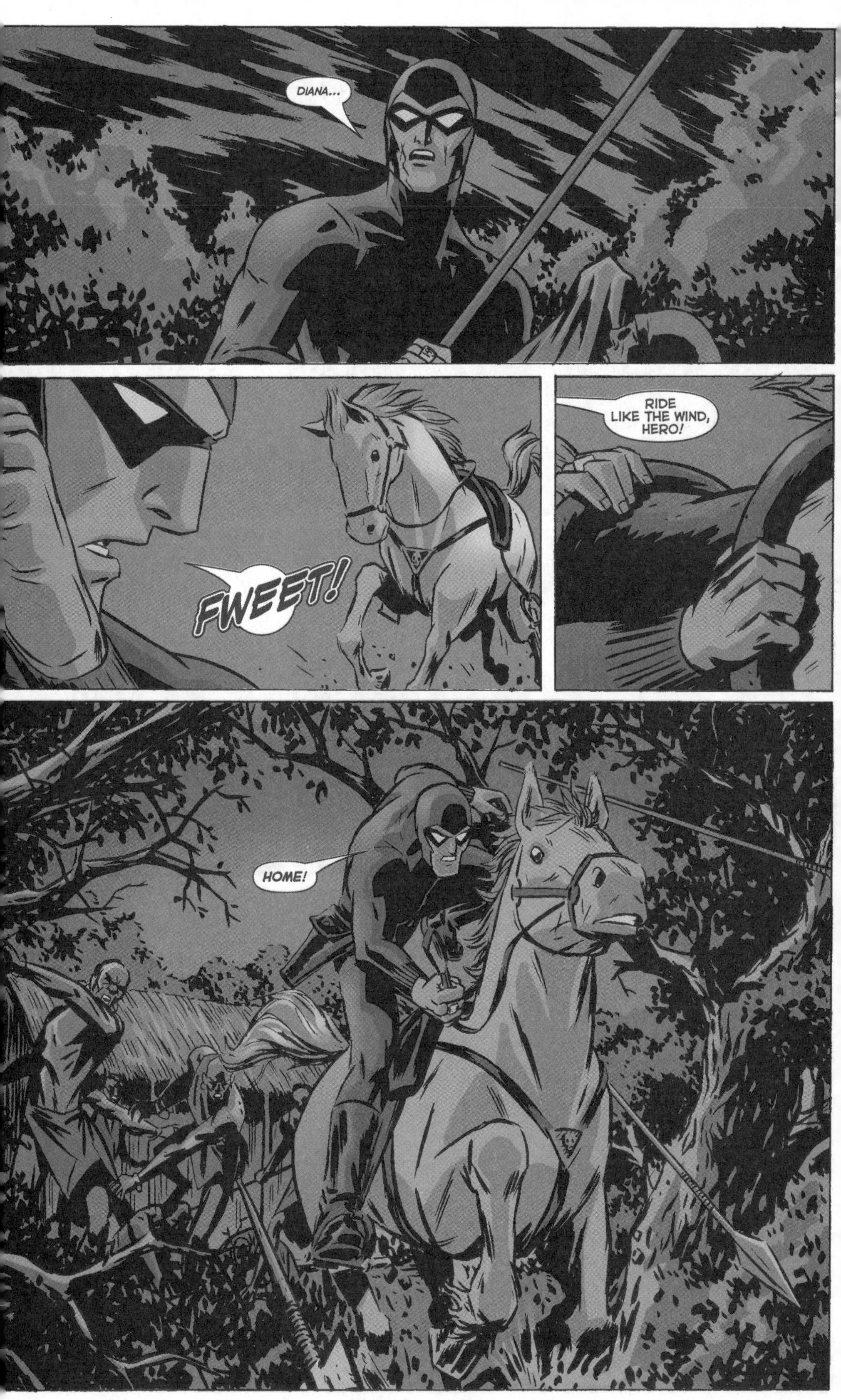
DIANA...
FWEET!
RIDE LIKE THE WIND, HERO!
HOME!

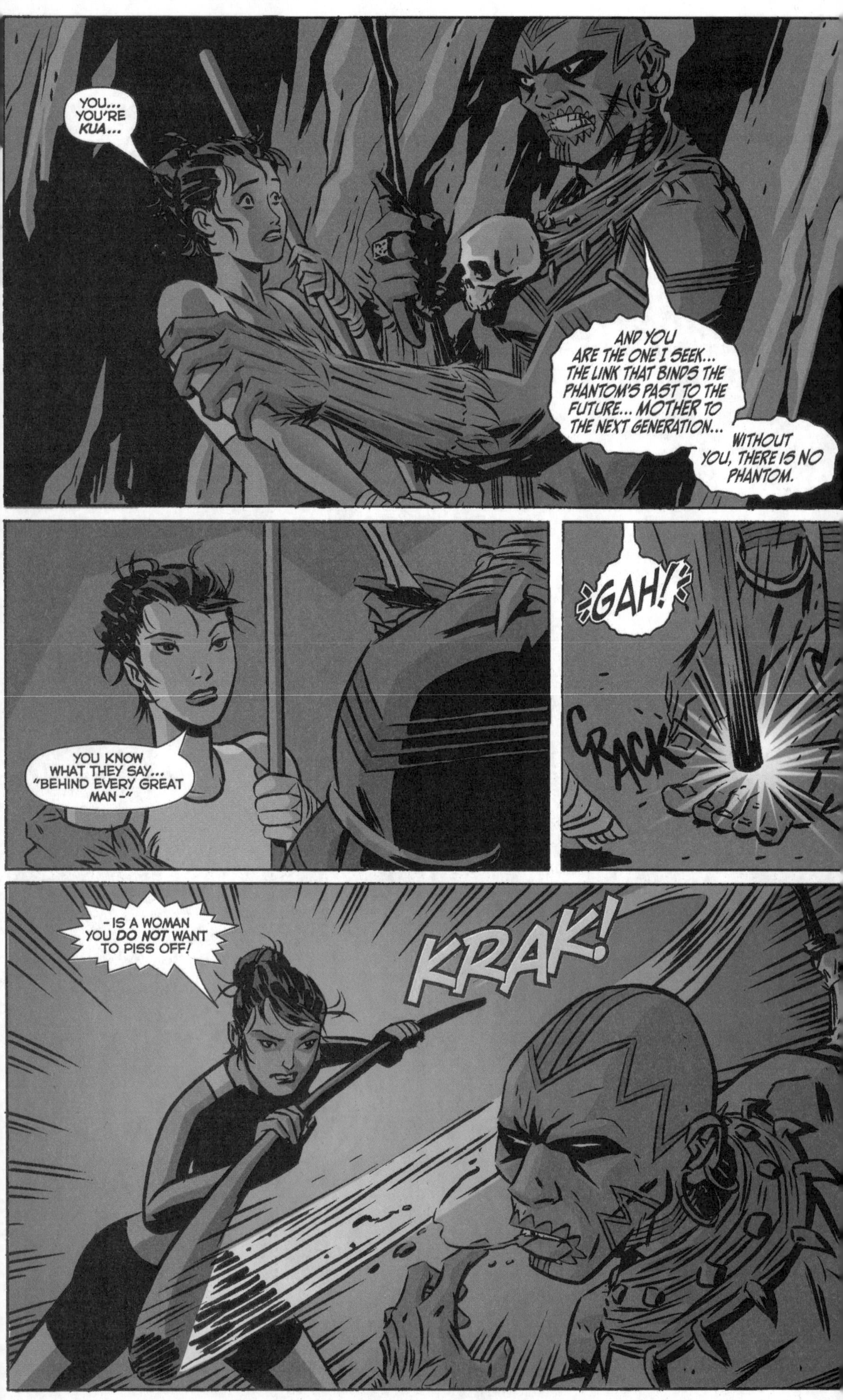
YOU... YOU'RE KUA...
AND YOU ARE THE ONE I SEEK... THE LINK THAT BINDS THE PHANTOM'S PAST TO THE FUTURE... MOTHER TO THE NEXT GENERATION...
WITHOUT YOU, THERE IS NO PHANTOM.
YOU KNOW WHAT THEY SAY... "BEHIND EVERY GREAT MAN-"
GAH!
CRACK
-IS A WOMAN YOU DO NOT WANT TO PISS OFF!
KRAK!

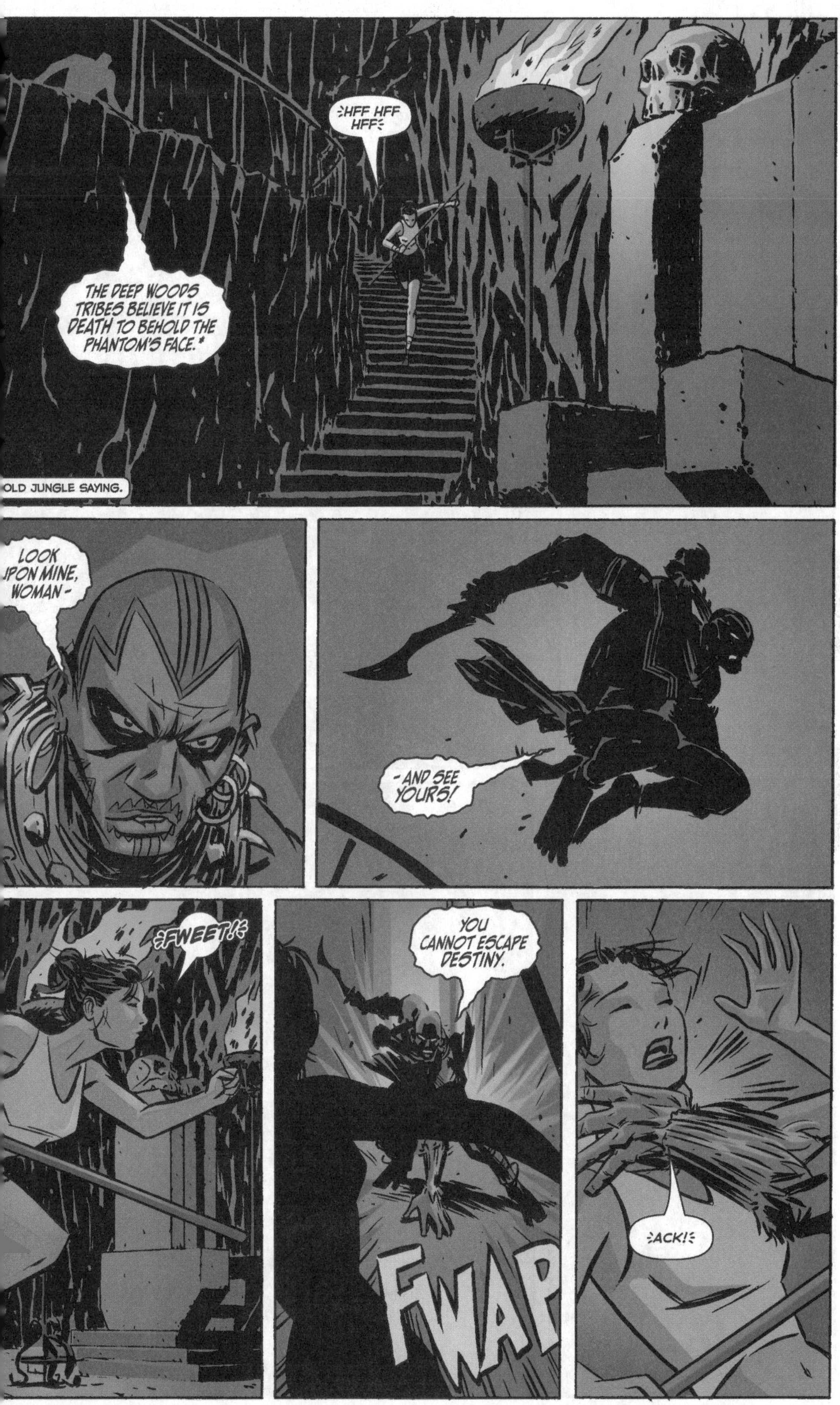
THE DEEP WOODS TRIBES BELIEVE IT IS DEATH TO BEHOLD THE PHANTOM'S FACE.*
HFF HFF HFF
OLD JUNGLE SAYING.
LOOK UPON MINE, WOMAN -
- AND SEE YOURS!
FWEET!
YOU CANNOT ESCAPE DESTINY.
FWAP
ACK!

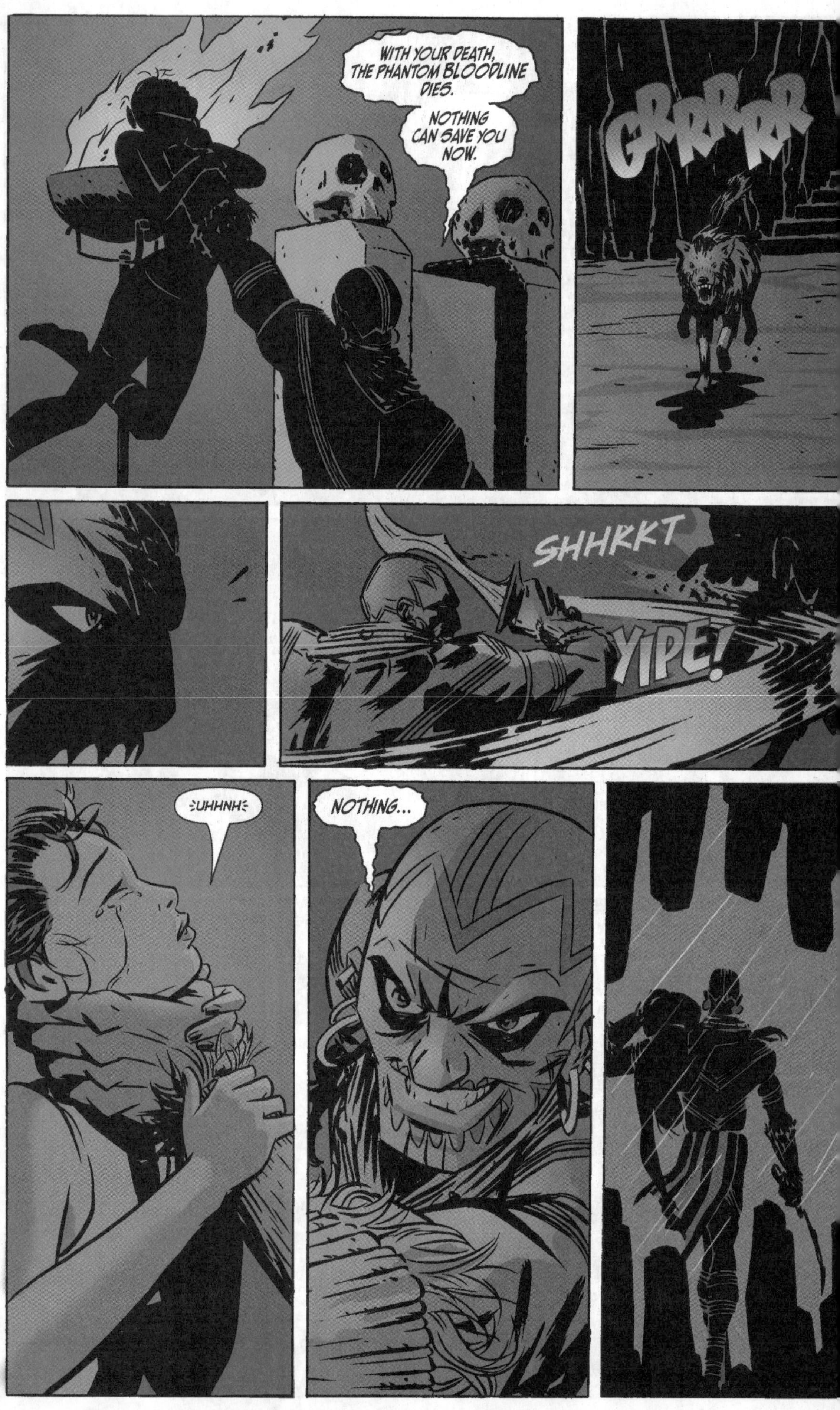
WITH YOUR DEATH, THE PHANTOM BLOODLINE DIES.
NOTHING CAN SAVE YOU NOW.
GRRRRR
SHHKKT
YIPE!
UHHNH
NOTHING...

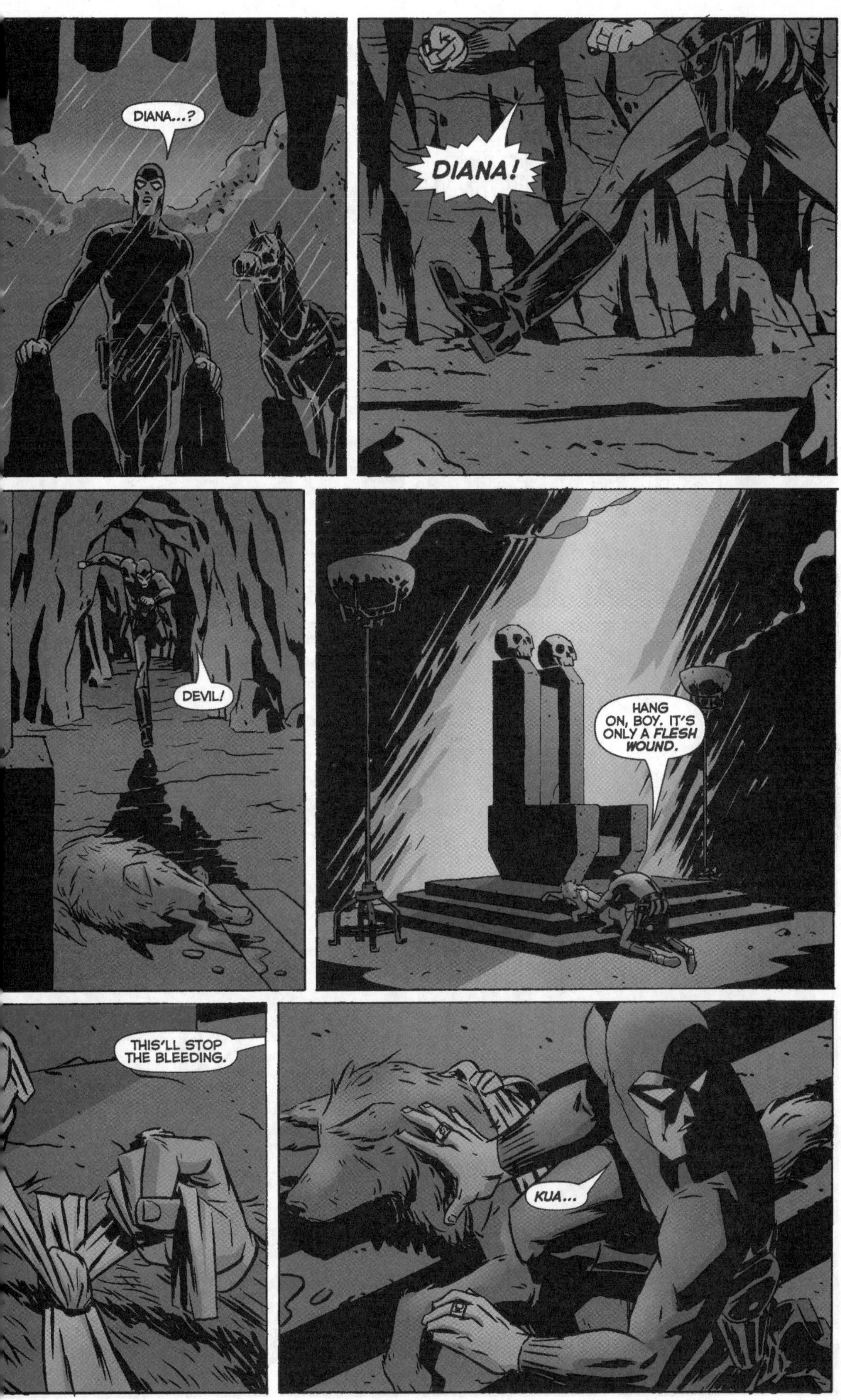
DIANA...?
DIANA!
DEVIL!
HANG ON, BOY. IT'S ONLY A FLESH WOUND.
THIS'LL STOP THE BLEEDING.
KUA...

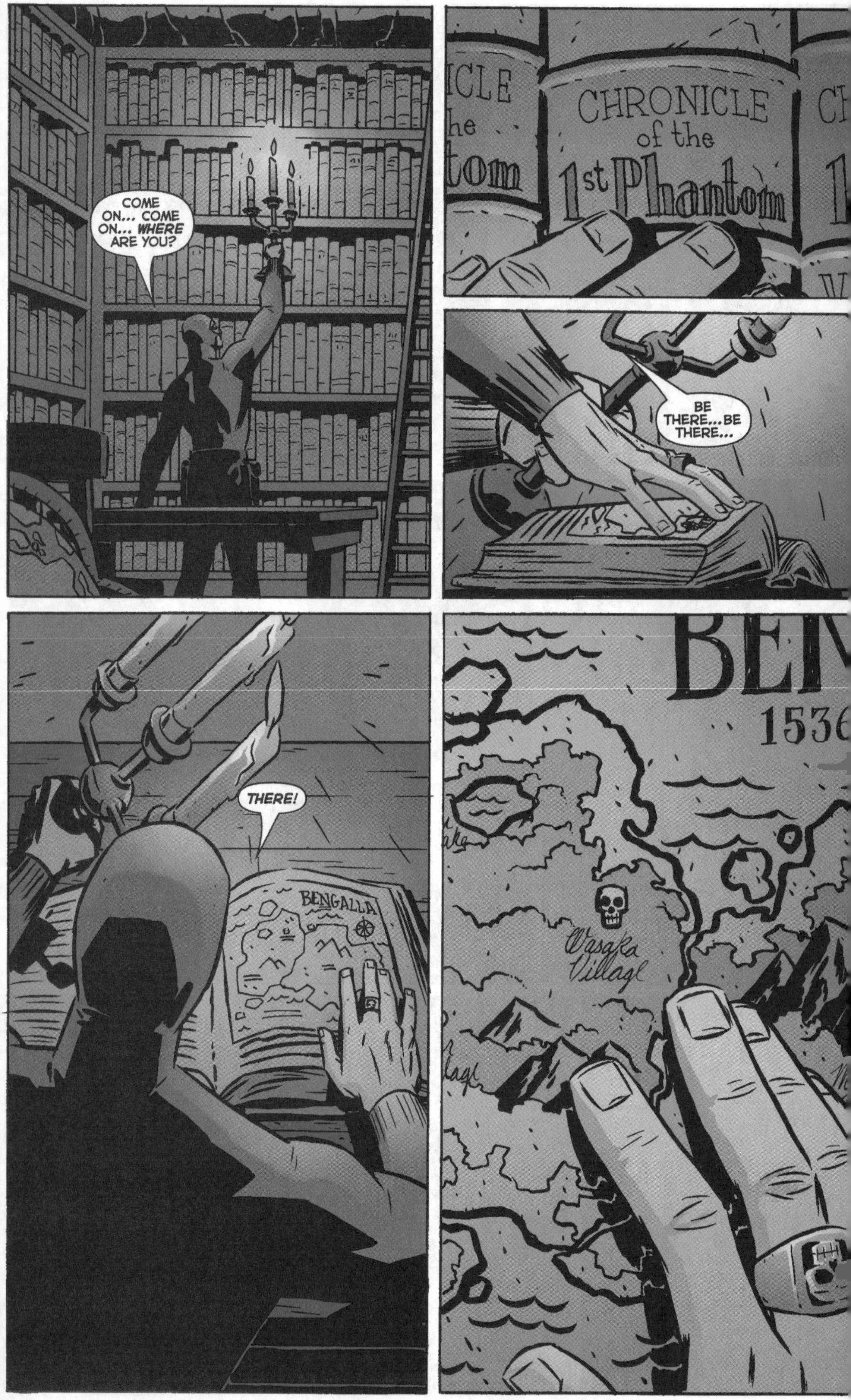
COME ON... COME ON... WHERE ARE YOU?
CHRONICLE of the 1st Phantom
BE THERE...BE THERE...
THERE!
BENGALLA
1536
Wasaka Village

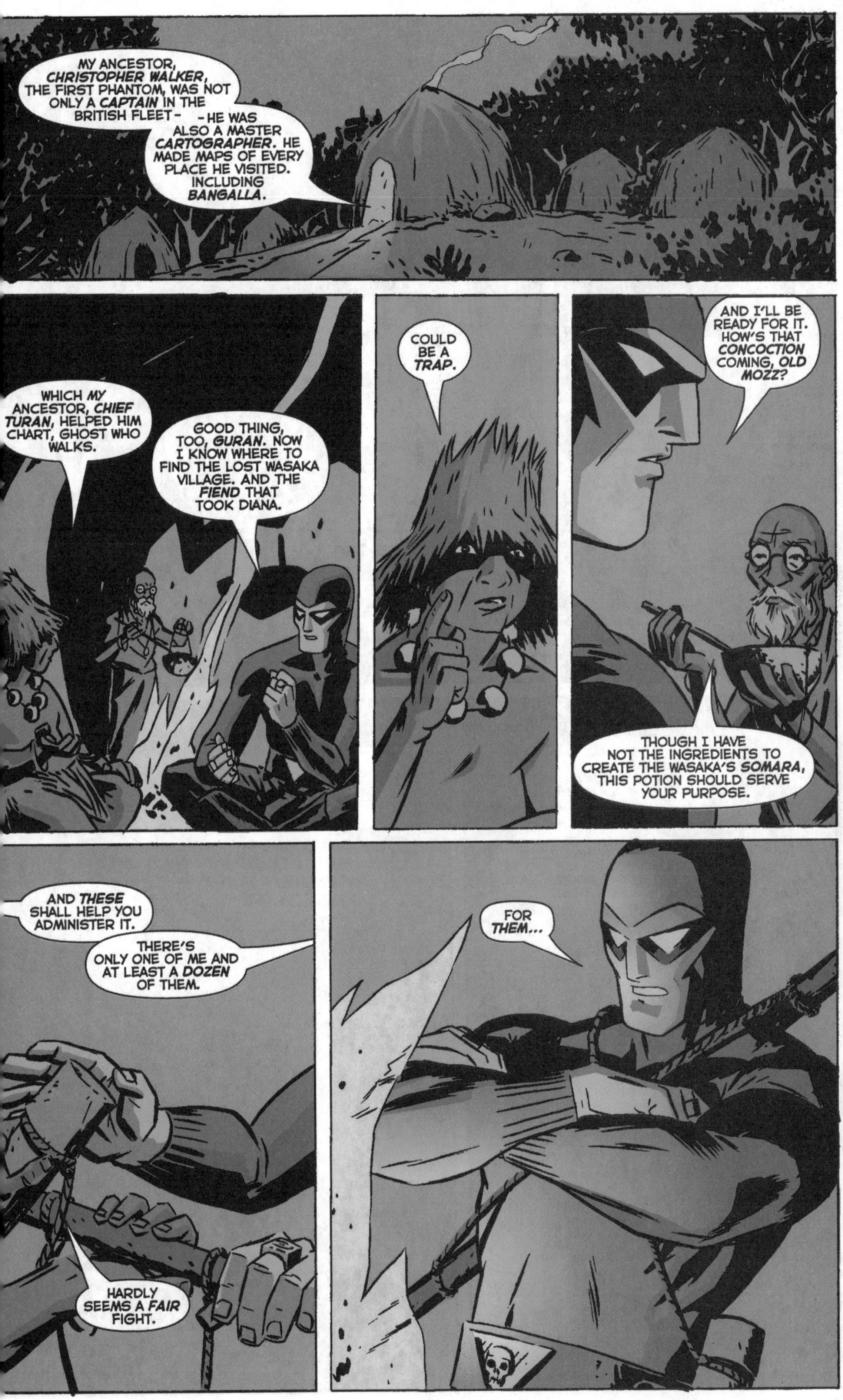
MY ANCESTOR, CHRISTOPHER WALKER, THE FIRST PHANTOM, WAS NOT ONLY A CAPTAIN IN THE BRITISH FLEET-
-HE WAS ALSO A MASTER CARTOGRAPHER. HE MADE MAPS OF EVERY PLACE HE VISITED. INCLUDING BANGALLA.
WHICH MY ANCESTOR, CHIEF TURAN, HELPED HIM CHART, GHOST WHO WALKS.
GOOD THING, TOO, GURAN. NOW I KNOW WHERE TO FIND THE LOST WASAKA VILLAGE. AND THE FIEND THAT TOOK DIANA.
COULD BE A TRAP.
AND I'LL BE READY FOR IT. HOW'S THAT CONCOCTION COMING, OLD MOZZ?
THOUGH I HAVE NOT THE INGREDIENTS TO CREATE THE WASAKA'S SOMARA, THIS POTION SHOULD SERVE YOUR PURPOSE.
AND THESE SHALL HELP YOU ADMINISTER IT.
THERE'S ONLY ONE OF ME AND AT LEAST A DOZEN OF THEM.
HARDLY SEEMS A FAIR FIGHT.
FOR THEM...

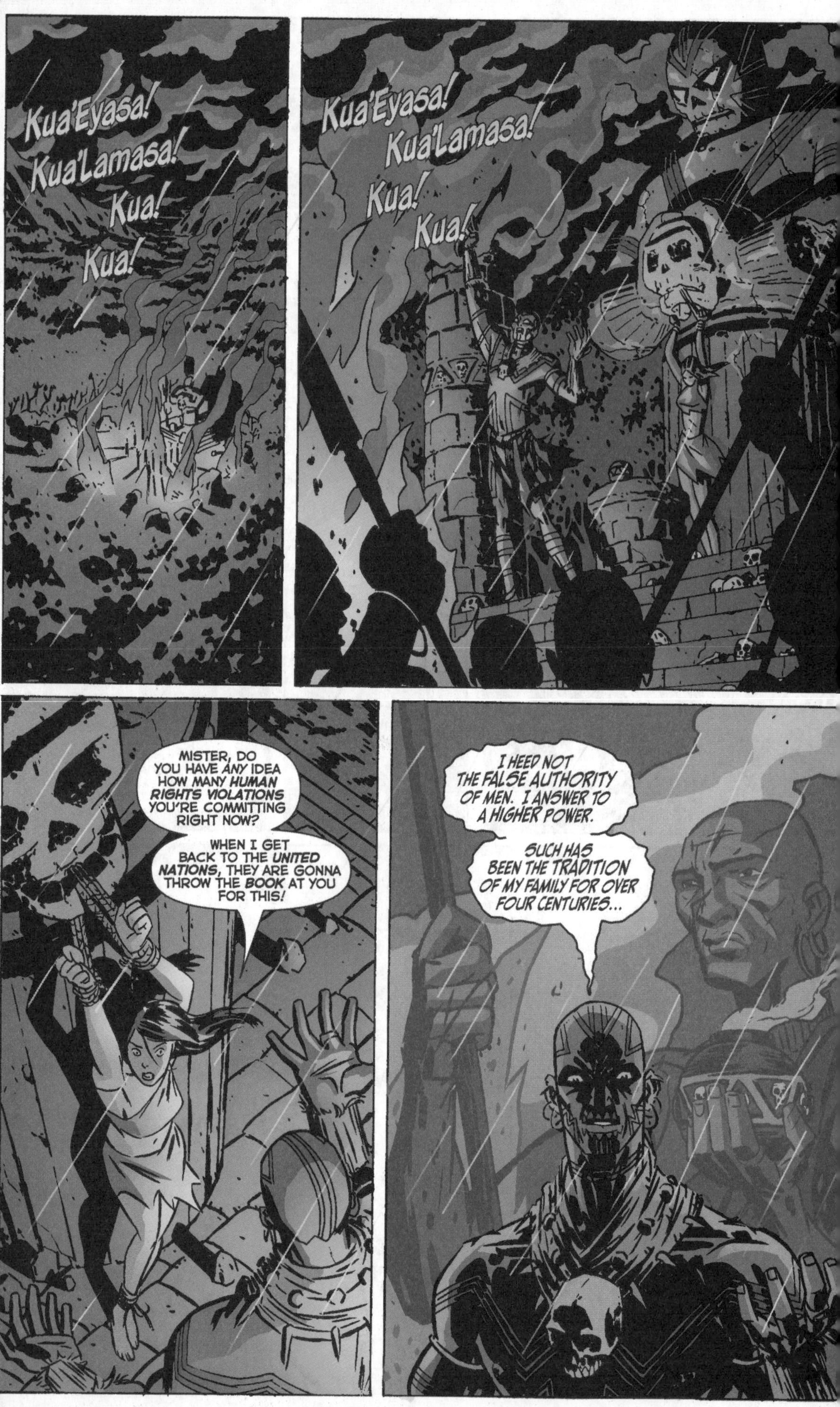
Kua'Eyasa!
Kua'Lamasa!
Kua!
Kua!
Kua'Eyasa!
Kua'Lamasa!
Kua!
Kua!
MISTER, DO YOU HAVE ANY IDEA HOW MANY HUMAN RIGHTS VIOLATIONS YOU'RE COMMITTING RIGHT NOW?
WHEN I GET BACK TO THE UNITED NATIONS, THEY ARE GONNA THROW THE BOOK AT YOU FOR THIS!
I HEED NOT THE FALSE AUTHORITY OF MEN. I ANSWER TO A HIGHER POWER.
SUCH HAS BEEN THE TRADITION OF MY FAMILY FOR OVER FOUR CENTURIES...

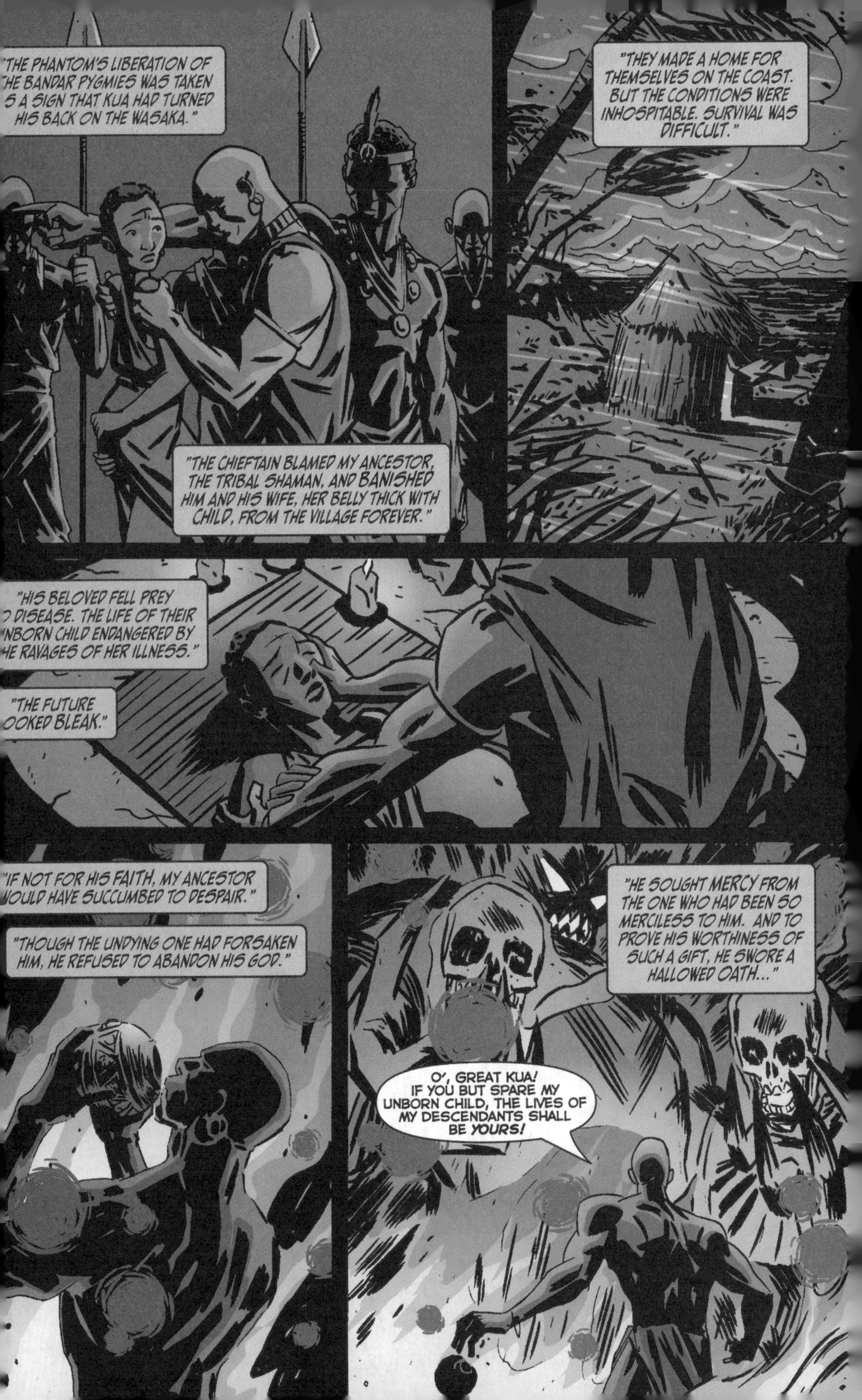
"THE PHANTOM'S LIBERATION OF THE BANDAR PYGMIES WAS TAKEN S A SIGN THAT KUA HAD TURNED HIS BACK ON THE WASAKA."
"THE CHIEFTAIN BLAMED MY ANCESTOR, THE TRIBAL SHAMAN, AND BANISHED HIM AND HIS WIFE, HER BELLY THICK WITH CHILD, FROM THE VILLAGE FOREVER."
"THEY MADE A HOME FOR THEMSELVES ON THE COAST. BUT THE CONDITIONS WERE INHOSPITABLE. SURVIVAL WAS DIFFICULT."
"HIS BELOVED FELL PREY O DISEASE. THE LIFE OF THEIR NBORN CHILD ENDANGERED BY HE RAVAGES OF HER ILLNESS."
"THE FUTURE OOKED BLEAK."
"IF NOT FOR HIS FAITH, MY ANCESTOR VOULD HAVE SUCCUMBED TO DESPAIR."
"THOUGH THE UNDYING ONE HAD FORSAKEN HIM, HE REFUSED TO ABANDON HIS GOD."
"HE SOUGHT MERCY FROM THE ONE WHO HAD BEEN SO MERCILESS TO HIM. AND TO PROVE HIS WORTHINESS OF SUCH A GIFT, HE SWORE A HALLOWED OATH..."
O', GREAT KUA! IF YOU BUT SPARE MY UNBORN CHILD, THE LIVES OF MY DESCENDANTS SHALL BE YOURS!

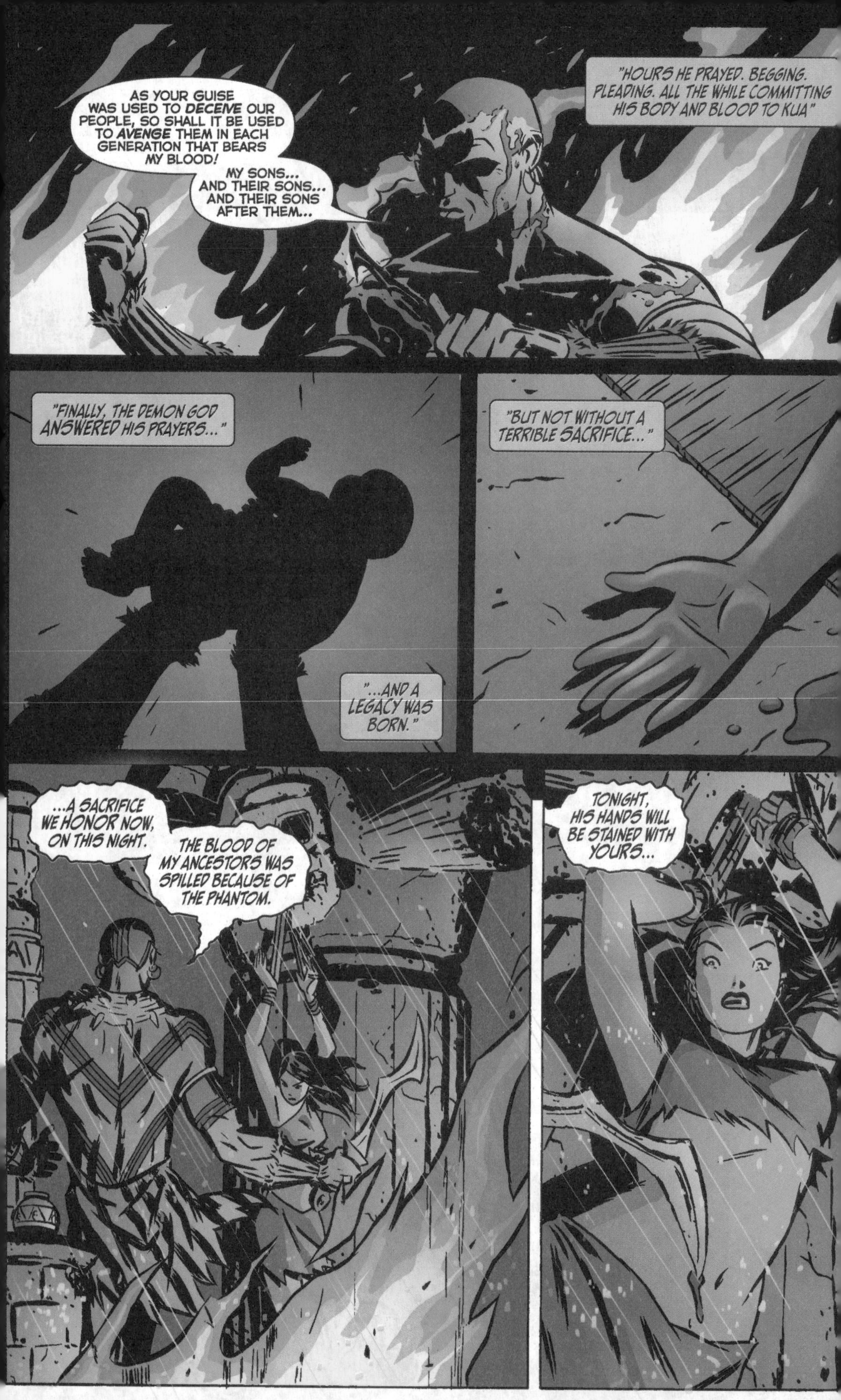
"HOURS HE PRAYED. BEGGING. PLEADING. ALL THE WHILE COMMITTING HIS BODY AND BLOOD TO KUA"
AS YOUR GUISE WAS USED TO DECEIVE OUR PEOPLE, SO SHALL IT BE USED TO AVENGE THEM IN EACH GENERATION THAT BEARS MY BLOOD!
MY SONS... AND THEIR SONS... AND THEIR SONS AFTER THEM...
"FINALLY, THE DEMON GOD ANSWERED HIS PRAYERS..."
"...AND A LEGACY WAS BORN."
"BUT NOT WITHOUT A TERRIBLE SACRIFICE..."
...A SACRIFICE WE HONOR NOW, ON THIS NIGHT.
THE BLOOD OF MY ANCESTORS WAS SPILLED BECAUSE OF THE PHANTOM.
TONIGHT, HIS HANDS WILL BE STAINED WITH YOURS...

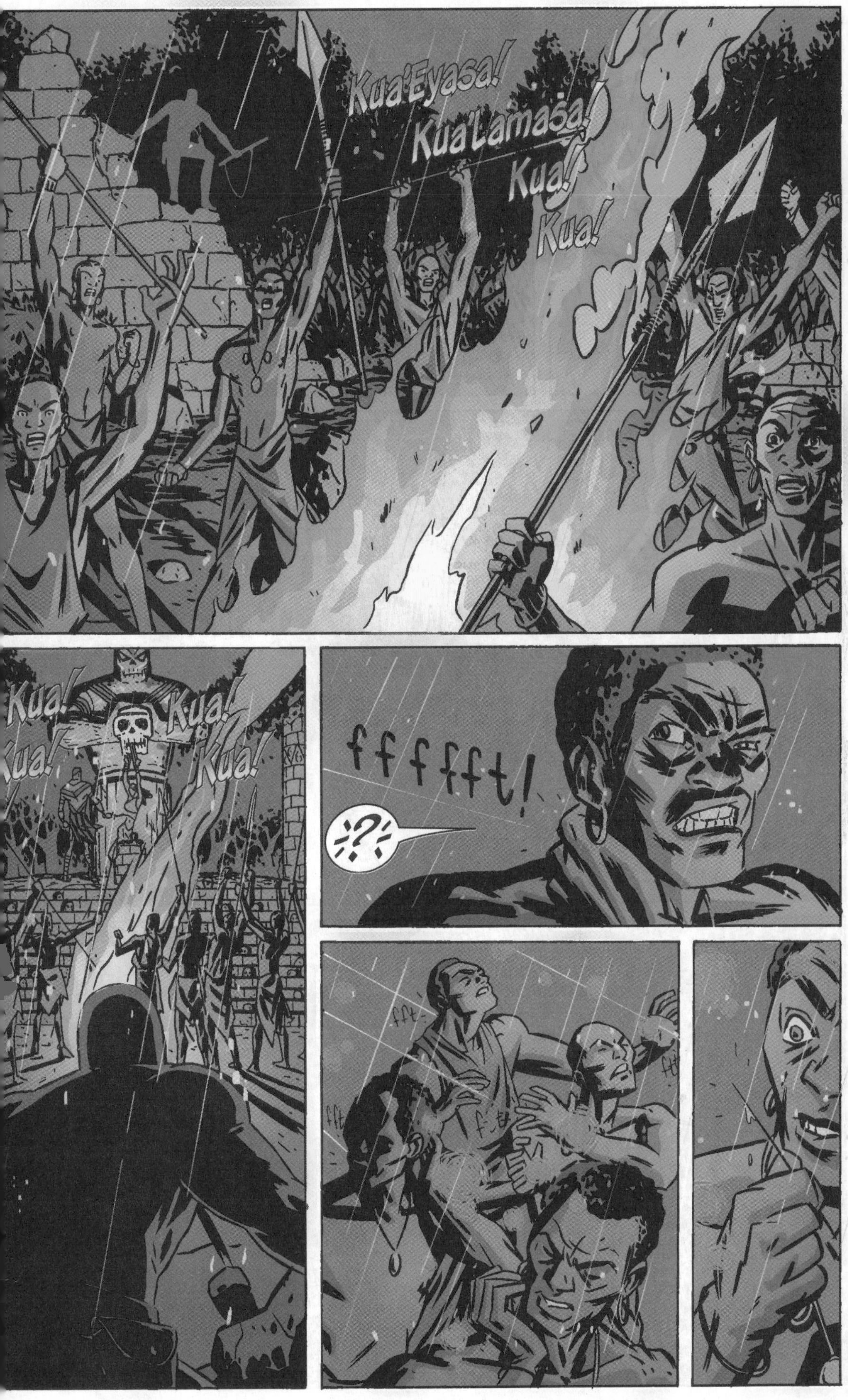

Kua'Eyasa!
Kua'Lamasa!
Kua!
Kua!
Kua!
Kua!
Kua!
Kua!
ffffft!
?
fft
fft
fft

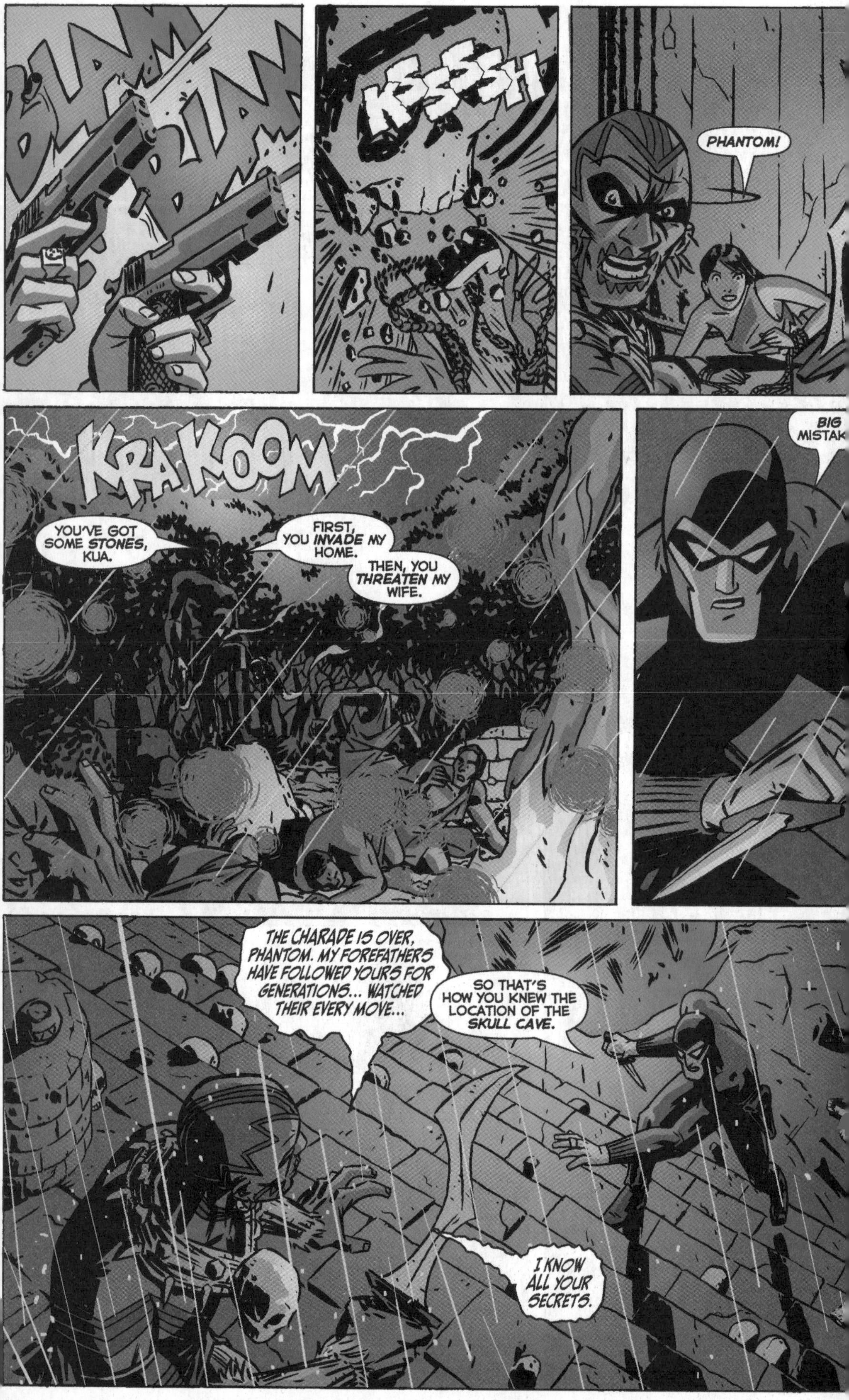
BLAM
BLAM
KSSSSH
PHANTOM!
KRAKOOM
YOU'VE GOT SOME STONES, KUA.
FIRST, YOU INVADE MY HOME.
THEN, YOU THREATEN MY WIFE.
BIG MISTAK
THE CHARADE IS OVER, PHANTOM. MY FOREFATHERS HAVE FOLLOWED YOURS FOR GENERATIONS... WATCHED THEIR EVERY MOVE...
SO THAT'S HOW YOU KNEW THE LOCATION OF THE SKULL CAVE.
I KNOW ALL YOUR SECRETS.

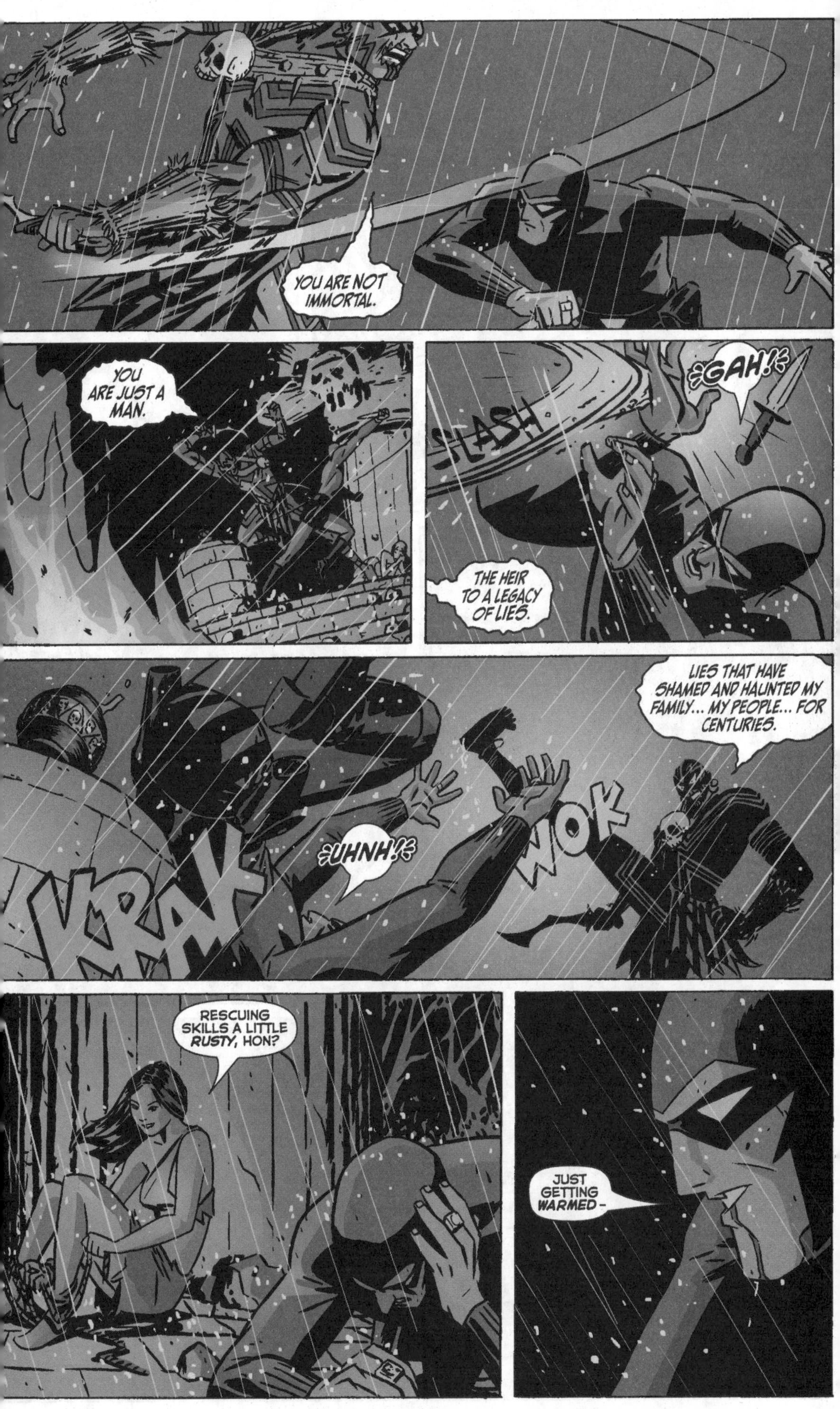

YOU ARE NOT IMMORTAL.
YOU ARE JUST A MAN.
SLASH
GAH!
THE HEIR TO A LEGACY OF LIES.
LIES THAT HAVE SHAMED AND HAUNTED MY FAMILY... MY PEOPLE... FOR CENTURIES.
WOK
UHNH!
KRAK
RESCUING SKILLS A LITTLE RUSTY, HON?
JUST GETTING WARMED -

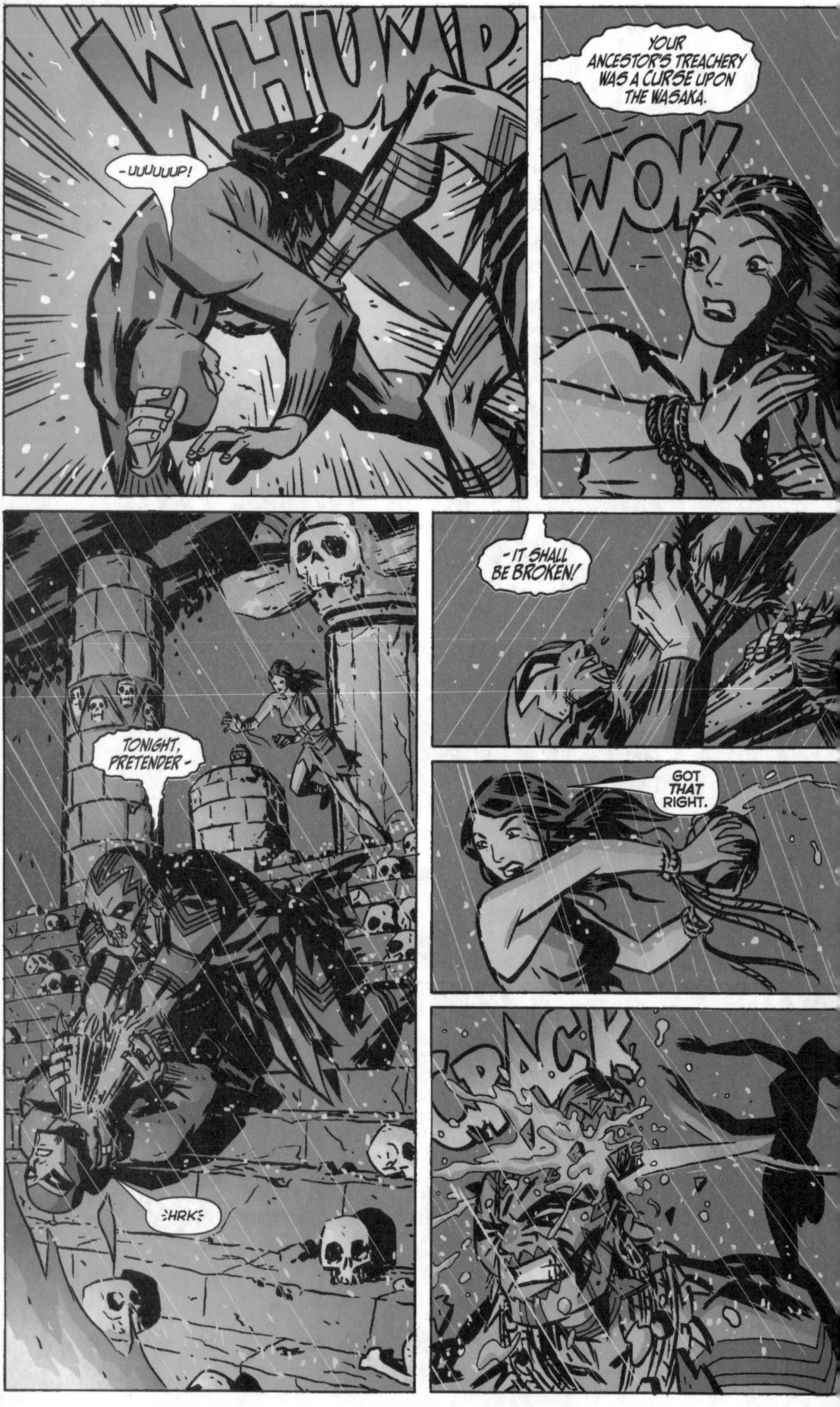
WHUMP
-UUUUUUP!
YOUR ANCESTOR'S TREACHERY WAS A CURSE UPON THE WASAKA.
WOK
TONIGHT, PRETENDER-
-IT SHALL BE BROKEN!
HRK
GOT THAT RIGHT.
PACK

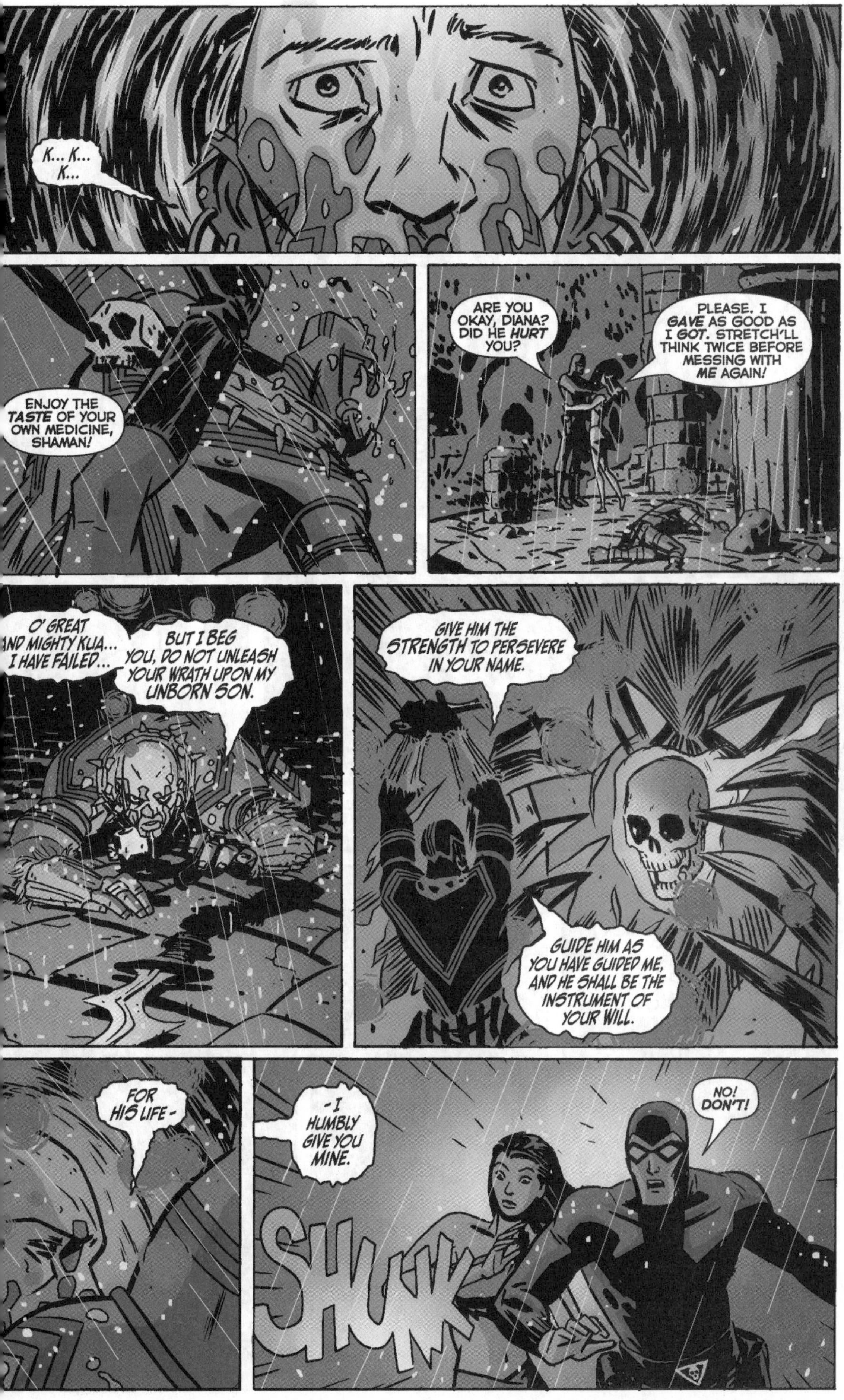
K... K... K...
ENJOY THE TASTE OF YOUR OWN MEDICINE, SHAMAN!
ARE YOU OKAY, DIANA? DID HE HURT YOU?
PLEASE. I GAVE AS GOOD AS I GOT. STRETCH'LL THINK TWICE BEFORE MESSING WITH ME AGAIN!
O' GREAT AND MIGHTY KUA... I HAVE FAILED...
BUT I BEG YOU, DO NOT UNLEASH YOUR WRATH UPON MY UNBORN SON.
GIVE HIM THE STRENGTH TO PERSEVERE IN YOUR NAME.
GUIDE HIM AS YOU HAVE GUIDED ME, AND HE SHALL BE THE INSTRUMENT OF YOUR WILL.
FOR HIS LIFE -
- I HUMBLY GIVE YOU MINE.
NO! DON'T!
SHUNK

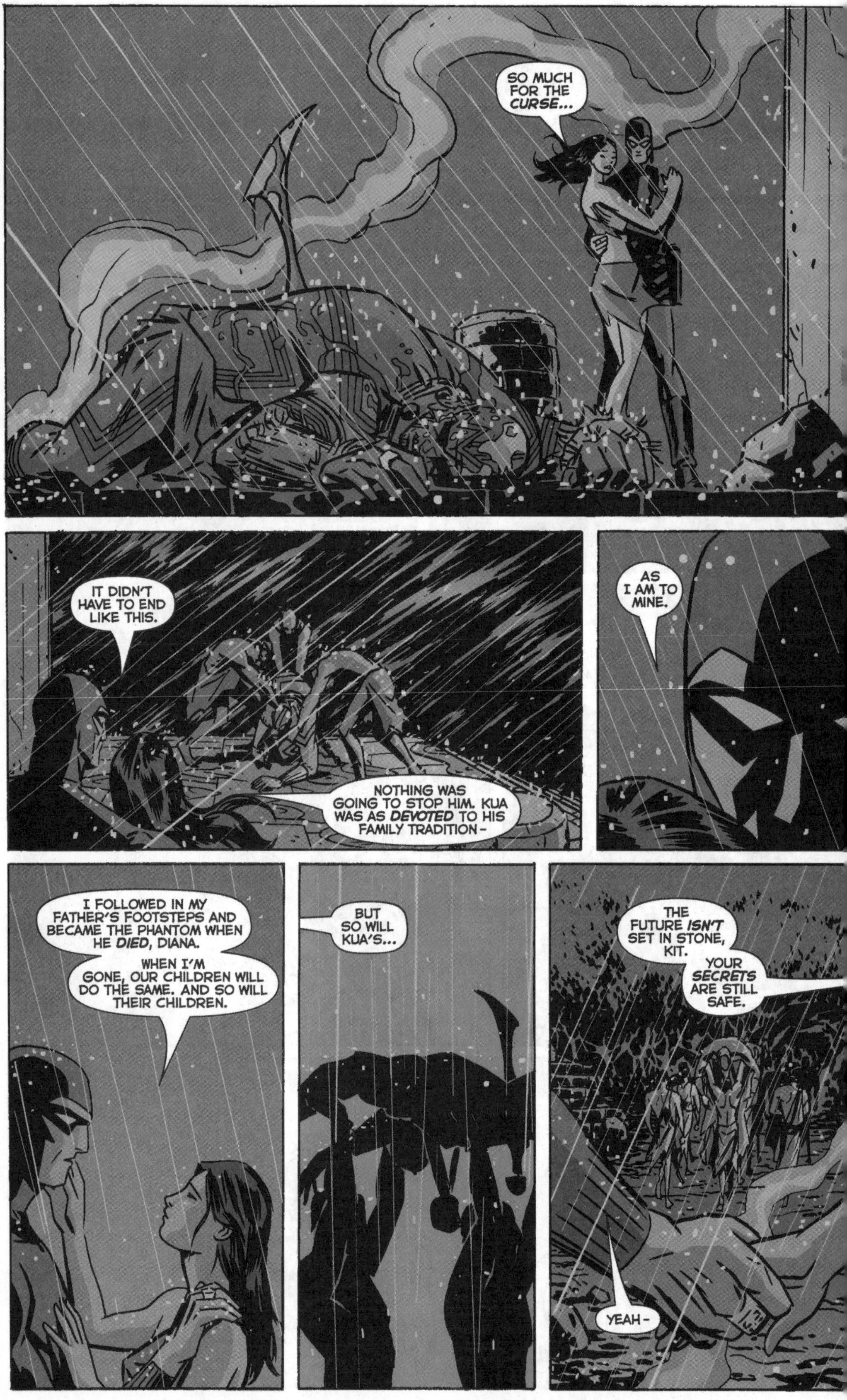
SO MUCH FOR THE CURSE...
IT DIDN'T HAVE TO END LIKE THIS.
NOTHING WAS GOING TO STOP HIM. KUA WAS AS DEVOTED TO HIS FAMILY TRADITION-
AS I AM TO MINE.
I FOLLOWED IN MY FATHER'S FOOTSTEPS AND BECAME THE PHANTOM WHEN HE DIED, DIANA.
WHEN I'M GONE, OUR CHILDREN WILL DO THE SAME. AND SO WILL THEIR CHILDREN.
BUT SO WILL KUA'S...
THE FUTURE ISN'T SET IN STONE, KIT.
YOUR SECRETS ARE STILL SAFE.
YEAH-

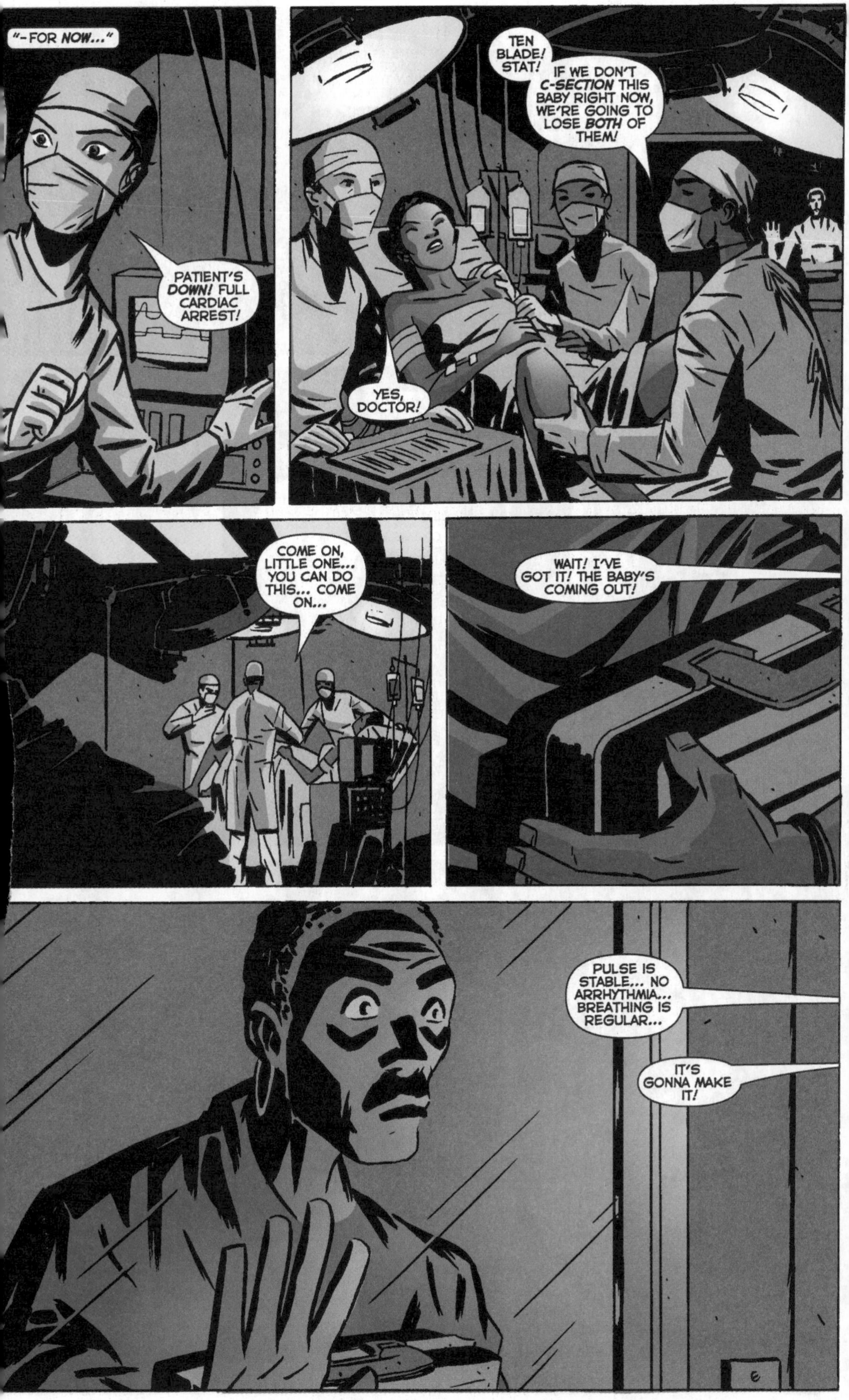
"-FOR NOW..."
PATIENT'S DOWN! FULL CARDIAC ARREST!
TEN BLADE! STAT!
IF WE DON'T C-SECTION THIS BABY RIGHT NOW, WE'RE GOING TO LOSE BOTH OF THEM!
YES, DOCTOR!
COME ON, LITTLE ONE... YOU CAN DO THIS... COME ON...
WAIT! I'VE GOT IT! THE BABY'S COMING OUT!
PULSE IS STABLE... NO ARRHYTHMIA... BREATHING IS REGULAR...
IT'S GONNA MAKE IT!

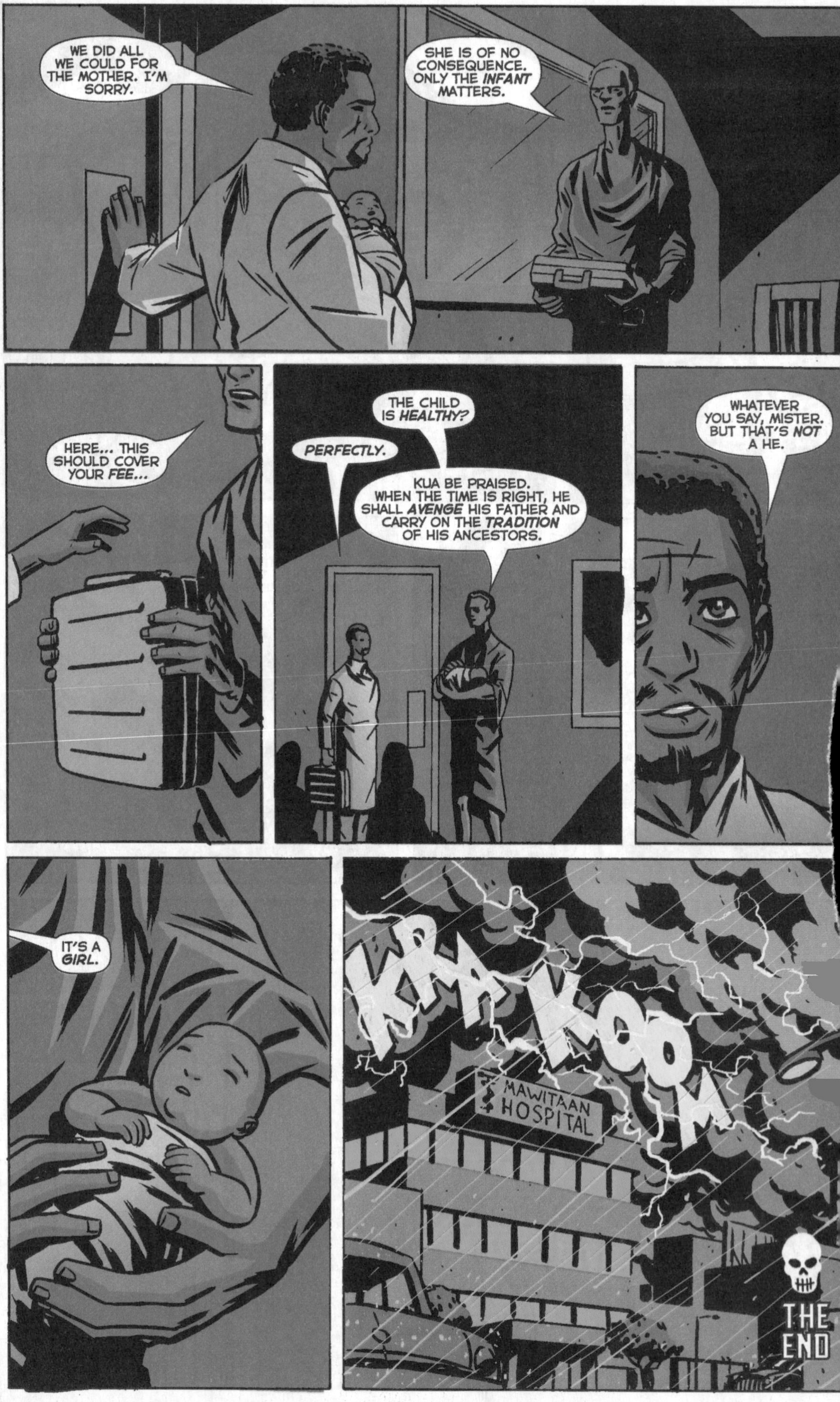
WE DID ALL WE COULD FOR THE MOTHER. I'M SORRY.
SHE IS OF NO CONSEQUENCE. ONLY THE *INFANT* MATTERS.
HERE... THIS SHOULD COVER YOUR *FEE*...
THE CHILD IS *HEALTHY?*
PERFECTLY.
KUA BE PRAISED. WHEN THE TIME IS RIGHT, HE SHALL *AVENGE* HIS FATHER AND CARRY ON THE *TRADITION* OF HIS ANCESTORS.
WHATEVER YOU SAY, MISTER. BUT THAT'S *NOT* A HE.
IT'S A *GIRL*.
KRA KOOM
MAWITAAN HOSPITAL
THE END